MORE ESSAYS FROM THE WORLD OF MUSIC

The author with his wife

VOLUME TWO

More Essays from the World of Music

ERNEST NEWMAN

Essays from the 'Sunday Times'

Selected by

FELIX APRAHAMIAN

JOHN CALDER

LONDON

First published in Great Britain 1958 by John Calder (Publishers) Ltd.,
18 Brewer Street London W1R 4AS
Re-issued in 1976.

ISBN 0 7145 3549 4 Casebound
ISBN 0 7145 3598 2 Paper

These articles are published with the permission of *The Sunday Times* and are printed from writings by Ernest Newman during the last fifty-six years.

Front panel and frontispiece photographs by Felix Aprahamian

Printed and bound by Billing & Sons Limited
London, Guildford and Worcester

CONTENTS

To

VERA

INTRODUCTION

Mr Newman's own introduction to these reprinted essays from The Sunday Times *will be found in the first volume of* From the World of Music. *Perhaps this second volume calls for a word from the compiler to answer the general cry of 'Why none of the essays on Mahler, Strauss, Wolf, Berlioz?'. This constituted a valid criticism of the contents of the first volume, for neither my revered senior colleague nor I had offered any explanation of their absence.*

When I first suggested the reprinting of some of his Sunday articles, Mr Newman pointed out that many of them—dealing with, precisely, Mahler, Strauss, Wolf, Berlioz—represented sketches for or pendants to larger works in progress on those composers and were, therefore, not available. My task was to prove that even without the proscribed essays there was more than enough material. The present volume affords additional proof of this, and, happily, there is more to come.

FELIX APRAHAMIAN

London, December 1957

PART I

CONDUCTORS

THE CONDUCTOR

I

24th July 1949

Is a conductor really necessary? When and how did he become really necessary? These are questions grave enough to occupy an idle hour.

The conductor's function today is obviously two-fold, firstly to keep the performers together, secondly to 'interpret' the work to the audience. (I employ the questionable term 'interpret' purely for convenience' sake. As I have pointed out before, an interpreter, strictly speaking, is one who does us the service of translating something for us out of a language we do not understand into one we do. Manifestly nothing of that sort happens in the case of a musical performance.) Of the two functions I have mentioned, the former is of course the older, because the more basic; we see a conductor at work in this way in several ancient representations of mass music-making.

He gave the time (as he did, indeed, in our concert rooms and opera houses until comparatively recently) by clapping with his hands and stamping with his feet. It is probable, however, that even in the earliest days he aimed also at something which we would describe today as rudimentary interpretation, not merely indicating the strong beats or calling for varying degrees of loud and soft but suggesting certain little refinements of expression with his hands or fingers. The impulse to do this is innate in mankind; which of us has not been moved at some time or other to convey outwardly our sense of the curve of a gracious melody by drawing a line in space with our hands?

The second, and to the modern mind the most important, function of the conductor came more and more to the forefront as both the performers and the impassioned listener gradually realised that more goes to the ideal performance of music than everyone playing the right note at the right moment. 'Expression' came to be regarded as the truly vital thing. It was felt that the changing emotions of the music, or varieties in the shading of the same emotion, could be brought out only by substituting for the metronomic beat and the uniform tone something of the flexibility of line and variety of tone colour of emotional speech. A distinction was soon perceived, if not definitely formulated, between objective rhythm, the business of which is simply to impose uniformity of note values and metres on the whole body of the performers, and subjective rhythm, which tenses or relaxes in accordance with the nature or the urgency of the feeling. Musicians became fully aware of the need for the latter kind of rhythm at the beginning of the seventeenth century, when composers were wearying of the classical contrapuntal type of vocal texture—in which the words were mostly unintelligible owing to the overlapping of the voices—and giving their melodies a shape suggested by the sentiment of the words.

As the 'new' madrigal became more 'expressive' the need was felt for a mode of performance corresponding in elasticity of tempo, variety of nuance, and range of dynamics to the art of the actor or orator. The baroque doctrine of the potency of the 'affetti' (the 'Affekte', the 'passions') was already beginning to take shape. We find Frescobaldi, in 1614, insisting that the old formal regularity of time was inappropriate to the 'new' madrigal, for obviously we do not languish, for example, at the same pace as we rage. Monteverdi, of course, got to grips with this matter as he did with every other distinguishing characteristic of the 'new' music of his day.

In his 'madrigali guerrieri et amorosi' of 1638 there is a 'madrigale rappresentativo', in three sections—'Non avea Febo ancora'—the middle one of which is a 'lamento della ninfa' over her betrayal by her lover; it is accompanied or punctuated by sympathetic ejaculation from the three male voices which explain and comment on the situation in the first and third section of the work.

In a prefatory note the composer tells his performers how he wishes the madrigal to be 'represented'. He has printed only the separate parts for the three male voices in the first and third sections, he says, because these are to be sung simply 'al tempo de la mano', that is to say, according to the hand-beat; whereas in the lament 'the three voices that commiserate softly with the nymph are given in score (along with hers), so that they may follow her complaint, which is to be sung a tempo del "affetto del animo, e non a quello de la mano" '—i.e., not according to the regular beat but according to the passion of the soul.

In performance, then, the nymph would inflect her lament in a free subjective rhythm determined by the changing phases of her emotion, and it would be the business of whoever was directing the performance to see that the tempo of the other voices tightened or relaxed in conformity with this free rhythm of hers, in a way that a piano accompanist or a conductor today 'follows' the singer in a song or an Italian opera aria.

Here the new function of the conductor is coming clearly into view. Much ground had to be travelled, however, before he became the important person he is in our modern music-making.

II

31st July 1949

LIKE the good child he is, the modern conductor is seen, not heard—except, of course, in moments of Pythian inspiration when he sings with the orchestra. In the brave days of old, however, he was more heard than seen. Simple hand-waving might be harmless enough; but marking the time by hand-clapping or foot-stamping could be pandemonium. As early as the middle of the sixteenth century we find a writer on music putting in a plaintive plea for inaudibility on the part of the conductor. A hundred years later it was complained that opera audiences could not hear the singers for the noise of the conductor's baton hammering on the music stand, which by some opera audiences today would be regarded as being a matter for congratulation rather than censure.

'In the Italian opera', said a French writer of the latter half of the eighteenth century, 'the time is not beaten, but in place of that we have a most objectionable practice, the first fiddler stamping it out with his foot, throwing himself about, carrying on in general like one possessed with a devil, and keeping the orchestra together by means of such heavy attacks with his bow that they can be heard at the other end of the theatre; while the cembalist (doing a kind of conducting of his own at the keyboard) often marks the beat so noisily that he would be well advised to wear thick gloves so as not to break his fingers.'

But things were no better in France; Rousseau tells us that at the Paris Opéra people's hearing was damaged by 'the horrible and uninterrupted noise' made by the conductor's baton.

As orchestras and choirs grew larger the more necessity there was for an audible beat. It was as true then, of course, as it is now that in general a good orchestra could get on quite well without a conductor if it could rehearse a big work until it knew it inside out and everyone had arrived at the same notion of the meaning of the music, as is the case with string quartets today. It was by leathering away in this fashion at the 'Ninth Symphony' for a year or more that the Paris Conservatoire orchestra succeeded in making the baffling work intelligible to themselves and to their listeners. The self-conducted orchestra of today, however, is an impossibility, having regard to the enormous extent of the concert repertory and the growth of complexity in scores. A short cut to an overall conception of the work has to be found, by way of a conductor who studies it in the score, comes to his own conclusions about it, and gives unified direction to the whole huge machine.

In the early nineteenth century there were still two directors of a performance, one of them the cembalist, the other the leading violinist. The latter was a survival from the days when the upper strings were the most important factor in an orchestral ensemble. Memory of the practice survives in two quaint delusions of the ordinary concert-goer today. The first is that it is a great advantage to a conductor to have started life as a string player, especially a violinist. If that were the case, the two greatest conductors of the mid-nineteenth century, the founders of the modern art of conducting—Wagner and Berlioz—would have been disqualified, for neither of them could have played the simplest of tunes on a violin.

The second delusion is that the first of the first violins, who has gradually become so important a person in the eyes of the multitude that he has to make a separate entry on the platform and receive his round of applause, is in any sense whatever 'leader of the orchestra'. He was indeed that in days gone by; today, as Mr. Carse says, all he leads is the first violins.

Even after the absurdity of having two conductors of a performance had been recognised—the result was often contradictory tempi—the baton-using conductor could still be a nuisance sometimes. Foot-stamping fell out of fashion; but marking time with the baton on the desk was still practised, and batons, in those robust days, were batons, not the little fairy wands of today. When one of them hit the desk everyone heard it. Some conductors, it is true, used a roll of paper or a light stick, but there were still many batons such as might have been used by Lully, who, the reader will remember, died of an abscess in the foot caused by a blow from his baton when conducting.

Spontini's baton in the 1840s was a substantial ebony cosh, with ivory knobs, which he grasped not at the end but in the middle. The great Jullien's baton seems to have been adorned with jewels; anyhow his taste and his practice can be gauged from the description of the baton presented to him by some of his admirers in 1853—nearly two feet of maple wood with chased gold ringlets, two golden serpents each with a diamond in its head, seven other diamonds here and there, and a brilliant worth sixty guineas at the end.

By the third quarter of the nineteenth century the stage was set for the entry of the present-day conductor, the 'interpreter', a respectful worm's eye view of whom I shall permit myself in a final article.

III

7th August 1949

OLD Verdi spoke more wisely than he knew when he prophesied that the prima donna of the future would be the conductor. His vast increase in importance has been the result on the one hand of the growth in the size of the concert and operatic forces he has to control, on the other hand of the predominantly subjective nature of the music of the nineteenth century. Without a conductor, endless rehearsal would be required before even the best orchestra could arrive at a unified conception of a complex modern work. By means of a conductor that slow process is short-circuited. He alone needs to know the score as a whole; it is through him that the individual parts fit into the overall pattern.

That, of course, is the ideal; if it is not always realised it is because even a good conductor may be quite unfitted by temperament, range and quality of imagination, racial or cultural background and a dozen other things from seeing a given work as its creator saw it. As I think I have expressed it before now, horses for courses is not more of a truism in the racing world than conductors for works, or even conductors for composers, is in the musical. (The truism has been comically inverted in at least one instance. Of an eminent German conductor who is idolised in some quarters it was said by a devotee some years ago not that 'X is the ideal Beethoven conductor' but that 'Beethoven is the ideal X composer'.)

Important as he undoubtedly is, however, the conductor is not quite so all-important as the average member of the audience imagines him to be. The composer is surely entitled to some credit for the total result of a good evening's work. But as it is the conductor, not the composer, who comes into direct, white-hot contact with the public, it is hardly surprising that the unsophisticated music lover, in his true thankfulness for what he has just received, should regard him, rather than the creator of the work, as the onlie begetter of it all. The conductor would be more than human if, despite his natural modesty, he did not come to share this flattering opinion of his own contribution to the feast.

Always in musical history there has come a time when the prima donna, male or female, has advanced the claim, and had it admitted by the public, that it was he, not the composer, who had the prior claim to whatever laurels might be going. We find Plutarch, for example, pointing out, in connection with Greek music, that formerly the aulos players were subject to the poet; but the corrupt taste of a later day had brought in a more ornate kind of music, in the performance of which, we may be sure, the auletes staked out his own claim to applause.

Naturally a conductor here and there, if his head is not screwed on the right way, adopts this naïve view of his own importance and does all he can, when operating in the public eye, to drive it home that if the ship's course is as good as it is, that is because he, rather than some rival steersman, is at the helm. The ideal thing would be, from the musical listener's point of view, that the conductor should be unseen by the audience, so that we got the result of his mental activities without the sometimes distracting spectacle of the physical apparatus through which they function. The sight of the machine so hard at work is apt to bulldoze an uncritical audience into believing that everything the conductor does with his baton or his body is as vital to the music as it is to him.

As early as the sixteenth century we find one Philomathes waxing sarcastic at the expense of the conductor who not merely indicates the time but works himself up into a sort of dervish frenzy in his efforts to communicate his 'reading', as we would call it today, of a piece of music; he beats the air, says our author, with both hands and arms as if he were taking part in a fight, tosses his head about, stamps his feet like a frantic horse, and so on. I should like to read the comments of Philomathes on some of the conductors of today.

Perhaps we can divide conductors into three classes corresponding to those of the dignitaries of the old Roman empire, adopting Gibbon's nomenclature for them—(1) the Illustrious, (2) the Spectabiles, or Respectables, (3) the Clarissimi, or Honourables. (There is perhaps another class, which we might call the Untouchables, close contact with whom I do my best to avoid.) Of the first of the three ranks there are about half a dozen great representatives in the world today, and no words can express our indebtedness to them. The Respectables are a more numerous class, while the Honourables are more plentiful still. All three have their value for us, providing they and we hold fast to the basic principle that it is the composer, not the conductor, who really matters; occasionally it happens that it is one of the Respectables, or even Honourables, who, conducting a great work that suits his own imaginative wave length, brings us into closer touch with the mind of the composer than even one of the Illustrious, batting on a pitch that does not suit him, can do.

As for the effects, good and bad, of the present superabundance of conductors relatively to orchestras, that is a big subject, discussion of which had better be postponed to some later day.

IV

27th June 1948

Spies of mine who read the papers and keep me posted, without a similar painful effort on my part, as to what is going on in the world, inform me that the Island Race has recently been shaken from the soles of its leaden feet to the top of its wooden head by a revival of an old controversy—Is Britain Musical? Some people, I gather, have learned with shame that an outstanding genius like Sir Thomas Beecham had to cancel a concert because only a hundred tickets had been applied for. Others exult at the glorious news that at a recent concert in the Harringay Arena—'Arena!' blessed word with its exquisite reminiscent flavour of bread and circuses!—a conductor of the age of ten drew the Albert Hall's record crowd of 10,024. 'The largest known,' says a cutting that lies before me, 'at an indoor concert in England in recent years.' By all democratic standards, then (the counting of heads, regardless of what is inside them) this boy who wore (and perhaps this is where Sir Thomas Beecham fell down) 'black velvet with a white jabot and between each item hurried with his mother to his dressing room to sip grape-fruit juice', has saved our national credit.

Whatever may be happening to music in this country just now, there is no doubt that conductors are having the time of their lives. As the wise old Verdi foresaw two generations ago would be the case, the conductor has taken the place of the old-style prima donna. In the view of the simpler-minded members of the audience it is he who does everything at a concert. A casual observer might be inclined to jump to the conclusion that the seventy or so trained musicians in the orchestra, who know most of the works in the repertory so well that they could play them in their sleep, as, indeed, they have occasionally been known to do, deserve a little of the credit. Then there is the composer. It has never been computed with mathematical precision just how much of the pleasure we experience at a performance of the 'Eroica' or 'La Mer' can be rightfully credited to Beethoven or Debussy, but there seems to be ground for the suspicion, entertained in some quarters, that the composer may have had something to do with it.

But in view of the ordinary concert-goer, and certainly in that of the non-musical journalist, it is the conductor who does everything; and I am sure there are conductors who would be prepared to go to the stake to testify to their belief in that fundamental article of faith. According to a cutting that reached me the other day, XYZ 'told me . . . that he would not be away long'—an announcement which dispels our anxious fears on that score. 'Audiences in Johannesburg and Pretoria will have an opportunity to hear him conduct works by Vaughan Williams and Benjamin Britten as well as the more familiar classics.' XYZ, the chronicler continues, has just had a rather busy week in one place or another; 'in all he estimated his week's audiences at 35,000'. HIS audiences you will respectfully observe.

Hysterical women have written to me asking indignantly why I have never exactly boiled over with enthusiasm for a certain English conductor. For their part, they have assured me, his mere stepping upon the platform is ecstasy; as they put it, he at once 'communicates his magnetism' to not only the orchestra but the audience. This notion that conducting is a matter of magnetism seems to be prevalent among the unmusical. One of the joys of my boyhood days was to go to a music-hall and see a 'hypnotist' make a victim chew soap and candles while under the supposed influence. Now, it appears, the spellbinders have forsaken the music-halls for the halls of music; by their personal magic alone they throw the fiddlers and oboists and the rest of them into a catalyptic state in which, poor earthy clods as they would be if left to themselves, they utter Delphic oracles by the direct inspiration of this Apollo of the baton or that. One of the most treasured letters in my collection is from a man who asked me if I could help him to get some conducting. He had never done anything of the sort nor, he admitted, could he read a score, 'but,' he concluded modestly, 'I am conscious of possessing magnetism'.

Naturally the public cannot be told enough about these

irresistible hypnotists, as those wise men the publicity experts know. The other day I received from one of these gentlemen a number of interesting, nay, thrilling facts about a Spanish conductor. It appears that he gave a piano recital at the age of eight. In his spare time he was a bull-fighter. (This ought to make him an ideal conductor for 'Carmen'.) At eighteen, no doubt ambitious for fresh laurels, he forsook the bull-ring and became a conductor: as will be seen, he has a preference for dangerous occupations. The ladies, however, will be most interested in the information that he is now 'idolised by millions' and 'has 1,500 letters every week from fans, mostly women'. There's magnetism if you like!

I wanted to say something about boy conductors, but that august subject deserves an article to itself.

TESTS FOR CONDUCTORS

4th July 1948

THE public in general, and the sob brothers of the non-musical Press, who always come out in force when a child does some simple thing that older people have been doing for years without finding the mental strain unbearable, evidently have the quaintest notions about conducting. The conductor, as they see him, is a combination of the hypnotist and the lion-tamer. The orchestral players, however, do not see him in that light; apart from some half-dozen really great conductors, for whom, like the rest of us, they have a profound respect, they size him up as a man doing the easiest of musical jobs and not always doing it dazzlingly well.

Witness the old story of the player who couldn't tell an inquirer who had conducted that evening's concert because he had 'forgotten to look'. Only the other day a friend of mine told me that he had asked an eminent concert soloist who had recently been amusing himself with the baton how he enjoyed conducting. 'Not at all,' he replied, 'it's too easy after playing the ——.' (I omit the name of the instrument, as that might serve to identify him.) Or witness, again, the answer of a player in the London Symphony Orchestra who was asked what he thought of the talented boy from Italy. 'He's certainly the best conductor we've had this season,' a judgement which all concerned, including the public, can take in whatever sense they choose.

What is the *raison d'être* of the conductor? A string quartet manages without one, although the right performance of, say, the Beethoven C sharp minor quartet is a far more exciting business than that of the C minor symphony, and the second quartet of Ernest Bloch much more difficult, technically and intellectually, than the 'Oberon' overture or 'L'apprenti sorcier.' The string quartet manages without a human semaphore in front of it because it is made up of first-rate artists who know every nook and cranny of the work in hand, and by long association have learned to function as an organic unity. It is only when a great increase in the number of the players weakens the inner binding principle that some sort of external clamp becomes necessary.

This part of conducting is a routine that anyone can learn who will apply himself to it, though some, of course, will be better at it than others. But conducting in the greater sense means much more than this: it means fineness of spirit, a wide musical culture that enables the possessor of it to distinguish between the mind of one composer and that of another, and between different orders of musical imagination, and an experience of life that makes him imaginatively one, with all that a great composer has felt and suffered and said in his music. It stands to reason that no child, however gifted, can possibly be a conductor in this greater sense of the term.

Conducting a few standard works which the orchestra knows by heart is a feat well within the powers of any naturally musical boy. What anyone can do by going through the business of practising it is not surely a matter for blank amazement, and the age at which we can expect a child to be able to do this or that in music is progressively falling as educational methods improve. Has the reader heard the story of old Moriz Rosenthal and the fond mother who was convinced that her boy was a pianistic wonder such as the world had never yet seen? At last Rosenthal consented to hear the prodigy, and something like the following dialogue ensued. 'So you are going to play to me?' 'Please sir, yes sir.' 'And what are you going to play?' 'Please sir, the "Tchaikovsky Concerto in B flat minor." ' 'Oh that? And how old are you?' 'Please sir, four-and-a-half sir.' 'Four-and-a-half? Too old!'

I myself will begin to be amazed at a conductor of tender age when he shows his quality not in a few standard works well known to the orchestra but in the rehearsal and first performance of a new symphony by a living composer. If he comes brilliantly through that test he can be sure of counting on me among his warmest admirers. And while we are on the subject of tests, why not arrange for one for conductors in general, that might decide whether those people are right or wrong who say that, ruling out some half-dozen really great conductors, an audience would be hard put to it to distinguish between ninety per cent of the others if it did not see them? Will one of our orchestras be a sport and give us a concert something after this fashion? Let the orchestra (invisible to us) play three times without a conductor some standard work or other, and, in between, play it under three conductors—no age or sex barred—without our seeing them or being told their names. After that, let the audience try to decide which performance was which. It ought to be good fun—if the conductors chosen will consent.

THE SINS OF CONDUCTORS

14th October 1954

I HOPE I need not assure my readers that in saying what I am going to say on the subject of conductors I have no prejudice against these gentlemen as a class, or that I am oblivious of the fact that even the worst of them may have his good moments. My attitude towards conducting resembles in its humbler way, that of a certain street orator, whose pitch I passed one evening on my way to Queen's Hall, towards the science of chemistry. What this gentleman's main theme was I do not know, but as I hurried past him I caught a sentence which has remained in my memory ever since as the ideal expression of one of the most magnanimous sentiments in the world's history. 'Mind you,' said this generous fellow, 'I've nothin' agenst chemistry.'

I, for my part, have 'nothin' agenst' conducting, I approach that blend of art and business with the splendid tolerance of one of the brightest of my Press colleagues, who, entering the dining room of a hotel after a festival concert, found there a well-known conductor with some of whose readings he had unfortunately been unable to agree in the course of his journalistic work. The conductor, humanely anxious not to make even a musical critic too acutely conscious of his own inferiority in the presence of his betters, invited my friend to sit at his table, adding graciously, in order to set the man quite at his ease, 'You know, I don't mind criticism.' 'That's all right,' the critic replied, taking the chair to which he had been motioned, 'I don't mind conducting.' It would be hard to decide to which of the two the palm of magnanimity should have been awarded.

I choose conductors, rather than musical performers in general, as the text for this article because, in the main, the latter do not call for the same liberal exercise of the spirit of forgiveness on the critic's part. It is not so much that the fiddlers, the pianists, and so on are frequently more skilled workmen in their own line. It is rather that they do not have the same opportunities to do wrong, nor are subject to the same temptations to do wrong, as the conductor. Except when they tackle one of the great sonatas, they are mostly concerned, during the hours of public business, with small-scale works that involve no particular principle of architecture; and it is in the matter of architecture that so many conductors crash.

Few of them, I am sorry to say after a lifetime's experience of the species, have any real sense of what is often the most vital factor in a great orchestral or operatic work. Ample proof of this lack on the part of some of them is to be found in the cocksure way in which they substitute their own ideas of what is fit and proper for those of the composer, who, one would have thought, is the person entitled to have both the first and the last word on all matters connected with the performance of his work.

The gravamen of my complaint against some of the people is that they will not leave the masterpieces alone, will not let the great work speak for itself. I contend that we have the right to demand of a conductor that he shall give the composer the credit of knowing just what he wanted, and that *he* shall not presume to know better; and my grievance against some of these gentry is that they are evidently unable to see the big work as its creator saw it. They are mostly too intent on decorative details, of the kind that win them the admiration of the crowd, to be able to reproduce the proportions or the informing idea of the work as the musician who has studied it knows them to be.

Elgar more than once spoke bitterly to me on this point. 'The "expression" is all there is in my music,' he would say, 'if only people would be content to play the music as it is set down in the score.' What he meant was that he himself had provided in advance, in his lay-out of the details, for every point upon which the conductor feels it necessary to lay a special emphasis of his own, with the inevitable result that he achieves only over-emphasis. The necessary shading of an Elgarian emotion is already provided for in the shape of the melody, the nature of the harmony, and the peculiar timbre of the instruments employed at that point. But the conductor, realising that here is a super-sensitive episode with which he can make an 'effect' of his own, applies his own shop recipe for effect to the playing of it, the result being that the sentiment at once slobbers over into sentimentality—a sentimentality for which Elgar is wrongly blamed.

Few composers, indeed, suffer as much in this way from their uncomprehending interpreters as Elgar does; his exquisite sensitiveness is turned into sentimentality, his high spirits into vulgarity, his *nobilmente* into theatrical bombast—all because the conductor does not know where to stop, does not see that what he is doing is to add up Elgar's plain two and two and make the answer a highly-coloured six.

But it is a vital matter of architecture that most conductors fail us in the great large-scale works, because not being architects themselves but only painters and decorators, they cannot see that all the effects of contrast and transition at which they are aiming for their own glory's sake are already there in the music. The conductors who fail us in this respect may not know it but in acting as they sometimes do they are merely guilty of bland impertinence towards a much greater mind than their own. It is surely, one would suppose, a reasonable assumption that when an architect of the very first order, such as Beethoven, has spent a year or two brooding and sweating over the proportions of a symphony, he, who knows best what the work is all about, has finally provided *in the music* itself for every point of contrast and transition, of tension and release, of contraction and expansion, of slackening and tightening, the slow drawing back of the arm and the swift delivery of the mighty blow.

But certain conductors seem to find this assumption anything but reasonable. *They* know better than Beethoven what Beethoven wanted and how it is to be achieved. And so in a passage of obvious relaxation of the tension or broadening out of the feeling, they slow the music down in order to get what *they* deem to be the right measure of contrast between what has gone before and what is to come after: they are ignorant of the fact that, as Elgar would have said, all that they are aiming at, for the sake of 'effect' on the audience is already there in the music itself, and that what they are doing is not to establish the proportions of the work but to pervert them.

Almost invariably they begin a rallentando, an accelerando, a crescendo, or a diminuendo a few bars before it is marked in the score, because they feel that, within the limits Beethoven has set them, there is insufficient scope for hitting the audience between the eyes with a stunning 'effect'. If the conductor happens to be an outsize in this type of mountebankery, he will begin, for instance, the allegro theme of the 'Leonore No. 3' in the most tenuous of pianissimi in order to make a greater 'effect' with the ensuing crescendo and fortissimo.

We have an abundance of good draftsmen, sculptors, colourists, and surface decorators among conductors, but the architects among them are rare. If some of them had a better sense of the architectonic in music they would not cut certain works as they do; it really does not follow as they innocently appear to imagine, that because a certain page in the work does not appeal to them it has therefore no *raison d'être* in the composer's far-flung design. Possessed as they are with the notion of the supreme importance of their own 'personality', they are apt to forget that we go to concerts not to listen to them but to listen to the composer.

I can see no remedy for this exasperating condition of things but a few outbreaks of ruthless violence on the part of the real musicians in the audience. The other evening a listener at one of the Promenades created a mild sensation by protesting against the omission of a crescendo in an aria by Handel. Whether he was right or wrong in this particular instance I do not know. But we certainly want more listeners who will follow a performance of, say, a Beethoven or an Elgar, or a Sibelius symphony with the score, and if I may use the profane expression in a Sunday paper, raise hell, not at the end of the performance, but there and then, at each and every departure from the composer's plain text. The audience that can permit, for example, a performance of the 'Leonore No. 3' to proceed two bars beyond the point at which the opening theme has been misrepresented in the flagrant way I have described is past praying for. What it ought to do is to stop the performance there and then and insist on a fresh start.

The ironic feature of the matter is that if any critic were to call the conductor who disorganises a masterpiece a fool, he would lay himself open to an action for libel, whereas the conductor, who has virtually called the composer a fool, by implying that he did not know how to write his own music, not only gets away with safety but becomes a popular idol!

WORKS AND PERFORMERS

23rd January 1944

I HINTED a week or two ago that the seasoned musician is becoming so critical of performances that it is difficult to drag him to a concert: he prefers, he will tell you, his knowledge of the score, his own imagination, his memories of this or that great performance in the past, to hearing one of his best-loved masterpieces reeled off by an orchestra that obviously regards the thing just as another job to be got through, under a conductor who, as likely as not, does not thrill to the work as he does. I recommend anyone who is interested in this subject to read a brilliant article by Mr. Arthur Hutchings in the October number of the *Musical Times*. Mr. Hutchings is mostly concerned with the performance of Mozart, about which he has some searching things to say. But the question is really much wider than that. First-rate Wagner or Beethoven or Berlioz or Elgar performances are just as rare as first-rate Mozart performances, though for different reasons in each case: the quality that makes a given composer's mind and art what they are is something wholly personal to him, and the methods of performance that suit one composer to the life may be completely wrong where another is concerned. To conduct Mozart as if he were Wagner or Beethoven is a sad mistake, but really no sadder than to conduct Wagner as if he were Mozart or Verdi.

Conductors in general do not always realise this: they trust too implicitly to their taste, their temperament and so on. But while taste, temperament, and, if we can get it, genius in the performer are extremely valuable, even they do not constitute everything that is sometimes required. For the right handling of the music of the seventeenth and eighteenth centuries some knowledge of the practice of the period, and the mentality underlying the practice, is essential. I am not pleading for 'antiquarianism' simply for its own sake, but for a complex of knowledge that can be wrought into the tissue of the present-day performer and listener. We have to recognise frankly that it is impossible now for us to play or sing in public much of the older music as its contemporaries played or sang it, because the world can never hear it with the ears and the minds of those contemporaries. The 'Messiah' sung as it was in Handel's day would sound comic to us. Our grandfathers, even as late as the mid-nineteenth century, found a dramatic expressiveness in coloratura the sense of which it is vain for us to try to recapture; and we have grown so used to playing Bach's clavier music literally according to the printed notes that when Dolmetsch—having shown conclusively, in his notable book, that the eighteenth century wrote down its music in one way but played it, to some extent, in another—played Bach as Bach himself would have done, it merely struck the ordinary listener as 'all wrong'.

To retrace our steps in some directions, then, purely for the sake of historical authenticity, is practically out of the question now; and I am not suggesting that concert-givers should try. But I do contend that unless the performer has some knowledge of the aesthetic of the past, of the way in which our ancestors apprehended the music of their own day, he will do many things with an old work which he should not have done, or fail to do many a thing he should.

Take, by way of simple illustration, the exquisite orchestral passage in thirds and sixths that precedes and then interweaves itself with Donna Anna's words 'Calma il tuo tormento' in the aria 'Non mi dir' in 'Don Giovanni'. Never yet, and I have heard many a performance of that opera, have I heard this music given its proper expressiveness, for the reason that neither conductors nor players have realised what it meant to Mozart and his contemporary listeners. I am far from holding that a mere book knowledge of historical aesthetic will of itself furnish anyone with the golden key to the ideal performance of the older music. If the conductor is by nature a clod, no amount of knowledge of that kind will suffice to de-clod him. He must first absorb it into himself and then subconsciously use it as material for the evocation of his own sensitivity, for the play of his own genius upon the music. But the knowledge, I maintain, is an indispensable prerequisite.

GENIUS AND THE CLASSICS

1st March 1931

I FIND that by my last week's article I have been taken to mean that I approve of the conductor—whom I propose to take as representative of executive artists in general—dealing in his own way with a work, and especially an old work, in order to give it a modern vitality in performance. On the contrary; apart from the alterations occasionally necessary in an old piece of orchestration to make it sound as the composer must have really wanted it to sound, nothing should be done with the actual notes of the work but play them as they are. The conductor's function is not to re-write the work but to re-think and re-feel it, and to make us re-think and re-feel it with him. I sympathise with the English composer who recently complained to me that a broadcast of one of his works by a certain well-known foreign pianist-composer was like anything in the world but the work itself. 'It was a pianistic achievement,' he wrote me, 'but it was not my ——. Where it was marked *p* he played *f*: he altered the value of the notes, put in all sorts of pauses and other extravagances, with the result that there was no continuity in the work. . . . He said he hoped I would not be annoyed at his interpretation, which was quite unlike my own. His excuse was that he conceived the piece as 'a highly nervous work'! and that as he had played it as such all over the Continent, and always had an enormous success with it, he thought his interpretation was justified. I told him that X's interpretation was more in accordance with my own intentions, and his answer was that X, not being a composer, could not feel the work as it ought to be felt!! Queer logic!

'Not long since,' his letter continued, 'I was asked to meet a woman pianist in Berlin who wanted to play my works to me. First of all, she treated me to a long speech in which she said that the composers themselves were quite unaware of what their works really signified, that the expression marks were usually all wrong, and so on and so forth. Then she played me my —— as *she* conceived it. I never heard such a noise in my life!' I could only give my friend my sympathy and exhort him to bear up: he should try to imagine what Mozart and Beethoven and Wagner and Berlioz and a few more of them must suffer when the ether bears to them their own music as the famous X, or the infamous Y, or the notorious Z plays or conducts it for us. The last time I heard a notorious virtuoso conduct a Beethoven symphony without a baton (it was *not* Sir Thomas Beecham, by the way), I was moved to the mournful comment that I should have enjoyed the work much more if he had conducted it without an orchestra.

The first thing the conductor has to do is modestly to admit at least the fair probability that the composer who wrote the work had some sort of notion of what it was he wanted to say and the best way of saying it. The second thing is to let the composer say it in his own way, as regards notes, time values, pauses, rallentandi, accelerandi, crescendi, diminuendi, and dynamics in general. Since these markings are, for the composer who knows his job, blood of the blood of the work that has slowly travailed its way into life within him, we must pay him the compliment of believing that the first approach to the work must be by way of a scrupulous regard for his markings. It is astonishing what light is often thrown on a work by a study of the markings alone, astonishing, we may cynically put it, how much composers know about the works they have composed.

I had a blinding light thrown on this simple but too often forgotten truth during Toscanini's performance of 'Tristan' at Bayreuth last summer. I thought I knew that work from end to end and from outside to inside; but I was amazed to find, here and there, a passage coming on me as a new revelation and going through me like a dagger stroke. What, I asked myself, has Toscanini done here? I took a mental note of the passages, and looked them up in the orchestral score when I got home. Then I found that all, or practically all, that he had done was to play the notes just as Wagner directs them to be played. Here is a case in point; the quotation is from page 42 of the Schott vocal score:

There have been three terrific orchestral volleyings of the theme of 'the sick Tristan' as the maddened Isolde tells Brangaene of her wrongs; then, as she speaks of how her impulse to revenge faded out of her when the wounded man turned his helpless eyes on her, we get the passage I have quoted.

A musical friend to whom I played the passage on the piano as nearly as I could in Toscanini's way declared that he had heard 'Tristan' fifty times, but had never noticed that passage before. Nor had I, particularly. Yet all that Toscanini did was to realise what Wagner has marked in the score! The melody is given not to the violins but to the violas; the violins are underneath these. The viola marking is *weich* (soft, smooth). The dotted contrabass notes are marked *sehr weich*. The cello part (here shown as the tenor) is marked *sehr zart* (very tenderly, delicately, sensitively). All that Toscanini did was to play the passage as Wagner conceived it: he got just the right strength and the right colour out of the violas at the top and the contrabasses at the bottom; he gave a strange significance to the cutting-off of the bass notes; and above all he gave us that curious succession of slurs following dots in the cellos as I had never heard it before. The total effect was indescribable: I shall remember it and thrill to it to my dying day; there was nothing in the whole marvellous work that surpassed it for poignancy.

Yet it goes without saying that Toscanini *must* have done something more than merely play with the right time-durations, the right nuances, and the right colour a few bars that in most performances are passed over as being of no particular significance. What, then, was that something more? I take it to have been the imagination of Toscanini piercing to the very heart of Wagner's poetic meaning in the passage, the genius of this poetic perception translating itself into a certain delicacy and intimacy of handling, and this again passing over by the sheer magnetism of genius into the players. It is in this way, not by mountebank 'readings' of this or that classic that has lost a trifle of its first blood-heat for us, that the conductor of genius must revivify or recreate it for us today.

THE PROBLEM OF INTERPRETATION

7th November 1937

THE question of conducting, of course, is only a part of the general question of interpretation; the conductor is simply a performer like the singer or the pianist or the violinist, except that he plays not upon one instrument but upon a large number simultaneously. Unfortunately the problem of interpretation, like every other problem in music, becomes more difficult the more we reflect upon it. There are few first principles in connection with it on which anything like general agreement can be found; the most we can do is to narrow the problem down to its essentials, and then grope our way as best we can among these.

The two extremes of opinion on the matter are (1) that interpretation is an affair mainly of personality on the part of the interpreter, (2) that since the composer, in most instances, can be credited with knowing best what he wanted to say and has indicated to us, in his markings, how he wishes it to be said, the one thing needed is to play the music just as it is written. But neither of these extremes 'works' by itself, in practice. What we call personality or genius in the player is as a rule only one narrow human faculty in a high state of development, and it can go completely wrong in practical music-making if it is entirely left to itself and the possessor of it has too comprehensive a belief in himself and in it.

We all know the type of performer, whether conductor, singer, or what not, who has certain formulae of style and expression which he applies as a matter of course to every kind of music. If the music happens to suit the particular composer or work of the moment, well and good; if it does not—if Wolf or Mahler is sung as if he were Schubert, or if a Wagner opera is played as if Verdi had written it—we who listen find ourselves at cross-purposes with the performer. On the other hand, a mere faithful observance of just what is written in the score gets us nowhere; without genius on the part of the performer the result can still be utterly flat and futile. But if we bring our two theoretical extremes nearer and nearer to each other we at last reach a point—a purely ideal point, no doubt—at which they meet; and that point is genius of the highest order placing itself wholly at the service of the composer, not using him as a medium through which he can exploit his own personality, but regarding himself as merely one more instrument in the composer's hands.

When we have reached this point, however, we find that even yet we have not solved our problem; as a matter of fact, it now confronts us in a more baffling form than before. The situation is very much like the one that is always presenting itself to us in criticism. The latest theory of criticism—I am referring now not only to musical criticism but to criticism in general—is that the critic, instead of performing a fantasia on his own 'reactions' to a work (writing about himself, as Anatole France said *à propos* of so-and-so), should place himself at the point of view of the author or artist when he was creating his work. The fallacy of this theory resides in the fact that even when the critic conscientiously tries to do all this, and as conscientiously believes that he is doing it, he is not really looking at the work through the creator's eyes but through his own, through a prism that lets certain rays go through quite straight while it blocks or deflects others. The history of musical criticism in particular is strewn with the corpses of critics who have perished in an attack on a fortress that is impregnable: they have worked out to their own satisfaction the most perfect system of definition of what constitutes good art, and then failed lamentably when they came to apply their principles to a particular case in hand.

Read, for instance, what Berlioz had to say about the 'music of the future'. His argument, in effect, was this—if good music means this, that and the other, then this music is bad music. Our reply to him is that we fully agree with him in his statement of what is necessary to a work of art to make it good, and completely disagree with him in his denial that these elements are to be found in the music of Wagner. Berlioz's error was that of the naïve gentleman who writes to the papers to assure us that 'every right-minded person' must feel so-and-so about such a question: he soon discovers that a number of people differ diametrically from him on the matter, yet are convinced that *their* view of it is the one that must appeal to all right-minded persons. Try as we will, then, to 'see the work as its creator saw it', we still cannot see it in any other terms but those of our own eyes, with all their individual variations of long-sight, short-sight, clear-sight, squint-sight, and so on.

So with the performer. He may honestly believe that after prolonged study of a symphony or an opera he is interpreting it just as the composer imagined it, but in this he may be deluding himself; try as he will, he is still interpreting it not wholly in terms of the work but in large part in terms of himself. Is the upshot of it all, then, that any one performance of general intelligence and technical competence is as good as any other, since there are as many conceptions of what is 'right' in music as there are music lovers? In the very last resort, perhaps, we may be driven to that funk-hole of aesthetic nihilism. In practice, however, the situation is not quite so desperate as this. Because an absolute solution of a problem that in its entirety is perhaps finally insoluble is beyond us, that is no reason why we should not seek out a relative solution that will work as reasonably well as can be expected. In the matter of interpretation that relative solution, I think, is to be sought by bringing our theoretical extremes to meet in a very narrow point of compromise. In the first place, performers in general should realise that, with exceptions so rare that they could be counted on the fingers of one hand, nature has not fitted them to perform all kinds of music equally well. This may seem a counsel of perfection, and I am far from believing that it will ever be put into practice: conductors especially are compelled, for obvious reasons, to conduct almost everybody and everything. Nevertheless no harm will be done by the kind suggestion that the bad results they so often achieve, at the expense both of works, composers and listeners, are due to the fact that the mental world of this or that composer lies so completely outside their own that they will never win access to it if they live to be a thousand. The sooner the vast majority of them realise this the better it will be for them and for all of us.

In the second place, I would suggest that performers in general, and conductors in particular, might with advantage devote more time and care to the study of the minds of the composers with whom they have most temperamental sympathy. They will no doubt tell me that study of this kind is not necessary in their case, that their feeling and the light of their genius are sufficient guides to how the music should be interpreted. I respectfully suggest to them that they are wrong. Their mere feeling can, and often does, mislead them woefully.

The most valuable work of musicology during the last thirty years or so has been in connection with the intensive study of the structure and the workings of a few great composers' minds, and with the fine distinctions, historical and aesthetic, between styles or genres. How many conductors, to say nothing of smaller performers, have even a bowing acquaintance with this vast field of research? They all conduct Beethoven, let us say, and some of them conduct him, by the pure light of genius, fairly well. But when the pure light of genius fails them, as it is so often bound to do, they come to grief. All that is implied in Beethoven's notes and markings is not to be understood by merely looking at these in the score: there are a thousand subtle little points of phrasing, of historical style, of personal style, of meaning in relation to the habits of the composer's day as well as of his own mental habit, the problems in connection with which can be perceived and solved only by intensive study. How many conductors have either the time or the inclination for this study? And if they cannot or will not address their minds to it, can they wonder that while their technical virtuosity, or their ardour of imagination, or their sensitiveness of nuance imposes itself on the simple public, the gulf between them and the scholar and the student is widening alarmingly?

Our public music-making in general, in fact, is not based on anything like the proper amount of study, and the right kind of study, on the part of performers. One remedy for our ills would be, of course, fewer concerts and recitals and better ones, and a more intensive specialisation on the part of everyone, including the listener—for, strange as it may seem, not every lover of music is qualified by nature to be a listener to every kind of music. Leaving the listener out of the question for the moment, however, I would still urge that the vast majority of musical performers would be doing more real service to the art if they would attempt less and think harder about what they do attempt. But this, I fear, is only another counsel of perfection: the acceptance of it would imply a general adoption of the view that music is primarily an art, not a business.

PART II

COMPOSERS AND THEIR WORKS

BACH: THE MIRACLE MAN OF MUSIC

I

15th September 1946

BACH is usually regarded as one of those artists who are fortunate in being hardly known to us except through their work. That, however, is not the case; the scraps of information we have about him build up into quite a substantial total, and it was a happy idea of an American scholar, Dr. Hans T. David, to collect them in a volume which includes also a sound critical study of Bach as an artist by Dr. David, and an appendix giving the solution of the riddle canons which Bach delighted in writing for his friends and colleagues.*

Dr. David rejects the portrait of Bach given us in a well-known passage of Wagner's in which he calls him 'the miracle man of music':

> 'Look then upon this head, disguised in its absurd French full-bottomed wig, this master—a wretched cantor and organist wandering from one little Thuringian village to another, hardly known even by name, dragging out his existence in miserably paid posts, remaining so unknown that it took a whole century for his works to be retrieved from oblivion; even in music finding an art form already in existence that was externally the perfect picture of its time—dry, stiff, pedantic, like a wig and pigtail portrayed in notes. And now see what a world the inconceivably great Sebastian constructed out of these elements!'

The portrait, of course, is not strictly true to the original in detail: Wagner, writing in 1865, had no clear conception of what Bach's life had really been like, while, like everyone else at that time, he was unacquainted with nineteen-twentieths of Bach's work, for the Bach-Gesellschaft edition, which started in 1851, was not completed until 1900. But Wagner was right in the essentials of his thumbnail sketch: Bach lived what today would be called a very restricted life—as Dr. David puts it, 'his whole life was spent within one small area of Germany, bounded

* *The Bach Reader*, by Hans T. David and Arthur Mendel: Dent.

on the north by Lübeck and Hamburg, on the west by Cassel, on the south by Carlsbad, and on the east by Dresden'—and he did most of his work in art forms that not merely seemed stiff and dry and pedantic to the musical world of the nineteenth century but had tended to be all that in the hands of the rank-and-file of the German practitioners of the eighteenth.

That his life must have abounded in what the modern psychiatrist would call inhibitions is tolerably clear. In a wider and richer environment than that of petty German courts and organ lofts his tremendous mental and physical energy would surely have found quite other outlets. It does one good, for instance, to read the official account of his quarrel at Arnstadt, at the age of twenty, with the student Geyersbach. The said Geyersbach and five other students, he alleged, had 'set upon him with a stick calling him to account for having made abusive remarks about him'. (It was established that he had called Geyersbach 'a nanny-goat bassoonist'.) When he denied the charge, Geyersbach replied that

> 'if he had not abused him he had once abused his bassoon, and whoever abused his things abused him; Bach was a dirty dog; and with this he had at once struck out at him. Bach, for his part, had thereupon drawn his dagger, whereupon Geyersbach had fallen into his arms, and the two of them had tumbled about until the other students had thrown themselves between them.'

The thought of the future composer of the Matthew Passion and the Art of Fugue trying to put an end to a bassoonist with a knife is one that appeals to all that is best in human nature. There was evidently good stuff in this lad if it had been given its chance; with luck he might have become a second Benvenuto Cellini. By the way, was the 'silver dagger' that figures in the list of his belongings at his death the very one that might, with a bit more luck, have parted the nanny-goat Geyersbach for ever from his dear bassoon?

The over-riding impression given us by Bach biography is one of ant-like industry in an atmosphere of German provincial stuffiness. He was perhaps barely literate: 'he sometimes wrote a German,' says Dr. David, 'that is not even grammatical, let alone reasonably clear'; his style was 'often that of a provincial choirmaster, now ineptly wordy, now sputteringly inarticulate'. The mere titles of the books he left behind him send cold shudders down one's spine. (His library seems to have been mainly theological.) Tauler's *Sermons*, Pfeiffer's *Apple of the Evangelical Eye*, Müller's *Sermons on the Injuries of Joseph*, Jauckler's *Plumb Line of Christian Teachings*, Pfeiffer's *Anti-Calvin*, Rambach's *Reflections on the Tears of Jesus*, Gerhard's *School of Piety* (five volumes), Spener's *Zeal Against Popery*, Neumeister's *Doctrine of Holy Baptism*, Klinge's *Warning Against Desertion of the Lutheran Religion*, these are just a few of the snappier titles of the theological slush that, by some mysterious alchemy or other, became sublimated into the profound religious humanism of the Passions and the Chorale Preludes.

How then did it come about that a man of so little culture managed to cover so wide a range of feeling and thinking in his music? That is a question that may be worth considering next week, in connection not only with Bach but with the musical mind in general.

II

22nd September 1946

WHEN I suggested last week that Bach was 'barely literate' I meant this to be taken in the sense that he was far from being what today we would call a lettered man. What time, indeed, could he have ever had for general culture? It has been estimated that it would take a modern copyist about seventy years to transcribe his scores. Then there were his official duties —teaching choirboys, taking rehearsals, conducting church services, and so on; to say nothing of bringing up a family as large as his was. The last twenty-seven years of his life in Leipzig must have been spent mostly in or about St. Thomas's Church and School, among the pachydermatous fauna to be expected in such places. He probably knew next to nothing of the town outside his own narrow orbit. It must have been quite a lively place; the young Goethe, who went there as a student a few years after Bach's death, described it as 'a little Paris'. But Bach's particular bit of Leipzig must have been one of the drabbest, mustiest places on earth.

Any modern composer of genius would go mad in such an environment, committed day in and day out to such a round of routine hard labour. How then did this astonishing man succeed in doing what he did? It used to be a favourite thesis of historians that the musicians of the nineteenth century had the advantage over those of the eighteenth of being much more cultured. But did they write better music than Bach, Handel, Haydn or Mozart on that account? If not, then is culture really necessary to the composer? What *is* the artistic faculty? Is it just a knack, which some people are born with and others are not, for moving the counters of art—words, sounds, lines, colours—about in a particular way? We do not expect of a great billiards player or boxer that he shall have read Kant and Aeschylus, or understand the political problems of the Balkans. We do not even expect Mr. Joseph Louis to have studied the rudiments of that science of the impact of forces upon moving masses upon the correct application of which his success depends. Indeed, were he and his like to try to get their results by reason, by 'culture', they would find themselves in the company of Mr. Belloc's nimble water-insect:

> If he ever stopped to think
> How he did it he would sink.

Here is Bach, a poor boy self-educated in music, with the minimum of culture even in his own domain, who never read a book on musical aesthetics or musical form in his life, for such things did not exist in his day, but who somehow managed, for all that, to demonstrate in his works all the architectonic possibilities of the flow and combination of any given set of musical sounds. Yet while achieving this wonder his mind was not merely working like a superlative machine; his genius for permutation and combination went hand in hand with an inexhaustible power of artistic creation of the most varied kind, each purely technical problem being solved not as it is in the books, by means of a portmanteau formula, but in terms of the particular aesthetic case in hand.

Are 'culture', then, and a capacity for other than purely musical thinking of no actual use to the composer who has the real thing in him by the grace of God? One hesitates to say that. The truth seems to be that there is no such thing as '*the* musical faculty'; there are musical faculties of various kinds. One kind is seen in a composer like Mozart, in whom it is complete, autonomous, self-nourishing, perfect from childhood. Wagner's is a musical faculty of a different kind; he writes mediocre music in his youth, and always develops slowly, because the music in him is a flowering of the whole man, the whole mind and its whole culture, so that after each accomplished stage of creation he has to wait and go through another long period of slow digestion, as it were, of all that life and books have taught him. Wagner's music without Wagner's culture, his experience of life, his capacity for reflection, would be unthinkable. Yet somehow or other a Bach or a Mozart manages to create just as rich and boundless a world of musical thought out of what seems, by comparison with the range of Wagner's intellectual processes, next to nothing. Truly, we have as yet barely the glimmer of an understanding of what 'the musical faculty' is, and how it works.

THE BARTOK QUARTETS

11th November 1945

THE performances of the six Bartok quartets at the Boosey and Hawkes concerts during the last fortnight will have given those who heard them all some insight not only into these particular works but into Bartok's mind as a whole.

The quartets are a typical cross-section of his general development during the twenty years or so of his maturity. In the first two (1908 and 1915–17) he is still, to a great extent, working along traditional lines. In the third and fourth (1927 and 1928) he has virtually cut the cable between himself and the past: sentiment—to give a convenient name to a quality of music which none of us can define but which all of us know when we see it—has almost disappeared from his field of interest, and he concentrates now on following up the logical consequences of a train of thought with the most ruthless disregard of the pleasantness or disagreeableness of the sounds he makes in the process. In the fifth (1934) and the sixth (1939), while the logic of the thinking is maintained at the old high pressure, there is a certain easing of the rigours of the texture; the actual sounds may still hurt the ear at times, but not so cruelly as in some parts of the third and fourth; while he sometimes takes us for a minute or two into a world of strange beauty, as in the adagio and the andante of the No. 5 and in some pages of the No. 6. In the final section of the latter one catches hints of a return of his mind to the 'sentiment' of Nos. 1 and 2, though of course in a subtler and more individual form.

* * *

Already in the first two quartets we see that dichotomy of his mind that puzzles most listeners. In these two remarkable works as a whole, and more especially in their long first movements, we feel, for the first time in the chamber music of the last hundred years, that the challenge to music launched in the posthumous quartets of Beethoven has been taken up, not self-consciously, of course, but out of an inner creative impulse. It is no longer 'themes' that are being 'developed' in the older formal way but a frame of mind that is being explored to its recesses, the music not being made out of preconceived thematic elements but rather precipitating these, as it were, in the course of its flow, as in the first movements of the Beethoven E flat major and C sharp minor quartets. It is true that Bartok is still, at this stage, swimming in the nineteenth century romantic sea; again and again we feel that we might be in Kareol with Tristan or in Monsalvat with Parsifal and Amfortas, though there is nowhere anything that could be called a definite Wagnerian reminiscence.

But there was another factor in Bartok's make-up—perhaps the purely Hungarian factor, with its liking for obstinately reiterative or convulsive rhythms and for angular gesture and even grimace—that was in time to edge him further and further away from the older emotional world of Western music and make him concentrate, at all costs, on quasi-geometrical problems in the working out of which the actual sounds produced become a matter of indifference to him. The beginning of this tendency can be seen in the second movement of the second quartet. After that his quartets become a fascinating and, on paper, a perfectly logical play of lines and rhythms. But it is only through the actual sounds that the ordinary listener can take it all in, and these sounds he often finds it impossible to assimilate. The notes of the score project and group themselves and go through their gyrations very much like the particles of matter in what are known to students of acoustics as Chladni figures—grains of matter on a glass or metal plate are set in motion by stroking the plate with a bow, and they group themselves into all sorts of designs. Neither to the bow nor the plate nor the laws of energy does it matter in the smallest degree whether the particles are of gold or of grit; the figures and the dance are the thing, the unfolding of natural law.

That, at any rate, is how I myself feel when I alternately read and listen to the Bartok quartets of the middle period. Merely to watch, in the score, how the tonal particles behave on the plate in obedience to the vibrational energy let loose in them under the strokes of the master demonstrator's bow is fascinating; but when the figures are taken out of the field of the abstract and converted into actual sound the physical ear cannot do otherwise, it seems to me, than pronounce some of the effects repulsively ugly. Will the ear of the musical world in general ever accommodate itself to such sounds to the extent of finding them beautiful? Will it ever accept them as the lawfully begotten heirs of the harmony we have hitherto known? That remains to be seen. We must leave it to the future to decide whether Bartok's discords are only a new and higher form of concord, his ear being a couple of generations in advance of that of his time, or whether he was a visionary and solitary so preoccupied at times in pursuing a tonal abstraction to its logical theoretical end that he forgot that for the rest of us music has a physical as well as a geometrical side to it.

BELLINI AND 'NORMA'

2nd June 1929

There is one fatal flaw common to the many admirable books that in recent years have taught us How To Listen To Music; they do not teach us how to listen to music. Or rather they teach us how to listen to music in general but not to music in particular, to music in the abstract rather than in the concrete. Strictly speaking there is no such thing as 'music', in the sense of an art that is the same in all ages and for all ages, the rules of which and the laws of taste in which are agreed upon and can be formulated, and to which every listener, by learning the rules and the laws, has the same avenue and the same chance of approach. There is no such thing as 'music' in this sense; there are only composers, periods, styles, and genres, no two of whom or of which are alike; to no two of them do the same rules apply, to no two of them is the same method of approach possible. We realise this as soon as we are confronted with a genre the once-valid conventions of which have passed out of current use.

It soon became evident at last Tuesday's revival of 'Norma' that there were few people in the audience capable of listening to the work in the proper way. It begins well enough, with a short choral and orchestral prelude that adequately sets the general tone of the work and transports us into an atmosphere that, with a slight effort of the imagination, we can accept as Druidic; but as soon as the vacuous melody of 'Ite sul colle, o Druidi' came bouncing towards us a patronising smile ran round the house; this, everyone realised, was not the kind of strain one could associate with any Druids, even those of Italian opera. Everyone was convinced that he was in for an evening in which the melancholy and slightly ridiculous ghosts of music would walk for few hours. Those who felt they could stand the spectacle and derive a certain amount of amusement from it lingered on and hoped for the best; others, outraged to the very depths of their soul at the discovery that Bellini was not Wagner, fled at the end of the first or the second act.

But most of those who endured to the end had a curious experience; they discovered that there was really something in this old work after all besides the superb Miss Ponselle. They found a steady crescendo of dramatic interest to the final note. The suspicion arose in them that, old-fashioned as the idiom is, the composer knew his job; and they began to understand how it is that 'Norma' has kept the stage for a hundred years, and why many of the greatest of operatic singers during all that time have found the fullest scope for their art in it; Lilli Lehmann, for instance, who had sung almost every operatic part there was to sing, from the great Wagner and Gluck and Mozart and Verdi and Beethoven parts to those of Meyerbeer, Rossini, Donizetti, Auber, Offenbach, and a score of other composers, declared that 'Norma was ten times as exacting as Fidelio'. Norma is, indeed, one of the great figures of opera. But she would not have continued to be that for a century unless there were something more 'to it' than the drama alone; there must be something in the music also.

To listen in the right way to a work of this kind we have to do what the handbooks on How to Listen to Music never teach us to do—see the matter as the people saw it for whom this species of opera was not an old-fashioned thing to be condescended to but the most vital of contemporary forms. It is a fair assumption that our grandfathers were no bigger fools than we are, and that if they became particularly enthusiastic over a work there must have been something in it. Their conventions may seem ridiculous, indeed impossible, to us; but it is the fate of all opera to become a medley of outworn conventions to later generations, and those of the twentieth century will one day be as old-fashioned as those of Rameau, of Mozart, or of Meyerbeer. What we have to try to do is to pierce through the mould of convention that has slowly settled upon the operatic works of the past and get at the principle of life that was manifestly so strong within them in their own day. And we can do this, to some extent, by submitting ourselves to a special discipline before we judge these old works. We must purge our minds for a week or two, as well as we can, of the music that has been written since the epoch when the work was written, and try to listen to it with ears contemporary with itself.

When we have done that, it is surprising what a different aspect the work assumes, and how many good things one perceives in it that one had not suspected before. One acquires, as it were, a new sense of tactile values. One becomes like the shepherd whose eye can distinguish all kinds of differences between the faces of a flock, though to the townsman all the sheep seem alike. When one submits oneself to this discipline in the case of the older Italian opera one begins to sense what it was in this work or that that gave it its superior value in the eyes of its contemporaries. In the case of 'Norma', for instance, it becomes clear that, contrary to the current belief of today, Bellini had, for his time, a first-rate dramatic sense; and it must have been this that gave him his hold on his own epoch. We are accustomed to think of him as a saccharine and flaccid melodist and a poor musician; and it is true that few of his arias have much body in them today ('Casta diva' has a vigour and a variety that are very rare with him), that his harmonic range is restricted to a few of the more conventional chords, and that he was almost innocent of training in the ordinary technique of composition.

But to listen to him today with ears for the really vital things in him is to sweep the cavatinas aside as relatively negligible and concentrate on the lively dramatic imagination and the sense of the stage shown in a hundred passing little subtleties in the score. That he never lost sight of the stage even in the midst of his abandonment to his most sugary lyrical vein could be demonstrated from scores of passages in his works; always he manages to strike in at the right moment with an effect that is simple enough in itself, but invariably telling in virtue of its aptness and, above all, its perfect timing. In 'Romeo and Juliet', for example, the smooth conventional flow of the colloquy between Romeo, Tybald, Capulet, and the others is suddenly broken by a thrice-reiterated cry of 'Guerra' that must have made the audiences of Bellini's day jump out of their seats, so trenchant and unexpected is it, so perfectly calculated are the placing and the timing of it. It would be easy to cite similar examples by the score—effects that, to audiences that knew nothing of the shattering effects of later nineteenth century operatic music, must have been thoroughly startling.

Our modern ears, again, that have been brutalised by the more highly coloured music of later times, are insensitive, without a special training, to the finer shades of such music as this of Bellini's. We can re-develop this sensitiveness only by study and practice. Precisely because these old composers had so limited a range of effect to work in, they had to discriminate most delicately between adjacent tints of effect, tints so close to each other that the careless modern eye runs them all into one. I have been struck by the variety of forms and colours given by Bellini to what, to the casual eye, seems to be mainly the one monotonous accompaniment figure. He generally has something up his sleeve even here for the exceptional moment. An excellent instance is the curious sad sweetness of the chords —left floating in the upper air, as it were, after the pizzicato basses have faintly indicated the fundamental note—in the duet between Norma and Pollio ('Qual cor tradisti') near the end of the opera.

Verdi must surely have had a lingering memory of the musical atmosphere of this episode when he was writing the final scene of 'Aida', in which, as in 'Norma', two lovers who have blundered in life exult in the transcendentalism of death. A few pages later in 'Norma' comes still another variant upon the regular Italian-opera formula of accompaniment—a persistent, sobbing triplet figure in the violins, punctuated at the commencement of each bar with a single mournful note in the horns.

I have come to believe that the secret of Bellini's success in his own day was not his lyricism, which is generally commonplace, but his remarkable sense of the dramatic situation of the moment, revealing itself in all sorts of subtle touches that we have to train our modern ears to perceive. And it was in dramatic insight and dramatic technique, not in his cavatinas, that he developed as he grew older. In 'La Sonnambula' he turned even his little weaknesses to profit—his cuddling, snuggling thirds and sixths, for instance, are here the very thing for the homely characters and the situations—while in 'I Puritani' we see him reaching out towards a new technique in the concerted pieces. But throughout his work we are somewhere or other certain to come across some evidence of that sure control of all the dramatic elements of the scene, that steady leading up to the culminating point, that makes the final quarter-of-an-hour of 'Norma' so impressive. There was more talent in this young man than the modern world suspects. Let us not forget that he was only thirty when 'La Sonnambula' and 'Norma' were written, and that he was dead before he was thirty-four.

THE BLOCH QUINTET

9th October 1938

It is just about fifteen years since the Bloch piano quintet had its first performance in New York; but though no other piece of chamber music produced in any country during that period can be placed in the same class with it, it is still hardly known at all in this country. Yet it surely only requires a little 'plugging' on the part of our chamber music organisations to become popular. It has everything in its favour: the ear soon becomes habituated to its audacities, it is at the furthest imaginable remove from the dry abstractions which the musical public has shown so plainly it will not have at any price, it combines the maximum of passionate expression with the maximum of logical construction, and above all, while the vocabulary and the idiom of the work are 'modern', there is no cutting of the cables linking us with the language of the past.

Musical progress—by which I mean merely the occupying of new territory, the question of the relative values of the products of the old territory and of the new not coming up for consideration—has practically always been associated with, and therefore, presumably, dependent on the creation of new instruments or the discovery of new uses to which the old ones can be put. This was most obviously the case with the improvement of instruments of the viol type in the seventeenth century and with the displacement of the harpsichord by the piano in the late eighteenth: a combined change and extension of the sound-medium led to a vast change and extension of musical thinking. The double-keyboard piano will perhaps effect something of the same kind for piano music when two or three composers of genius—the Chopins, Schumanns and Liszts of the next generation—become aware of its enormous possibilities. I think I have already put forward in this column the proposition that the one real development of modern times, that of orchestral music, has been made possible because the orchestra, considered as a unity, has been an instrument capable of almost indefinite evolution. It is not that many new instruments have been added to it since Mozart's time, but simply that possibilities have been discovered in the old ones of which our fathers never dreamed. And Bloch has shown us, in this quintet of his, that four string instruments can be used in quite new ways.

Take, for instance, his liberal employment of the curious sounds obtained by bowing close to the bridge. It seems only the other day that the most authoritative treatises on orchestration were assuring us that the sul ponticello tones were not much more than a sort of freak effect used, it is true, once or twice by a great composer, but in very gingerly style, the said tones being 'painfully glassy and unpleasant', a 'not very pleasant sort of core of sound' being 'covered up by a thick layer of "scrape" ' and so on. It is evident enough now that the older composers made so little use of these sounds because they did not quite know how to use them for purposes of genuine composition: they were just 'effects', and rather suspicious effects at that, to be employed occasionally to suggest a certain strange atmosphere obtainable in no other way—as in the celebrated passage in the second act of 'Tristan'—but not as forming a constituent, organic part of the idea of a work.

But it is in this latter capacity that Bloch uses the ponticello tones in the quintet. They are not simply 'effects' designed to play upon the nerves through the ear, but, wherever they occur, the irreplaceable carriers at these points of the emotional and intellectual bloodstream of the music. Substitute anything else for them and you have not merely deprived yourself of an 'effect'; you have weakened the whole movement in which they occur. What Bloch has to say with these tones, both in and by themselves and in conjunction with other string timbres, is something that could not have been said in any other way whatever.

By means of them and of quarter-tones he has extended the range of nervous expression in music. The language of music is not purely artificial, as some people maintain. It is to a large extent the most natural of all languages; that is to say, there is a good deal in our melodic and harmonic procedure that is only a sophistication of the most primitive, even animal, ways of expressing strong emotion by means of a moan, a cry as the releaser of tension, and so on. It would be easy to illustrate this point by a series of gramophone examples, starting, say, with the simplest moan, and proceeding step by step down the ages through one melodic and harmonic intensification after another, down to the most heartrending passages in Wagner, Tchaikovsky, Mahler, Wolf and a dozen other moderns. Bloch, by his extraordinary use of ponticello sounds, harmonics, and so on, has extended still further the range of this kind of expression. He has done so, again, with his quarter-tones in the quintet. If music were perfectly free to move on to the next logical stage of its evolution, it is obvious that the emotional finesses reached at one time or another in its history by the subtler and subtler exploitation of semitones would now be carried on into the still subtler medium of quarter-tones. But unfortunately music is not free to do the simply logical thing just when reason tells it that the time has come to do it.

If we could imagine musical thought being passed on from the brain of the creator to that of the receiver by no other medium than some kind of spiritual wave, we should by this time have been well on the way towards quarter-tone music. But unfortunately the sound-symbols in which a composer's thought is notated can reach the receiving mind only through the physical medium of instruments; and the time comes when, like other middlemen, the middleman-instrument is as much a hindrance as a help. Not only are most of our instruments—and especially the domestic instrument, the piano—now fixed in their structure, with immense commercial interests vitally concerned in maintaining that structure, but the daily dependence on these instruments has netted humanity in certain tonal prepossessions from which it will find it hard to escape. It is difficult enough for the plain Western man even to *hear* quarter-tones, so coarsened has his ear become by having for so long accepted the semitone as the smallest division of sound to which he need address his perceptions: a musical *language* of quarter-tones, with its new vocabulary and its new grammar, could such a thing be created now, would be utterly beyond his capacity to follow, and is likely to be so for a very long time to come.

Bloch, in the quintet, makes no attempt to construct a complete quarter-tone language; he only uses quarter-tones here and there to put a finer edge on a sensation than the too customary semitone could do today. But that these quarter-tones, like his other string 'effects', are not merely something arbitrarily foisted upon the surface of the music but an organic part of the musical thinking, anyone can convince himself by the simple process of substituting, either in his imagination or actually on an instrument, the relative semitones for Bloch's quarter-tones. He will find that in so doing he has not merely made the music *sound* differently, in the purely physical sense, but made it think differently.

To the out-and-out quarter-tonists, of course, this way of introducing the new interval is only a regrettable and unfruitful compromise: quarter-tone music, they hold, should be complete in itself, homogeneous; the quarter-tone as just a slice off the half-tone, inflecting here and there the line of a single instrument while the supporting harmony is obviously of the traditional kind, is not the real thing. Of course it is not, in the abstract. But in the concrete it justifies itself for the time being: it gives a finer point to our sensation, while not attempting to decoy us into realms of harmonic hypothesis in which we would soon be lost. It is only a timid feeler put out into the dark unknown; but does any sensible person contend that in the dark unknown we ought to move any further than we can feel? Nor is it only in this matter of the sound-material of the musical language that Bloch moves so cautiously in his quintet. He is equally conservative in his use of consonance as a factor in the design of a work that to the ordinary listener may seem, at first, mostly dissonance. The discussion of this subject, however, will necessitate another article.

BRAHMS AND THE SERPENT

I

6th July 1941

I SEEM to have read somewhere lately, though I cannot recall where, that some publisher or other has brought out an English edition of the Four Piano Pieces constituting Brahms's op. 119. It is a pity that we so seldom hear at recitals any of these miniatures of Brahms's middle and final periods, for all in all they are the most flawless of his instrumental works, their conciseness enabling him to dispense with the padding with which he has occasionally to stuff out his larger structures. I would like to see an English edition in one volume of the five sets of small piano pieces ranging from op. 76 to op. 119; for it is in some of these that the composer throws his spear furthest into the future.

Why they are so neglected by recitalists I do not know. One reason may be that there are so many women pianists and young pianists about; and, speaking generally, Brahms at his most mature is not the stuff for women of any age or for the young of either sex. They may 'like' him, but few of them understand him; there is something in the music of the final Brahms, as there is in the poetry of the final Hardy, which opens out horizons to those who have passed middle age that are hidden from the view of those who are so unfortunate as not yet to have reached that dividing line. There is little, of course, in most of these pieces—nothing at all in some of them—to attract the pianist whose prime purpose is to make it clear to his audience that he has a technique; which may be one of his reasons for neglecting them. They call for intellectual qualities which few even of the 'star' pianists possess: out of a hundred specimens of this superabundant fauna picked up by a drag net any afternoon in Piccadilly or on Broadway who could dazzle us in a Liszt rhapsody or the more difficult of the Chopin studies, it might be hard to find a single one who could play the simple, easy little B minor Intermezzo of op. 119 as it should be played.

But these miniatures have an even deeper interest than the emotional or philosophical. They show Brahms getting really to grips with that problem of unbroken continuity of tissue which too often baffled him in his bigger instrumental works. The creative musical imagination at its best, its most logical, should work as Coleridge described Shakespeare's imagination working: he 'goes on creating', says Coleridge, 'and evolving B out of A, and C out of B, and so on, just as a serpent moves, which makes a fulcrum of its own body, and seems for ever twisting and untwisting its own strength'. That, perhaps, will be the ideal of the instrumental music of the future; the way to it, indeed, seems at last to be opening out before modern composers in proportion as they discard the last tiresome vestiges of sonata form. This, from being what it was originally, the natural mode of expression of a certain eighteenth century way of thinking in music, became in the nineteenth century a drag upon both individual thinking and the free unfolding of the inner vital force of an idea, and is now simply a shop device by which a bad composer may persuade himself and the innocent reader of textbooks that he is a good one.

The kind of composition so admirably described by Coleridge is an entirely different thing from the so-called 'development' of sonata form, and infinitely more difficult—so difficult, indeed, that the greatest masters have very rarely achieved it, and then only for a few minutes at a time. An ideal example of it is the C major Capriccio of Brahms's op. 76 (No. 8). This plays for some two and a half minutes, which seems to be about as long as the most gifted nineteenth century composer could continue on this principle of the serpent and his own fulcrum. As the student may like to look into the matter further for himself, with a few concrete examples to refer to, I will enlarge upon it next week.

II

13th July 1941

I SAID in my last article that it was in some of the piano miniatures of his middle and last period that Brahms threw his spear furthest into the future. Were the history of an art, as some people suppose, a record of continuous progress, the instrumental music of the nineteenth century would have gone straight on from the final Beethoven to the conquest of fresh territories. What happened was that instrumental composers, finding it impossible to continue the advance along that line, because, for one thing, their brains were not of the calibre of Beethoven's, went back to an earlier phase of his genius which he himself had outgrown, and made that a starting-point for safe excursions of their own. For all the effect they had on the instrumental practice of the nineteenth century the masterpieces of Beethoven's last years might almost as well have never been written.

It ought to have been evident to the self-styled 'classicists', at least, that if Beethoven himself could not carry any further his own older type of structure it was hardly likely that they would be able to do so. In certain sections of the quartets and the piano sonatas of his last period Beethoven was manifestly feeling his way towards a quite new method of musical weaving. We can only smile now at the despairing attempts of the puzzled theorists to analyse some of these movements of his in terms of what they call 'condensed' sonata form. The very essence, the very significance of them for us today is that they foreshadow a new principle of the unfolding of all the latent possibilities of a musical idea, the principle, as Coleridge expressed it, of the serpent and his own fulcrum. The traces of sonata form found here and there in the sections to which I am referring are no more than temporary retreats on the great artist's part; when even his titanic strength failed him for a moment in his attack on a problem so new as this, he 'stalled', as a modern sportsman would say—he fell back on a safe routine to get breath for a fresh assault on new lines.

The type of weaving which I am trying to describe is something quite different from that of sonata form even at its finest. Coleridge speaks, in connection with Shakespeare's peculiar art, of the ceaseless coiling and uncoiling from within the organism that produces B out of A and C out of B. This is an entirely different thing from the virtual *compulsion* upon a composer, in sonata 'development', to say a particular, forecastable B after he has said a particular A. The first hundred bars or so of the Beethoven No. 5 are a perfect example of this species of musical logic: we can not only see just how the thing is done but we can even do it ourselves in many another connection—so far, of course, as mere externals are concerned! But a composition like the Capriccio of Brahms's op. 76 (No. 8) is something wholly different. Here everything that happens to the idea is unforeseen and unforeseeable, a secret possessed only by the composer, and one that is valid only for that particular idea. The texture woven is so beautifully, flawlessly one that at no point could we insert a knife-edge between one phrase and another. Were we to cut the organism it would bleed.

This is the hardest thing of all to achieve in music, which is the reason why so far it has been done so seldom and on so tiny a scale. There are fleeting hints of it in Haydn, and longish stretches of it in the final Beethoven. Then it virtually disappeared until an intuition of it came to Brahms; and the difficulty of it cannot be better demonstrated than by the fact that after the superb C major Capriccio of op. 76, which dates from 1879, it practically disappears from his work until we reach the next set of miniatures in 1892–93.

BRAHMS AND WOLF

18th August 1940

'HE can't jubilate,' was Hugo Wolf's rather peevish complaint about Brahms. Recalling this, I wondered last Wednesday what Wolf would have had to say about the Alto Rhapsody had it been his duty to 'cover' the Promenade concert of that evening for the Vienna 'Salonblatt'. Having discovered that he had actually written about the work on 11th April 1886, I was astonished to find him declaring it to be one of Brahms's best—astonished not only because very little that Brahms had written up to then (he died, by the way, in 1897) had commended itself to Wolf, but because there is certainly none of the 'jubilation' in it the lack of which in Brahms's music as a whole Wolf found so repellent. He even went so far as to suggest that the Rhapsody was hardly the sort of thing the Vienna Brahmsians expected from their idol, for it came nowhere near 'the freezing point of imagination and sensibility' reached in 'the latest works of this industrious composer'.

Much of Wolf's fury against Brahms, one suspects now, came not so much from temperamental alienation from a good deal of his music—though there was something, of course, of this—as from exasperation with the more stupid of the official Brahmins, from Hanslick downwards. Not only did these people claim too much for Brahms, but sometimes they claimed the wrong things for him. It was a mistake for the Brahmins to proclaim that Brahms was 'the heir of Beethoven', the divinely appointed warden of 'the great classical tradition', and so on. The musical world of today sees clearly that Brahms had the minimum of affiliation with Beethoven, either as thinker or as craftsman. Nowhere in any of his works has Brahms the smallest point of contact with the far-reaching developments which the giant mind of Beethoven fought so frantically, if not always quite successfully, to compass during the last few years of his life. And the ultimate verdict of history upon Brahms may possibly be that in spite of the heroic efforts he made from time to time to achieve organic symphonic structure on a large scale

—efforts sometimes decidedly successful for long stretches, at others too obviously eked out with mere academic makeshift and padding—he was essentially a miniaturist. It was this quality that made him the incomparable master of the variation. To this quality, again, we owe not only dozens of lovely songs and small-scale piano pieces of his, but also many of the finest episodes in the larger works, such as the exquisite coda to the first movement of the second symphony, which amply compensates us for so much that is the merest class room mechanics in the 'symphonic' manipulation of that movement as a whole.

Wolf's revolt, again, was in large part against the foolish attempts of the temple Brahmins to make of their idol not merely a great composer but a solemn high priest of art. Hanslick, for instance, stressed admiringly his 'austerity'—as if 'austerity' in itself were a virtue in art, irrespective of what was being said with the corners of the mouth turned so austerely down! Actually what gives Brahms his strong hold on music lovers today is not the restraint and aloofness for which the sillier of his contemporary German and English partisans commended him but the grateful warmth and approachability of his humanism. There were times, it is true, when, lending too credulous an ear to that Brahms clique of which he himself was never really a member, he tried too obviously to live up to the role of seer and prophet for which he had been cast by the anti-Wagnerians and anti-Lisztians; and when he does that he can be woefully empty and exceedingly tiresome. But when he is content to be just what nature made him—an artist responsive to a few simple but profound and universal emotions for the perfect expression of which his technique as a miniaturist was extraordinarily adapted—he touches us in a way peculiarly his own.

His case is probably unique in music in that he says very much the same things in his last works as in his first, the only difference being the greater *approfondissement* of the expression in the later ones and the more consummate art in the weaving of the texture through which that expression is made manifest. He was truly a philosopher, if on a somewhat limited scale, by far the best of his philosophising being an emanation from the pensive melancholy that was the basis of his spiritual being. Moving works like the 'Alto Rhapsody' (1870), the 'Song of Destiny' (1871), and the 'Nänie' (1881) show us this fundamental strain of his moral and artistic nature in the middle period of its evolution. For the final and perfect expression of it we have to go to some of the exquisite pianoforte miniatures of his last years, such as the A major Intermezzo of op. 118 (1893), or, best of all, perhaps the B minor Intermezzo of op. 119 (also 1893). But things like this were so authentically the voice not of Johannes Brahms alone but of all that was best in the soul of Germany in that epoch, that here and there in them it is almost impossible today to distinguish that voice from the voice of the later Wagner or from that of Wolf himself.

BRUCKNER

24th November 1929

A DISTINGUISHED dramatic critic, in a letter from which I quoted in one of my recent articles, referred to 'those colossal bores, Bruckner and Mahler'. In a month or so the London public will have an opportunity to hear Mahler's 'Lied von der Erde'; and if the audience on that occasion declares the composer of that moving work to be a colossal bore I shall give up musical criticism. Later in the season we shall hear his eighth symphony; it is certainly colossal, but whether our public will find it boring or not remains to be seen. Bruckner is virtually unknown to the present London musical generation, so that it was a bold venture on the part of Herr Klemperer to plunge it at once into one of the longest of the Bruckner symphonies—the eighth, which plays for about seventy minutes. I can well believe that a great many people were rather tired at the end of it, but the state of mind of the few with whom I have been able to talk after the concert could hardly be described as boredom.

It has to be admitted that, outside certain circles in Austria and Germany, Bruckner's music still makes little headway. But there is a substantial German literature dealing with him, and his admirers have always included among them many people whose taste and judgement we must respect. Wagner may be presumed to have known something about music. He had nothing at all of Liszt's oily complaisancy in the matter of other men's work; there was little of it that appealed to him, and he often carried frankness with regard to it to the point of rudeness. He declined to accept the dedication of a Bruckner symphony until he had satisfied himself that the work was deserving of that honour; he studied the manuscripts of the third and the fourth, and then enthusiastically accepted the dedication of the former. The critical Hugo Wolf was a strong Brucknerian, though he was not blind to the man's faults; and since his day there have been too many good musicians on the side of Bruckner to permit of our rubbing him off the slate with a single contemptuous gesture.

One of the reasons for the failure of Bruckner to establish himself in our concert-rooms is the sad fact that he is a composer with a unique faculty for tailing-off. Few of his movements are quite as good at the end as they promised to be at the start, and the finale of each of his symphonies is the weakest section of it. The public does not as yet know him well enough to be able to exercise the same charity towards him as it does towards other composers who also have a tendency to strain its endurance now and then. If Wagner or Beethoven or Bach or Brahms or Strauss strikes a dull patch, we set our teeth and wait till he is through with it, knowing that before long something will come to more than compensate us for our suffering. But as yet the plain man does not know his Bruckner well enough for that; and in any case there is the unfortunate fact to which I have just referred, that it is generally in the last quarter of an hour or so that Bruckner deflates our enthusiasm.

But there is so much fine stuff in his work that it is worth while making an effort to establish him in the repertory. I would suggest beginning either with the third symphony (the 'Tragic') or the fourth (the 'Romantic'), each of which has the maximum of Bruckner's virtues and the minimum of his defects; or even—though the idea may horrify some people—giving now and then an isolated movement at a concert. It would be impossible, I am sure, for the average music-lover to hear the opening movement of the third or that of the fourth symphony, or the Scherzi of the fourth and the eighth, or the impressive adagio of the seventh (written in foreboding of the death of Bruckner's adored Wagner), without realising that here is a composer who, with all his faults, is deserving of more serious attention than has yet been given him in this country.

His faults are so obvious in themselves and so faithfully reproduced in one work after another that it takes only a little time to familiarise ourselves with them and to turn a tolerant ear on them. Bruckner the musician was as naïve as Bruckner the man. His mental world was not a very wide one, yet he seems to have been constitutionally incapable of exercising within it that self-criticism that is even more essential to the naïve artist than to the subtle and complex artist, for the reason that in the former case there is bound to be less of that element of surprise that in the other cases will suddenly take us out of ourselves and make us oblivious of patches of routine dullness.

We need not dwell on the more obvious mannerisms of Bruckner's music, such as his liking for phrases (especially in his second subjects) made up of two crotchets followed by a group of three crotchets with the value of two. As I have recently remarked, every composer, great or small, is in the depths of his subconsciousness a machine functioning blindly according to rule and expressing himself in persistently recurrent formulæ. A formula such as this of Bruckner's merely arouses general comment because there is no missing it by the most casual listener; but there is no composer whatever without his formulæ. The difference between a composer like Beethoven or Wagner or Chopin or Strauss and one like Bruckner is not that the latter is the slave of mannerisms while the former is free of them, but that a Beethoven, while unconsciously employing the same basic formula again and again for what is basically the same mood, will give it each time so new a turn that the average listener never suspects the presence of a formula, whereas a Bruckner uses the formula time after time in terms so little different from each other that it is instantly recognised and labelled as a mannerism.

The question is not whether a composer is a machine or not —for all composers are that over a considerable area of their minds—but the extent to which the machine can be made to present varying aspects of thought. It is here that a Beethoven shows his range and a Bruckner his limitations. A few simple ideas and antitheses sufficed Bruckner from first to last. Dr. Alfred Einstein, in his admirable article in the new *Grove*, tells us that 'above all else, Bruckner's symphonic idea is pure music, quite untouched by the poetic or "programme" influences of his time'. On the other hand, Dr. Ernst Decsey, in his notes for last Wednesday's concert, expounds the eighth symphony in terms of a programme. Both are right, and both wrong. Bruckner may not have worked to a consciously formulated programme, but undoubtedly all his music was controlled by a simple sequence of ideas that can be roughly paraphrased along some such lines as those adopted by Dr. Decsey.

The German commentators who sum Bruckner's music up as

being in about equal parts the expression of Nature and of God have got as near the root of the matter as anyone can hope to do in words. The basis of this music is a certain racial or ancestral mentality that is nourished by a strong feeling for nature and an equally strong sense of the conventional relations between God and man, or between man and the world. Always we come upon the same impression of struggle, defeat, victory, of difficulty and doubt ended by religious consolation or philosophical illumination. Almost always there is the same leaning towards the chorale or the flashing fanfare at certain points in the structure of the first movement, the same simple joy, as it were, in the indulgence of the hunting or the dancing instinct in the scherzo.

Where Bruckner misses real greatness, in spite of the beauty and the high-mindedness of so many of his pages, is in his structure. He generally plans on a bigger scale than his naïve genius will allow him to carry out. Sometimes he throws up pillars as huge and as widely spaced as those of Beethoven on the first movement of the Ninth; but he can neither plan the consistent filling of the spaces between nor bring to them material strong enough to stand the strain. His sequences, his repetitions, his pauses, his rhetorical gestures, his sudden bursts of energy, no doubt corresponded to something more or less definitely programmatic at the back of his mind. But whatever the basic non-musical idea may have been, it has not been fully transformed into the substance of music before being committed to paper, and so, instead of growing organically from point to point *qua* music, conveying its own logic to the musical consciousness of the listener, it merely uses music as best it can to do its work for it. It is this frequent failure to make the musical tissue coherent and consistent in itself that baffles and tires the hearer in a long Bruckner movement, as in the far-flung first movement of the fifth symphony, for example. But the case against him in this respect must not be pressed too harshly. When all his failures have been written off, there remains enough good music to justify more frequent performance of his symphonies than they receive at present.

BUSONI AND THE OPERA

I

7th March 1937

In view of the concert performance of Busoni's opera 'Doktor Faust' by the B.B.C. on the 17th of this month, some preliminary remarks on that work, and on Busoni's attitude towards opera in general, may be of interest to those of my readers who intend to listen-in that evening.

Busoni died in July, 1924, so that his brochure of 1926 on the possibilities of opera ('Über die Möglichkeiten der Oper und über die Partitur des "Doktor Faust" ') is a posthumous publication. One gathers that it was written, or at any rate drafted, in whole or in part, some four or five years earlier. There was a good deal of discussion of the problem of opera going on in Germany about that time: in 1925 Ernst Krenek published an interesting essay on the subject, while in the following year the late Hermann Abert, the leading European authority on Mozart, brought out a suggestive brochure entitled 'Grundprobleme der Operngeschichte'. The opera question, in fact, was once more in the air, as indeed it has been now, intermittently, for over three hundred years.

I am not sure, for a reason that will be given later in this article, that all our talk about the problem of opera gets us very much nearer to a solution of it: but a problem of opera there always has been and always will be. I think I have already, in some article or other, put forward the thesis that opera is the most vital of all musical genres, because it confronts practitioners and listeners with ever new problems. This is because of the number of its constitutive elements and of their possible permutations and combinations. It is compounded of vocal music, orchestral music, words, dramatic motives, dramatic action, scenery and miming: and not only are these prime factors capable of various mixtures at any one period but each of them varies, both in itself and in relation to the others, from generation to generation. What we may call the problem of opera, then—the best way of making these factors co-operate—

will never be finally solved; for the factors themselves are perpetually changing. Each artistic epoch in turn despises, or is patronisingly tolerant of, the opera form of its predecessors, and more especially of its immediate predecessor; and the mocker soon becomes, in its turn, the mocked. New ideals spring up with new culture-conditions; each epoch fondly believes that it, at last, has solved the problem for good; and each supposedly final solution proves, in time, to have been only a temporary solution.

Progress in art is possible only by any given epoch concentrating on one or two factors at the expense of the others. In this way a disequilibrium is in time produced; and then the instincts both of the creative artists and of thoughtful spectators lead them to concentrate on some other factor. This in turn becomes, in consequence, relatively over-developed; then an attempt at a new equilibrium becomes necessary; and so *ad infinitum.* The first essays in opera aimed at dramatic continuity without what we of today would call an organic form. When the sense of form asserted itself the musical units in opera became stylised, and in the end mechanical and tyrannic. These stylised forms were then found to be something of a hindrance to the naturalistic element in drama; and to give this freer play the forms were deprived of some of their old excess of authority.

In the last great historical development—the Wagnerian music drama—we find ourselves at the furthest end of the swing of the pendulum from, say, the Handelian opera. This latter was static, formal, stylised, both dramatically and musically; Wagner's aim was to make opera dynamic, which he did by giving the drama more rights, or at any rate new rights, and by making the music continuous from the beginning to the end of each act. But we now see that the Wagnerian form is not necessarily law-giving for all time; it was in part the product of the impact of a number of historical forces upon each other in a particular epoch, in part the personal expression of a man of highly individual genius. Wagner himself would have been the first to deny that he had fixed the final form of opera, or that any vital new development could come by other people adopting his methods: it was one of his theses, indeed, that the new spirit of each age must make its own art out of its own material and its own necessities, and that only stagnation can ensue when artists imitate older forms without being themselves part and parcel of the historic conditions that had evolved those forms by an inner organic process.

It is as natural and right, therefore, that the progressive thinkers of today should be seeking for a new form of opera as that Wagner, Gluck and others should have revolted against the typical eighteenth century form, or that the Italians of the second half of the seventeenth century should have turned their backs on the Florentines and Monteverdi, or that these latter should have tried to establish a different relation between words and music than was possible in sixteenth century polyphonic music. And as Wagner laid such stress on the drama in his own opera, it is a perfectly natural present-day development that the pendulum should now be swinging back, at any rate in theory, towards the musical element in opera. This will prove in the long run, on historical analogy, to be only a temporal phase; but for the moment it seems to be the vital phase.

The musicians are everywhere claiming that the new opera will have to be born out of the spirit of music: Krenek, in his very suggestive essay, claims that the inner life of the musical tissue of the new opera will have to determine everything else in the work—not only the drama and the words but the acting, the lighting, the setting, and so on. Unfortunately he neglects either to tell us exactly how this is to be done or to provide us with a demonstration of how it can be done, or what it will all look and sound like when it is. Still, his essay is interesting as indicative of a trend. What all the theorists fail to perceive is that no amount of mere talk will solve the newest problem of opera. The solution, as was the case with Wagner, will come only from some creator of genius.

For more than a hundred years before Wagner the thinkers of Italy and Germany had been demonstrating in the most logical way what was wrong with contemporary opera and the ways in which it might be reformed: in the actual year of Wagner's birth one Mosel published a book that contained, in embryo, practically everything that Wagner had to say on the subject later. But all this brave talk would have come to nothing but for the dual fact that meanwhile the developments of *symphonic* music had been supplying the modern opera writer with a wealth of new material and new resource, and that nature happened to throw up in the post-Beethoven epoch, in the person of Wagner, the one man who was capable of using this material and these resources to supply the music drama with the vitamin it needed for the next stage of its growth. And we may take it for granted that, let the theoreticians speculate as they will, the newest problem of opera will not be solved until some supreme creative artist solves it not by reasoning but by intuition.

Meanwhile, however, the speculations are very interesting as far as they go. Busoni, of course, gets no nearer a valid solution than any of the others. He never really solved any problem, not even his own most pressing individual ones: what he does, in all his prose writings, is to throw out a number of penetrating remarks on aesthetics, along with a number of other remarks that are more noticeable for their oddity than for their seminal quality. He lays it down, for instance, that 'a love duet on the stage is not only shameless but downright false'. His strange argument is that anyone who has ever been in the company of two lovers has felt that he is *de trop*, and that in a theatre the audience is just a big multiplication of that third person who is not company! He assures us that in the older opera there are no love duets—an *obiter dictum* that prompts us to ask whether he had ever seen a score, for instance, of Handel's 'Giulio Cesare'; nor does he pause to ask himself whether this ban of his ought not to be extended, by parity of reasoning, to many other situations in opera in which two or more people who are ostensibly concerned only with themselves are made to open a window in their souls for the benefit of the spectator. The fact is that Busoni is here, as everywhere else, merely generalising from his own artistic bias: he is obeying the natural impulse of the artist to make himself, with all his prepossessions and prejudices, the norm for all other artists. So again with his verdict that the ideal opera is the 'Magic Flute'; that dictum is merely the product of the craving for satisfaction of certain mystical elements in his own complex nature during his last years.

But if Busoni's brochure, with its alternation of pure absurdities and flashes of the most piercing insight, does not carry us very far in our search for the ideal form and contents of the opera of the future, his own attempt to solve the problem in his 'Doktor Faust' is both interesting and instructive. I will deal with the dramatic plan of that work in a following article.

II

14th March 1937

THERE are few composers who have not had, at some time or another, the idea of either making an opera or a symphony or a symphonic poem out of the Faust subject; it has an almost irresistible attraction for the philosophical mind. For all that, we may doubt whether, in its entirety, it is really a good subject for opera. I say in its entirety, because the more popular treatments of it, such as those of Berlioz, Liszt, and Gounod, confine themselves to the First Part of Goethe's enormous work—the romantic story of a man, a maid and a devil. As readers of Goethe's Second Part know it is only after the Gretchen episode is finished with that Faust becomes a real subject for philosophical poetry. But this Second Part has so far defied reduction to operatic form, though Schuman wrote some fine music for certain episodes from it.

The subject could not fail to attract a mind so given to philosophical brooding as Busoni's. His thinking about the problem of opera seems to have led him to much the same conclusion with regard to it as the well-known one of Wagner, who laid it down that the best field for opera is the myth, in which we see life in its most 'purely human' form. (The 'Meistersinger', of course, is not derived from a myth; but Wagner's later practice did not all correspond to his earlier theories.) Busoni saw that the ideal opera subject, for him at any rate, would have to deal with some figure historically remote enough from us of today to have to become generalised, quintessentialised, yet near enough to us to permit of our seeing ourselves and him. He thought in turn of Merlin, Don Juan, and the Faust of Goethe. The Don Juan theme he rejected because of its association with Mozart's great music, though, as he rightly says, a modern treatment of the Don Juan legend is conceivable in which the many episodes not dealt with by Da Ponte could be turned to good use.

The pull of Goethe's poem upon Busoni was very strong, but he was appalled, as he well might be, by the difficulty of the task of reducing that huge mass to the dimensions of music. In the end the Faust subject forced itself irresistibly upon him; but he thought to solve his problem by making a 'Faust' of his own, not out of Goethe's work but out of the puppet plays that had been so popular in Germany for three hundred years, and the verbal traditions of which have been sought out by various scholars during the second half of the nineteenth century. Reconstruction of these puppet plays was difficult, because each touring troup guarded its own dialogue jealously from possible plagiarism by others.

But though Busoni went back directly to the Puppenspiele for his incidents, he could not, of course, escape Goethe's influence upon the philosophy of his drama. That influence of itself was sufficient to create certain difficulties for him, because the operatic form of a single evening does not suffice for a convincing elaboration of the 'Faust' psychology as we moderns conceive it. Upon this point I shall touch later. Meanwhile it has to be noted that the puppet play itself piled up a number of difficulties for Busoni. It does not appear to have been observed that the puppet play was such a roaring success with the populace precisely because it was a puppet play; that is to say, it was a perfect adaptation of certain episodes to a certain stage technique. It is not too much to say that only the puppet stage *can* present the traditional 'Faust' story adequately. The sudden appearances and exits of the characters, and certain incidents in the handling of the story, were the easiest thing imaginable when all that was required was the jerking of a string; but there is no place for them on the ordinary stage. At the point, for instance, when Faust was to sign the compact with Mephistopheles, Busoni makes a raven fly in with a pen in its beak. This is typical of the kind of action that was simplicity itself on a puppet stage, but that raises a smile in the spectator of a modern Faust drama.

The puppet stage, again, could deal with complete ease with the various episodes—the raising of Herod and Salome, Samson and Delilah, Helen of Troy, Lucretia, Judith and Holofernes, and so on—that are designed to demonstrate Faust's magic powers. But in the first place this kind of thing is in itself never very successful on the ordinary stage; and in the second place, as these episodes have to be made acceptable to us, have to be psychologically inwrought with the substance of the drama, the stage playwright has either to spend an excessive amount of time in setting forth to us the inner meaning of them or to present them in mere sequence, the connection of which is not, and cannot be, made clear to us. Busoni failed to solve this central problem.

His drama opens with a symphonic prelude, followed by a chorus, behind the scenes, singing an Easter hymn. Then the curtain rises and we see the poet, who recites ten stanzas in which Busoni expounds his views upon Opera and gives us his reasons for having finally settled on the Faust subject after having rejected those of Merlin and Don Juan. The first scene proper of the play takes place in Faust's study in Wittenberg. Three mysterious students from Cracow enter and present Faust with the magic book—*Clavis Astartis Magica*—a key, and some title deeds. Later Mephistopheles appears and offers him riches and power, the joys of love, universal fame, in return for the surrender of his soul in due time. Busoni seems to me to have been not quite clear as to his own Faust at this stage. He presents him, at one moment, as a mere arrogant, revengeful thirster after magical power, almost a second Alberich; moreover a man of dubious life who needs Mephistopheles' assistance to help him outrun the constable; he has offended the priests, his cheated creditors are at his heels, his life is being sought by the soldier brothers of the girl he has seduced. Yet when Faust is thinking of accepting the aid of the devil he becomes a pure idealist, whose one desire is to embrace the world in his thought, to have genius and know the sufferings of genius, and so on. Busoni seems, in fact, to be oscillating between the cruder Faust of the puppet plays and the highly intellectualised, philosophical Faust of Goethe.

The next scene, a powerfully imaginative piece of work, shows the soldier in the minster invoking heaven's help in the slaying of his sister's betrayer. Mephistopheles, disguised as a monk, plays cruelly with the wretched man, who is ultimately killed by an armed patrol.

The earliest scenes are styled by Busoni the Prelude, and the scene in the minster is described as an Intermezzo. His drama proper, we are given to understand, commences with the next scene. Following closely the puppet plays, Busoni now takes Faust to Parma. It is the wedding day of the Duke and Duchess. Faust exhibits his magic art, calling in turn Solomon and the Queen of Sheba, Samson and Delilah, and John the Baptist and Salome. In the last of these traditional tableaux the executioner has the lineaments of the Duke. As he raises his sword over the Baptist's head a cry breaks from the Duchess. Faust already has her in his ban. After the stage has been cleared of everyone the Duchess reappears alone wildly confessing her love for Faust, with whom she flies from Parma, Mephistopheles cynically counselling the bereaved Duke to find consolation in a fresh marriage for political purposes.

After a symphonic intermezzo—the Sarabande that occasionally appears in our concert programmes—we are plunged into a lively scene in a tavern in Wittenberg. There are some amusing disputes between the none too sober students. A Platonist smashes a plate by way of proving the Platonic doctrine of 'ideas': the plate, he says, is destroyed but does not the idea of a plate remain? There is much argumentative thrust and counter-thrust between him, a student of theology, a jurist, a physicist, a group of Protestants and one of Catholics. Faust, who until now has been silent, proposes the toast of Martin Luther, the inspired author of the couplet in praise of wine, woman and song. This leads to new disputes, which end with the Protestants goose-stepping out of the room.

Asked by the students to tell them about some of the women he must have met with in his travels, Faust begins to muse upon the episode, now nearly a year old, of the Duchess of Parma. He is interrupted by the entry of Mephistopheles, dressed as a dust-covered courier, who tells him that the Duchess is dead, throws the dead body of her new-born child at his feet, and tells the students the whole story in a ballad that seems to be dragged in by the hair of its head for purely operatic reasons. At the end of it he shows that the body is only a puppet of straw, which he consumes with fire. He promises Faust a still better adventure—with Helen of Troy, who, as in the puppet plays, now appears, only to vanish from Faust's sight when he tries to clasp the ideal in his arms.

It is now that Faust begins really to philosophise, in the true Goethean fashion, about life, its ends, its illusions, and if his sudden philosophising seems, dramatically speaking, to be insufficiently motivated, that impression increases in the final scene. It is a winter night in a street in Wittenberg by the minster; the streets are thick with snow, against a wall stands a life-size crucifix. The night-watchman, as in the Puppenspiele (and, we may add, in the 'Meistersinger'), passes by at intervals, singing his familiar exhortation to the burghers. We see and hear the students once more, this time congratulating Faust's former famulus, Wagner, on his inaugural address as Rector.

When the stage is at last empty Faust enters. He sees a beggar cowering against one of the houses, a child in her arms. It is the Duchess of Parma: she hands the child to Faust bidding him, before midnight, 'complete the work'—though we are given no clear idea of what the work is to be. She disappears. Faust, after a vain attempt to enter the church, sinks, with the child in his arms, before the crucifix. By the light of the lantern of the returning night-watchman he sees the crucified one metamorphosed into Helen. He becomes more and more mystical, expressing himself in phrases that might have come out of 'Tristan', and that are as untranslatable as those. He reaches out into the future, declaring himself 'an eternal will'. He dies. The night-watchman, who is now seen to be Mephistopheles, appears once more, throws his light on to the face of Faust, and ejaculates, 'This man seems to have come to grief!' Meanwhile, from the place where the dead child lay arises a naked body, who, with upraised hand holding a bough in blossom, goes slowly into the town and the night.

With due respect to Busoni, all this is the most egregious philosophical muddle that could be conceived. He never succeeds in making his mysticising clear to us, in large part because of the very nature of the construction of his drama he has to crowd it all into far too small a space in the end. Nor are matters much improved by the poet once more appearing on the stage and addressing the spectators, inviting them to fill out the symbolism of the story for themselves. Dramatically 'Doktor Faust' falls between too many stools to be a success.

HOLST: WORDS AND MUSIC

22nd April 1934

APART from its intrinsic merits, Holst's 'Choral Symphony' is of particular interest because of the questions it raises as to possible combinations of words and music in the opera of the future, or in some new form that may branch out of opera. This is perhaps the most fertile field for musical development now. It may be taken as an axiom that the more homogeneous, and therefore 'closed', an art form is, the sooner it will exhaust its latent possibilities, because of the relatively small number of permutations and combinations of which its few factors are capable; while in the nature of the case the composite forms are capable of more readjustments with regard to each other. For the time being it certainly looks as if purely instrumental music had come near the end of its formal resources: whereas opera keeps perpetually renewing itself, because there the co-operating factors of instrumental music, story, action, *mise en scène*, the sung word, the spoken word, and a genre that lies somewhere between the sung and the spoken, still make possible the creation of a large number of new forms. Let us glance at some of the future changes this principle may imply with regard to the relations between music and words.

There is a type of musical constitution, of course, to which questions of this kind are of no interest. This type of musician has a mind that is essentially melodic, and melodic in a rather narrow sense; being completely insensitive himself to the interest and the charm of the perfect blending of fine music and fine poetry or prose, he listens to Wolf, for example, with the expectation that the vocal line will be 'melodic' in the Handelian or Schubertian sense; not finding what he expects, he misses the very essence of the song, and, being himself not built by nature for the perception of this particular order of musical values, innocently assumes that the people who *are* sensitive to it are people of inferior musical taste to his own. That the deficiency may be in himself never occurs to him. The fact that those of us who like this kind of music are as sensitive as he is to the other kind—the more formally schematised melodic kind—ought at least, one would think, make him ask himself whether what he regards as a superfine palate in himself is not merely a deficiency in aesthetic digestion. But there it is; and we others can only extend to him the same large-handed consolation that Mr. George Robey, in a song of long ago, used to extend to those blessed souls who never miss the things they've never had. Leaving these musical unfortunates to God, let those of us who owe to the combination of poetry and music some of the richest moments of our aesthetic life look at one or two of the problems that Mr. Holst has posed for himself and for us.

Paradoxical as it may sound, the ordinary song-melody is not a vocal melody at all, but an instrumental one; ignoring the inner nerve of the words—if they have one—the refinements of accent or rhythm innate in them, it proceeds to shape and balance itself according to laws of its own; whence it comes about that a song or an aria like Handel's 'Ombra mai fu' or Schubert's 'Am Meer', or Mozart's 'Dies Bildnis ist bezaubernd schön' goes just as well on a solo instrument as with a voice. (How strong the pull of the old instrumental type of melody can be upon a modern composer is shown by Brahms's treatment of the Bible texts in his 'Vier ernste Gesänge'; the infinitely plastic prose is forced into the rectangular mould of abstract melody.)

But at an advanced stage in the development of vocal music both the composer and his listeners demand a type of vocal line which, while satisfying the musical ear, at the same time gives what I have called the inner nerve of the words its due. So the problem arises of finding a way of treating poetry (or imaginative prose) in music that will enable the composer and ourselves to draw upon the vast resources of our poetic sensibility while still not losing touch with music. But this problem will have to be solved in the future in a different way in each work according to the nature of the poem, the special kind of co-operation allotted to the music, and the general purpose of the whole. And it is already clear that a host of hitherto unsuspected difficulties will soon arise.

Mr. Holst begins his 'Choral Symphony' with a long quasi-recitation by the chorus, on a single note, of the lines of Keats's 'Invocation to Pan', the orchestra weaving a continuous tissue of its own above and under and around this level unison line. No other course was logically open to him. The moods and the images of the poem being an organic part of his musical emotion, he is justified in setting them before us. Yet a poem of this kind cannot possibly be set in the old complacent melodic way, for there are poems, and this is one of them, that defy that kind of treatment.

Mr. Holst himself unconsciously proves this by his later handling of some parts of the 'Ode on a Grecian Urn'—in the line for instance, 'Heard melodies are sweet'. Why, we ask ourselves in astonishment, make the voices rise a fifth on the 'mel', and again on the 'sweet'? No one would dream of *speaking* the words with an intonation even remotely resembling this, while as a melody pure and simple the vocal line does not bear within itself its own justification. The truth is that Mr. Holst has already settled upon that leap of a fifth as the cardinal feature in the *orchestral* figure upon which he has decided to construct this section of his movement. The orchestral idea is admirable in itself, and admirably worked out: but we part company both with poetic and with musical common sense when the vocal line is arbitrarily shaped in accordance with it.

Here, it seems to me, Mr. Holst falls back into the very slough from which, in so many other parts of his fine work, he is trying to rescue poetry. His procedure is more convincing when, as at the commencement, he just makes the chorus *intone* the poet's words, thus defining for us the imaginative world of the poem and leaving it to the orchestra to intensify the poetic suggestion in its own way. I can conceive expressive use being made of this device in a new genre of opera, in which fine music could be linked with the finest poetry. But at once a practical difficulty arises. Mr. Holst, who evidently has an exceptionally sensitive ear for the delicacies and subtleties of poetic rhythm—which, as our Shakespearean actors and actresses demonstrate, not one person in ten thousand has—writes out the one note of the chorus in crotchets, quavers, and semiquavers that approximately reproduce, in their totality, the way in which Keats's lines would be spoken by a reader with an exquisite sense of poetic accent and rhythm.

I say 'approximately' because, of course, these musical time-values, being based on set multiples of a metrical unit, cannot possibly indicate the refinements of time-values in rhythmic speech. If we were to chart out the rhythmic line made by a skilled reader of the poem we should indeed get, in broad outline, the time-values noted by Mr. Holst; but at every point they would be subtly modified in a way that is difficult, if not impossible, in music. The difficulty is increased when, as in the present instance, the delivery of the lines is entrusted not to a soloist but to a choir; for a choir can only keep in with itself and with the steady musical flow of the orchestral commentary by a certain amount of insistence on beats and bars, and this insistence, even if as slight as in the admirable delivery of the lines by the B.B.C. Chorus the other evening, jars somewhat upon the ear of a listener who is sensitive to the more esoteric subtleties of verbal rhythm.

I dwell upon this point not in order to disparage the fine effort Mr. Holst has made, in the 'Choral Symphony', to effect a new union of poetry and music, but merely to point out the extraordinary difficulties that are bound to arise for composers in this genre. Will these difficulties ever be overcome? And for whom, indeed, will they be overcome? A work in which these problems of the subtlest interfusion of poetry and music were solved would be a work for merely a handful of listeners who were themselves at once musicians and poets. 'La donna è mobile' and 'Celeste Aïda' will always, I am afraid, be the shortest cut of the greatest number to the greatest musical happiness.

KRSZMALY

17th March 1929

THE assiduous reader of this column—apparently there are still a few of them left, in spite of everything!—may have noticed sundry references of late to Krszmaly, whose works I have persistently pressed upon the attention of British music lovers. I find that the name of this composer is quite unknown here, and I have received letters from various parts of the country asking me for further information about him; I have even been approached by the musical adviser of one of our biggest and most enterprising concert organisations, which is anxious to include some of Krszmaly's work in its programmes. I had intended to reserve what I had to say about Krszmaly until I could treat him and his music at proper length in a book; but in view of the widespread interest that my brief references to him have evoked I have pleasure in giving a few particulars about him here.

Let me say, in passing, that I have been deeply wounded by a suggestion, on the part of a friend who, as the now silent Mr. Kurt Atterberg would say, 'has a sharp nose', that there is no such person—that I invented him, in fact. As if I would do such a thing! Not that there would be anything really unprofessional about such conduct; for most writers upon music have, in their time, discovered a composer who, since no one else has ever been aware of his existence, can be regarded only as the critic's own invention. Mr. Turner, for instance, frequently writes about a composer named Wagner who, I suspect, never existed outside Mr. Turner's imagination: at any rate he has nothing but the name in common with the Wagner *I* know. Then there is Sir Henry Hadow's Berlioz, again—a figment, surely, of that gifted humorist's fancy. And of course there is Mr. Kurt Atterberg, a quite original composer, if Mr. Atterberg's word is to be trusted, but whom I suspect to be the creation of Mr. Atterberg, the music critic.

There would be nothing, then, inconsistent with the loftiest principles of the craft were I also to invent a composer of my own. But what need is there for me to set my imagination to work when the Fates have provided me with Krszmaly ready to my hand? I must admit that I was on the look-out for a composer whom I could be the first to introduce to the British public, for only in that way can a critic hope to achieve fame. It is so difficult nowadays to say anything notable about a classical composer; besides, that could hardly be done without an exhaustive study of him off one's own bat, so to speak; and this sort of thing takes time. It is much easier to find a composer of whom no one else has heard and be his John the Baptist. I was looking round, then, for a new composer on whose shoulders I could climb to fame, or at any rate notoriety, when chance brought Krszmaly my way.

At once I saw my opportunity. For here is a composer who is not only, in my humble opinion, the greatest figure in the music of our own time but destined to have an enormous influence on the future. As a distinguished critic said some ten years ago, when announcing one of his own 'discoveries'—'a young man of thirty-six whom I do not know, whom I have never seen, and whom I regard as one of the most remarkable composers of his generation, a young man from whom may be expected not merely interesting works but works of the first order', etc., etc.—'I do not think there is any greater joy than that of discovering a new personality, a truly original temperament.' That is precisely how I feel about it. Everything else I have written will soon be forgotten; but one of these days I shall perhaps be asked to supply some biographical information about myself to a dictionary of music, and then I shall be able to point, with pride, to the fact that I was the first man in England to write on Krszmaly.

(The name, I hope, will not be an obstacle to his fame in this country. Franz Böhme, in his *Geschichte des Tanzes in Deutschland*, tells us of the sad fate of a Prague composer of about 1820 to whom the historians of music have never done elementary justice simply because no one could pronounce his name, which was Anton Krch. There ought to be no such difficulty with Krszmaly. The name is pronounced exactly as it is spelt—the 'Krsz' like krsz in krsz, and the 'a' broad with a slightly guttural inflection.)

Krszmaly, whom I regard as the greatest composer that Hungary has yet produced, is now in his twenty-fifth year. His father, an Albanian of the hills, was the commander of one of the largest submarines in the Swiss navy; his mother was a Dirne of the purest blood. Great men, as Schopenhauer pointed out, derive their genius from their mothers; and it was undoubtedly from his mother that Krszmaly drew not only his genius but that rich store of Latvian folk melody that, ripened and transformed in obedience to the necessities of the new time, was one day to make him the very incarnation of the Dalmatian national spirit in music. He was educated at the Leipzig Conservatoire; but even as a boy he rebelled against the sterile academicism of his teachers. He had to make his own technique if he was ever to express himself; and this he did by turning to new and unexpected uses the hitherto unsuspected harmonic wealth of the popular music of his native Illyria.

In no living composer, indeed, is the folk-element so strong as in Krszmaly: I need point, in proof of this statement, only to his 'Rhapsody Béotienne' for two flutes and xylophone, to which the most Bœotian-minded of present-day Bœotians cannot listen without feeling that the composer is the very soul, poetic as well as musical, of Bœotia. His already large output includes four string quartets, two operas—'Prc Zstvo Vêstcs' and 'Mrzovitl, Mrzovatl, Mrzovotl'—and no fewer than seven symphonies, of which the last, the 'Sinfonia Moronesque', has been accepted by all the inhabitants of Moronia as the truest expression yet achieved of the Moron mentality. It was after the first performance of this masterpiece that the King of the Morons made Krszmaly his Court Composer.

Outside Moronia, however, where his name is now a household word, this symphony drew upon Krszmaly's head the bitterest objurgation of the more reactionary critics of each country. Yet it was this very work, so daring, so original, so future-piercing, that made me his passionate admirer: it appealed irresistibly to the Sister Anne in me. A letter in which I poured forth my admiration won for me the privilege of his personal acquaintance, as the result of which I was allowed to be the sole hearer, besides the composer, of his revolutionary 'Concentus Silens'. In this astounding work Krszmaly has written *nothing but rests*. He was the first composer, indeed, to perceive and exploit the possibilities of the rest; and the mere sight of this score, with its many time-signatures, its syncopated rests, its cross-rhythm rests, its bewildering polyphony (if the term may be permitted me) of rests, should be enough to convince the most sceptical of the profound originality of Krszmaly's genius. The work was performed by a select choir of Trappist monks on 1st April 1927.

In his 'Chant du Fou' he has carried Schönberg's atonalism a stage further. 'Any one note of the twelve-tone scale', says Schönberg, 'is as good as another.' Krszmaly has clinched this with 'And better!' Here he has made music, for the first time, four-dimensional; no note means just what it purports to mean, but something quite different; and to pierce to the true meaning of it all, the notes have to be seen in their correct focus—which of course means an adjustment of the lens (if the term may be permitted me) of the ear of which few people are as yet capable. (The full score is not yet published; a simplified focal score has been issued, however, for the use of the layman.) It was this revolutionary work that led to the disgraceful exhibition of hooliganism at the last Festival (in Zagreb) of the International Society for Contemptible Music. Krszmaly, on that memorable occasion, learned what it means to a pioneer to be in advance of his time. Courageous as he is, sure of himself and his immortality as he is, the hostile reception of this masterpiece broke his heart. He flung himself sobbing on my shoulder: 'Prszbsl! Prszbsl!' ('Oh my God!') he wailed in his soft native Icelandic. It is this great work, however, by which Krszmaly is, I learn, to be introduced to the English public. It is to be broadcast at an early date: my suggestion for its performance was so strongly backed by the manufacturers of wireless receiving sets that the B.B.C., though with sore misgivings, had to yield to the clamour. I have no fear for Krszmaly in this country, for here we know how to honour great musicians. Has not the gifted composer of 'Sleep, baby, sleep', recently received a knighthood, while even the producer of relative trifles like 'Sea Drift', 'Paris', and 'The Mass of Life' has been awarded the lesser distinction of a Companionship of Honour?

A few days after the appearance of this article in the *Sunday Times* I received a letter purporting to come to me from Krszmaly himself, and running thus:

My kindest Mr. Newman:

Never has my good old *Sunday Times* seemed so good to me as this joyful morning when your so gracious article on my poor music lifted me the soul. Straightway and at once did flash upon me the—do you say?—simplification of my new style. Once more have I the inspirement to compose and is anybody more than my dear friend Mr. Newman worthy of granting to my poor self the dedification of my Fift String Quartet on A? After this is anything more able to compose in that genre? Is it not the last word spoken? No more again can I write for the Quartet—what yet remains for my inspiration is on the lapse of the gods!

Accept, my kindest Mr. Newman, the most best thanks of your verily regardful

PRSZBSE KRSZMALY.

I never discovered the identity of this accomplished joker.–E.N.

KRSZMALY:

DEATH OF A GENIUS

I

6th February 1949

ONE or two readers with long memories may recall that many years ago I contributed to the *Sunday Times* a brief biography and critical study of a great but quite unknown composer named Krszmaly. I pleaded his claim to recognition so eloquently, especially in connection with a string quartet of his, that I received from one of the more advanced thinkers at Broadcasting House an enquiry as to where the score of that revolutionary work could be obtained. I now grieve to have to announce the death of this great composer. The sad news reached me by secret channels some three weeks ago, when I was absorbed as usual in my morning devotions at the centre shrine of the Monte Carlo Casino; and the shock was so great that I had no heart to attend evensong there that day.

Since my return to England I have been searching for that old article of mine, in order to give my readers a few authentic details of Krszmaly's career. But I can't find it and I hesitate to write his biography afresh now for fear that if it should differ to any great extent from that of twenty years or so ago, as it conceivably might, a few uncharitable persons might accuse me of drawing upon my imagination for my facts. All that I can be sure of now is that Krszmaly, as his music so abundantly shows, had the good fortune to be free of any definitely national taint. His father, of Middle East origin, had had a distinguished career as Commander of a submarine in the Swiss navy, while his mother came from one of the most ancient of Viennese families, the Von und Zu Dirnen. Further back there were international complications in his heredity into which I cannot enter in detail now. His pedigree is a matter to which I attach great importance, as I have always held that the best results in music can come only from the crossing of breeds: Grieg, for instance, was half-Scottish, Beethoven was half-Flemish, Johann Strauss was half-Spanish, and Bruckner was half-witted.

In the years following the First World War, when musical geniuses who made Bach and Beethoven and Wagner look like ten cents were being discovered every month, there was a competition among our musical journalists for the honour of having been 'the first in this country to write about So-and-So'. No one, I think, will dispute my claim to have been not only the first but the only critic to discover Krszmaly. To me alone he showed, with me alone he discussed, his unpublished and unperformed masterpieces. I may even claim, without any lapse from modesty, to have been partly instrumental in setting him on his path, till then untrodden, that was to bring him at last to his greatest achievement, the 'Silent Symphony'.

It came about in this way. In the 1920s there used to be much talk among composers and critics about the need for a new music that would be free of the elephantiasis, as it was called, of those German masters whom the world, in its besotted ignorance, had till then mistakenly regarded as great.

'Too many notes!' was the cry, 'too spread-out forms! too much padding!' Krszmaly had long been working in solitude and secrecy along the new lines of compression and restraint, when one day he lighted on an article of mine on Mossolov's 'Music of Machines' and Honneger's 'Pacific 231'. The purpose of these works, I pointed out, was to rescue music from the tyranny of ideas and bring it back to its first and true function of being sound pure and simple. The two gifted composers I have mentioned had gone some distance in that direction, but not far enough. They had imitated to perfection the noises of the machines in a factory, a railway engine getting up steam, the grinding of brakes and so on. But they had made one fatal mistake—they had timorously approached the great modern problem of noise *via* music, of which there was still too much in their scores. The logical conclusion of it all, I argued, would be a sound-complex in which the noises would be left in and the music left out.

It was left to Krszmaly's inexorably logical mind to draw the right conclusion of which even I had not dreamed. If the fewer notes a work has the better, he argues, then obviously the perfect work will be one with no notes at all. He was influenced to some extent in this opinion by some lines he had come across in the great Turkish poet Ushabei Bhêbé: I will not quote them in the original, but a rough English equivalent would be Keats's 'Heard melodies are sweet, but those unheard are sweeter'. In a flash Krszmaly saw to the end of his problem: 'If', I remember him asking me one day in his quaint English, the fire of the born mystic blazing in his beautiful eyes—one pupil, by the way, was noticeably larger than the other—'if nobody hear the dam things, why for I go to trouble of write them?'

So he devoted the final years of his life to the working out of his magnum opus, the manuscript of which lies open before me as I write—the 'Silent Symphony', some notion of which I will try to convey to the reader in my next article. I earnestly commend it to the notice of the B.B.C.; it would make an ideal opening for the next development, now a little overdue at Broadcasting House—the Fourth Programme.

II

13th February 1949

I PROMISED last Sunday to tell my readers something about the crowning achievement of Krszmaly's last years, the 'Silent Symphony'. I have already described some of the influences that contributed to the making of that masterpiece. Underlying them all was the principle insisted on by all the best composers and critics of the nineteen-twenties, that there were too many notes in the classics; Bach, for example, positively spawned semiquavers. But it took a genius like Krszmaly to draw the logical conclusion from it all—that if, *ex hypothesi*, a wineglassful of notes is better than a bucketful, then the wineglassful must yield the palm to the thimbleful, and so, carrying the process of compression to its logical end, the ideal number of notes in a piece of modern music must be no notes at all.

It was the metaphysician and the mystic in Krszmaly that drove him on inexorably to this dazzling conclusion. Always he was in quest of the noumenon behind phenomena. I first became aware of this metaphysical-mystical strain in him when he began to collect holes, claiming that these were the true ultimate realities of space. What, he asked me one day, is a door or a window but the clumsy materialisation of a hole? The mind emancipated from the illusions of the empirical, he contended, ought to be able to conceive the size and shape and quality of a hole without the help of the customary material surround to it. What threw him into a mystical ecstasy was the concept of the hole *per se*, the *Loch an sich*, as Kant would have expressed it. In his later years Krszmaly collected holes as simpler-minded people collect stamps or netsuké, and he was never happier than when showing his collection to distinguished visitors; he was particularly proud of a hole, acquired at great expense, that was once in a sock of Mr. Gladstone's.

I could not always follow him in these daring metaphysical-mystical flights; but I am proud to think I contributed something to his theory of the quintessential abstract in art by bringing to his notice striking instances of the kind that cropped up in my own experience. I remember showing him one day a newspaper cutting that was entirely blank except for two small half-circles at the top. There wasn't a man of any culture in this country, I assured him, who would not recognise this at once as a quintessential portrait of Mr. George Robey. The eyebrows, I said, were the Robey noumenon, Robey *an sich*: a bare suggestion of these was enough, our imagination doing the rest. Krszmaly was greatly impressed by this triumph of abstraction in one of the visual arts. But his superb logical faculty at once carried the problem a stage further—why should not the art of abstraction go beyond even this, conjuring up Mr. Robey for us without even the trifling lapse into the representational implied in the semicircles?

I had to confess that I could not at the moment see how anything of this sort could be done in music. But Krszmaly's powerful brain never ceased to work at that problem, and one day, quite accidentally, I put him on the right path. I had been telling him of a famous English cat that by slow stages rid itself of materiality until nothing remained of it but a grin. (Krszmaly was ultimately able to add that grin to his collection of famous holes.) At last he saw the light; he would create a new species of music that would be to all previous music what the immaterial grin was to the material cat, a music which would scrap entirely the crude apparatus of sound and consist wholly of rests.

So, bit by painful bit, the 'Silent Symphony' came into being. (After all, he remarked jocularly to me one day, are not the rests the best part of a modern work?) But it cost him fifteen years of hard thinking to perfect the new genre. His problem was a triple one. First of all he had to create a new type of melody composed entirely of rests crystallising into exquisite designs. (Keats, I am sure, would have agreed with me that these silent melodies of Krszmaly's are the sweetest ever unheard.) Next he had to elaborate a harmony of rests based on the subtle natural differences between the consonances and dissonances of silence—diatonic rest-harmonies, chromatic, enharmonic, and all the rest of it: he was even working at a theory and practice of atonal rests when he died.

Last of all, and this was his greatest triumph, came an amazing counterpoint of rests. Only the photographic reproduction of a full page of the 'Silent Symphony', for which my editor churlishly refuses me a whole page of today's issue of the *Sunday Times*, could give the reader an idea of the ingenuity of this counterpoint, which makes the art of the old Netherlanders look like nursery stuff. Imagine the technical difficulties of imitation, inversion, augmentation, diminution, stretto, fugue, mirror fugue, canon, crab canon, lobster canon (this last ingenious device is Krszmaly's own invention) and so on, when transferred from the too easy sphere of material sound to the immaterial world of silence!

And now, I ask again, what are the B.B.C. going to do about it? Failing them, I look to the gramophone companies, and failing them the Arts Council. The problem, of course, will be to find a conductor who can get to the heart of the 'Silent Symphony' and an orchestra that can be trusted to count accurately through the soundless mazes of it.

MEYERBEER AND HIS EPOCH

28th February 1932

Mr. Van Dieren's recent articles in the *Daily Telegraph* on Meyerbeer raise some very interesting points. Whether it would be possible to get Meyerbeer into the ordinary English repertory, or, having got him there, to keep him there, may be open to doubt. But an occasional performance of one or two of his operas would surely be an attraction, if only the performances were adequate. A production such as the one we had of the 'Huguenots' at Covent Garden a few years ago is not merely useless, but harmful; the poor composer is damned for the all-round incompetence of his performers and producers. But a properly sung, properly played, properly staged performance of one of the operas would presumably be as successful in London as in any Continental or American town. It would certainly give the public something to think about, and the critics something to write about.

I heard 'Dinorah' and 'L'Africaine' in New York some years ago, and was strangely impressed by them. I found myself repelled by the man's mind, yet paradoxically unable to get away from it and the psychological problems it called up; the music seemed to me like those strange scents that create a faint nausea in us, but for some reason or other make it difficult for us to escape their unpleasantness by the simple process of keeping away from them. This view of Meyerbeer, of course, may be a purely personal one, though when I talked it over with one of my New York colleagues I found that he agreed with me. But I wonder whether Meyerbeer may not have affected his contemporary audiences to some extent in somewhat the same way—whether some people did not find the odour of the man's mind just a little unpleasant, but were still unable to shake themselves free of its curious fascination.

We shall never, of course, be able to hear Meyerbeer as his contemporaries heard him, for the times have changed, and we with them. But a little study of contemporary Meyerbeer criticism helps us to see the matter as the audiences of the eighteen-thirties and forties saw it, and so to understand how it was that Meyerbeer achieved so colossal a reputation in his own day. In one respect, indeed, his music is as remarkable now as it was then—in the strange beauty, the curiously searching quality, of some of his orchestral combinations. If these things surprise and fascinate us today, after a century of marvellous orchestral developments, we can imagine the effect they must have had on audiences to whom they were entirely new. But in the main, Meyerbeer's hold upon his own generation depended upon something that cannot possibly ever be reproduced for our generation or any succeeding one. He was the man of the moment, the incarnation of the spirit of the time. The world of the thirties and forties saw itself reflected in him more completely than in any other composer of the epoch. And precisely because he was the man of the moment, the very voice of the very soul of his generation, he has lost the bulk of his old significance, for we of today cannot bring to this music what the men of Meyerbeer's day brought to it.

A little research into the criticism of that period makes it quite clear that what mostly attracted people to Meyerbeer was the consciousness that he was the mirror of themselves and of the epoch. Heine, who was not specifically a musician, but was a shrewd observer of men and manners and social changes, has explained it all in a way that is as convincing now as it was a century ago. Heine, writing from Paris about 1837, says that Rossini's vogue was then declining somewhat. The predominant factor in Rossini's music, he says, is melody, which is the expression of man as individual; whereas the predominating factor in Meyerbeer's music is harmony, which expresses man in his communal aspects.

For this reason, he goes on to say, Rossini's music was the delight of, because it was the perfect expression of, the agitated and self-conscious humanity of the immediate post-Napoleon epoch, a humanity intent on its personal joys and sorrows, loves and hates, longings and despairs. But after the July Revolution (1830) a new consciousness had developed in Europe, a consciousness of the need for reconstruction in politics, in business, in social life, a consciousness of man as part of the community; and it was this new mentality that saw itself reflected in the Meyerbeer operas.

Rossini, says Heine, 'would never have obtained his huge popularity during the Revolution [of 1789] or the Empire'; he was emphatically the man of the Restoration epoch. The man of the new epoch that began about 1830 was Meyerbeer, in whose operas people saw the characters and the problems of their own world. Heine shows how it was that 'Robert the Devil' was such a stupendous success: in Robert the public saw themselves—'the hero who does not know precisely what it is he wants, who is in perpetual conflict with himself; he is a veracious portrait of the moral uncertainties of the epoch, that vacillated so restlessly and so painfully between virtue and vice, fretted itself in endeavours and galled itself against obstacles, and, like Robert, sometimes lacked the strength to withstand the assaults of the devil.' And again 'only when the great choruses of "Robert the Devil" and the "Huguenots" roared harmonically, rejoiced harmonically, sobbed harmonically, did men's hearts hearken and sob and rejoice and roar in inspired accord.' This, says Heine, is why Meyerbeer is 'the man of his epoch; and the epoch, which always knows its own man, has tumultuously raised him on its shield, proclaimed his overlordship, and celebrates in him its own joyous entry into possession.'

Other contemporary critics say much the same thing in other words. Meyerbeer was felt to be the man of the time because his operas were peopled with figures whose psychology was then new to opera. We have seen what psychological subtleties Heine read into Robert. Chorley points out that until the 'Huguenots', the Puritan (Marcel) had never been treated in opera. John of Leyden (in 'Le Prophète'), again, 'lover, son, fanatic, penitent', as Chorley describes him, was something new in a genre that had hitherto dealt mostly with stock figures or abstractions. The three Anabaptists in the 'Prophète' were a novel study in religious fanaticism. ' "Le Prophète", again', says Chorley, 'is peculiar as being the first serious opera relying for its principal female interest on the character of the mother.' And so on and so on: in each of his operas Meyerbeer gave his audiences the delighted feeling that they were being brought into touch with real life, that the characters they saw on the boards were men and women such as they might meet any day themselves, men and women caught up in such problems of morality or politics or social life as they themselves were interested in.

But in the long run, very little matters in an opera but the music. If that is good, it will sustain the most preposterous plot, the most primitive character drawing: if it is poor, the best plot and the most penetrating psychology of character will not keep the work alive. Meyerbeer's operas have perished, or live now only a half-life, because his musical gifts were not the equal of his general intelligence and culture. And in this simple fact we may perhaps read the impending doom of more than one opera of our own day that wins an immediate success by its truth to life, its contemporaneity of action and of psychology, rather than by reason of its musical excellence.

'He was, and is, the man of this his time,' said A. B. Marx of Meyerbeer in 1855. Marx then finds fault with Wagner for *not* being the man of his time, in that for his subjects and characters he went not to contemporary life but to saga and legend: '*this* drama the drama of the future? the Middle Ages a picture of our future, the already lived and outlived the child of our hopes? Impossible! These sagas and stories of the enchantress Venus and of the Holy Grail, with all their crash of honest heroes' weapons and their conflicts of justice among the gods, strike us now as merely an echo of long-dead states of mind that are alien to our own time.' Marx would be vastly astonished were he to return to earth today and find that the Wagnerian gods and heroes and myths and sagas are the staple fare of our opera audiences, while Robert and Raoul and Marcel and Vasco de Gama and John of Leyden and Auber's Masaniello and most of the other operatic characters that were at one time the last word in 'reality' have practically disappeared from the stage.

In our own day we have seen what looked like our own day's last word in reality, 'Johnny spielt auf', disappear from human ken in the course of a few short years. It will not be long before other 'mirrors of contemporary life', constructed by other 'men of the moment', follow that work into the limbo that awaits all operas that are richer in 'reality' than in music.

MOZART AND TWO SYMPHONIES:

CHANGING POINTS OF VIEW

9th September 1934

In *Love Among the Chickens* that profound student of human nature, Mr. P. G. Wodehouse, who is as great a philosopher as Emanuel Kant but twice as funny, poses for us one of the eternal problems of aesthetic criticism. 'It would be interesting to know,' he says, 'to what extent the work of authors is influenced by their private affairs. If life is flowing smoothly, are the novels they write in that period of content coloured with optimism? And if things are running crosswise, do they work off the resultant gloom on their faithful public? If, for instance,' continues Mr. Wodehouse, with a plunge into gloomy foreboding that is happily rare with him, 'if, for instance, Mr. W. W. Jacobs had toothache, would he write like Hugh Walpole?'

I am reminded of these luminous words of the greatest living Englishman by the fact that Mozart's E flat symphony was given at the Promenades a few days ago, while the G minor is set down for performance next Thursday. As the reader may remember, Mozart's three greatest symphonies, the E flat, the G minor, and the C major (the Jupiter) were all written in a few weeks between the June and the August of 1788. It was a time when the poor little man's affairs were at their worst; he was in ill-health, he was falling deeper and deeper into debt, and the future was as black as any man's could well be; and his letters of the period reveal the misery and despair that were eating their way into his soul. It has accordingly been one of the stock comments of the biographers that it is surprising that at a time like this he should have been able to write so 'gay' a work as the symphony in E flat. The current view of the matter is expressed in a programme note *à propos* of last week's performance, in which we were informed that 'there is no reflection in the E flat symphony of his mental tribulation. The music is as happy and gay as anything could be, and if it reflected anything at all, it was the youthful and optimistic side of the composer's nature.'

In that remark we meet with yet another proof of how sadly and, apparently, permanently Otto Jahn has misled the modern world as to the nature of the mind of Mozart. It is of no avail that during the last twenty years one German and French scholar after another has given us plentiful cause for believing that Jahn's reading of Mozart was a superficial one, or that in the new edition of his 'classical' work by Hermann Abert his errors have been so drastically corrected that, apart from the biographical portions, comparatively little of the original remains. Only the old Jahn has so far been translated into other languages, and so, in programme notes and elsewhere, we are still regaled with opinions about Mozart that no instructed student holds today. Jahn, Jahn, überall Jahn!

We know rather more now about the psychology of artists than we used to do, and so we no longer incline to the naïve belief that if a composer has quarrelled with his wife his next symphony will be a Pathétique, or that if his liver happens to be functioning normally he will produce a Hymn to Joy at the next Three Choirs' Festival. We know now that the creative imagination of a great artist functions too deep down within him to be greatly affected by anything that may happen on the surface of his life or his being. The subconscious is of much more importance in the artist than the conscious, and the subconscious proceeds by its own mysterious inner chemistry and obeys its own mysterious inner laws; the result being that if his daemon feels light the man will write light music even though the bailiffs be in the room below, while if his daemon is wrestling with the problem of the informing soul of the cosmos he will write a philosophical, and perhaps a pessimistic, work even though the glad news be brought him that his wife has left him.

We need not be in the least astonished, then, that Mozart, in this period of sore trial, should have been able to give his genius the free wing it has taken in the E flat symphony and the Jupiter: there is no need to assume that in June, when he was writing the E flat, life looked fairly bright to him, that it suddenly became so much darker that in July he simply had to write the G minor, while in August the clouds had cleared away again and, feeling less worried about Constanze and his creditors, the Jupiter followed as a natural consequence. Mozart the man was uniformly wretched throughout the whole of this period: the changes in the moods of the three works were due simply to changes in his aesthetic chemistry with which the experiences of his conscious mind had the minimum of connection.

But the nineteenth century, with its naïve psychology and its passion for sorting out the products of an artist's mind into neat parcels, each with a different label, made a further mistake over these works. It quite overlooked the fact that while the bulk of the E flat symphony is care-free in its expression, the adagio prelude is a tragic piece of work. Jahn is so occupied with telling us that the symphony is 'an expression of happiness' that he has neither eyes nor ears for this adagio: it did not fit conveniently into his neat verbal schematism for the three symphonies, so he blandly ignored it. Abert, on the other hand, rightly insists on the 'pathos' of the adagio, its 'gloom', its 'uncanny' quality, the 'profound pessimism' of it as a whole.

It is possible, after all, that Jahn, and others of his way of thinking, really saw nothing of all this in the adagio, that they misconceived Mozart as grossly here as they have done in so many other places—a misunderstanding that has latterly reached its climax in the truly comic theory that 'Don Giovanni' is an *opera buffa*. This and similar misunderstandings come mainly from the fact that early in the nineteenth century, owing to the great development of the technical resources of music under the romantics, the true feeling for the idiom and the aesthetic of the eighteenth century was lost. It has been the laborious business of the twentieth century, by *stilkritische* methods (I must apologise for not being able to find a convenient English equivalent of the term), to bring about a better understanding of the eighteenth—though this understanding, unfortunately, has not yet penetrated to most of our interpreters of Mozart.

The reader will be able to get an idea of the principle at stake if he will consider the various ways in which the G minor symphony has been looked at during the last century and a half. For listeners of its own day it contained something that made them shudder. Gradually the feeling for the tragic intensity of it, as for that of 'Don Giovanni', was lost; Schumann, for instance, took the almost incredible view of the symphony that in its 'light motion' it resembled 'a Greek Grace'. Even today there are conductors who regard it as a light and graceful work, and play it in exactly the same style as they would a symphony of Mozart in his most rococo mood. Among scholars, however, it is now recognised for what it is and always was, for what its contemporaries saw it to be—a 'daemonic' work, the expression of an unrest, a bitterness, a pessimism, that has few parallels in all music. The mere fact that a conductor 'feels' it to be a work of the other type is of no account whatever. Conductors as a rule are not scholars, but merely more or less sensitive musical instruments. They 'feel' an ancient work in a particular way because that is the way of their own temperament, and they play it accordingly. They do not pause to ask themselves whether that way may not be a complete error, due to the unconscious substitution, in our own epoch, of quite another set of aesthetic concepts for those of a bygone age.

It is the scholar, and the scholar alone, who can help us to see that old music as its composer and his contemporaries saw it. He can do this in three ways. In the first place, by an examination of the theoretical speculations and the musical criticism of the epoch he can discover what the aesthetic of that epoch really was, in what a very different way from ours they looked at music, what it was they held it to be the function of music to express, the means by which they thought this expression could be achieved, and so on. In the second place, he can restore for us, to some degree, the perception the modern world has lost of language-values and idiom-values in certain old music: he can show us, for example, that, owing to the enormous development of the harmonic vocabulary during the last hundred years, certain harmonies, or certain successions of notes, no longer have for us the startling or lacerating quality they had when they were brand new. In the third place, by *stilkritische* methods he can show that certain typical procedures on the part of an ancient composer were invariably the outcome of certain moods in him.

Armed with this knowledge in the case, for example, of the G minor symphony or 'Don Giovanni', the scholar can show that the fund of feeling in the work is very much deeper and richer than is imagined by the average modern performer, who approaches it with no solid backing of historical musical culture, and so can do nothing more with this or any other old work than play it as he 'feels' it, blissfully unsuspicious that his 'feeling', owing to the changes in the vocabulary of music between the composer's day and now, may be the most unreliable guide imaginable to what the work meant to the composer and to those who heard it in its first freshness. It is quite possible that, even after all the Mozart research of the last twenty years or so, conductors will continue to play the G minor as if it were a 'Greek Grace', in which case there are sure to be listeners who will enjoy it in that form and innocently imagine they are listening to genuine Mozart. And if the mere scholars who happen to be in the audience become furious at the perversion, well, scholars are always bound to be in the minority where public music is concerned, and they can be conveniently written off as cranks.

THE LAST PUCCINI

12th June 1927

We are given to regretting the early deaths of composers like Mozart, Schubert, Purcell and Pergolesi; but the seemingly paradoxical proposition could be maintained that the composers who died too young were Wagner, at the age of seventy, Beethoven, at fifty-seven, Brahms, at sixty-four, and Verdi, at eighty-eight. It might be argued that there is no particular reason to suppose that any of the composers whose early deaths we lament would have gone on developing after their middle youth. There may be something in flawed physical stocks like Mozart and Pergolesi that implies, as a matter of course, early fruition and if, not early mental decay, an early mental standstill; and I have already suggested in this column, as an interesting subject for speculation, the probable position of Mozart about 1830 had he survived Beethoven, as he could quite easily have done without being a very old man. Where would he have stood as regards his own work in the years that saw the Eroica, the No. 5, the No. 9, the Mass in D, and the last piano sonatas and quartets of Beethoven? Would he have been able to hold his own against these, to grow as Beethoven grew, to transform himself from the purest type of the eighteenth century composer to the type that alone could express the needs of the early nineteenth; or would he have lived on to find himself superseded?

But while there is a reasonable doubt whether the minds of some of these early-deceased men would have grown greatly with length of years, there is no doubt at all as to the tremendous growth of minds like those of Wagner and Verdi: between 'Rienzi' and 'Parsifal', between 'Nabucco' or 'Ernani' and 'Falstaff', the distance is so great that no spectator of the earliest work of these two men could have had the slightest inkling of how far they would travel before the end. And by all appearances Puccini, dying at the age of sixty-six, died too soon; for who, after the evidence of 'Gianni Schicchi' and

'Turandot', can doubt that his brain had the same capacity for steady growth as Verdi's?

Most of what we heard in the crush-room during the intervals of 'Turandot' last Tuesday was precisely what we should have expected to hear on an occasion of this kind. Skilled practitioners in the obvious were reminded of the 'Mikado' and 'Chu Chin Chow', and quite naturally; for is not the setting of each of these three plays in an alleged China of some sort or another, and does not the milieu, for some people, reduce everything that may be shown in it to the same common denominator? Others shook a wise head and told us that 'Turandot' was of mixed quality: specially daring and original stylists even said something about a curate's egg. That there is something of the old Puccini along with the new is not to be wondered at; the surprising thing would be were it otherwise, for Puccini was still in search of his last and best self even here.

People who are shocked to find that now and then, after exhibiting a style to which there is no parallel in his earlier works, the Puccini of 'Turandot' reminds us of the Puccini of 'La Bohème' and 'Madame Butterfly', would do well to spend an hour or two in an intensive examination of the early and late work of certain other long-lived composers—Verdi, for example. They would then discover that not only are there obvious traces of the earlier Verdian idiom in the latest works, but that Verdi all through his career kept harking back to certain formulae; so strong is the pull of early habits upon the musical as upon the moral man, so prone is the most original mind, the mind most capable of growth, to take unconsciously the line of least resistance. The phrase to which Manrico, in 'Trovatore', sings 'Prima che d'altri vivere' is virtually that to which, thirty-five years later, Otello will sing his moving 'Spento è quel sol, quel sorriso, quel raggio'. The melodic line of Manrico's 'A chi desia, a chi desia morir', in the Miserere scene, is that of Aida's 'O patria mia, non ti vedrò mai più'. In the 'Oberto' of 1839 (Verdi's first opera) will be found the essentials of Gilda's 'Infelice core, cor tradito, per angoscia non scoppiare' in the 'Rigoletto' quartet of 1851. Violetta's cry of 'Amami, Alfredo, amami quant' io t'amo' in the 'Traviata' of 1853 is plainly a reminiscence of Lida's 'Ma Dio mi volle' in

'La Battaglia di Legnano' (1849); while Arrigo's 'Ah no, ah no, trafitto esangue' in the last-named opera is practically the same phrase as Manrico's famous 'Ah che la morte ognora'. An accompaniment figure in 'La Battaglia di Legnano' is met with again, slightly altered, in 'Aida', as accompaniment to Amonasro's 'Quest assisa ch'io vesto via dica'. A love-motive in 'Un Ballo in Maschera' (1859) is plainly the sister of Violetta's 'Amami, Alfredo'.

Other analogies could be cited by the dozen. The point in connection with them is that they are not deliberate employments, for economy's sake, by Verdi of phrases that have already served him well, but subconscious reversions to type. It is the shallowest of criticism, then, to try to disparage 'Turandot' by saying that the old Puccini is still visible here and there in the score; as a matter of fact he has succeeded very much better in getting away from his old self here than Verdi did in getting away from his old self in 'Otello', the marvellous development of which from the Verdi of 'Trovatore' is never questioned. And, like the later Verdi, when the later Puccini harks back unconsciously for a moment to his earlier idiom it is with a great spiritual difference. It may be only Violetta's cry to Alfredo that we hear once more in Desdemona's moving 'Ah, Emilia, Emilia, addio!' but more than thirty years of refinement of the spirit lie between the two expressions of the same mood.

When the Puccini of 'Turandot' reminds us of the Puccini of the earlier works it is with the same sense of change. One way of realising how vastly he had grown is by comparing his own writing in 'Turandot' with Alfano's finish to the opera. I do not know to what extent Alfano has here worked upon sketches left by Puccini, but even if some of the actual material is the latter's how profound is the difference between the general tissue, the soul more than the body, of this last scene and Puccini's first and second acts! The opera suffers sadly from not having been finished by its creator: only he could have given it the spiritualised ending we feel is now lacking to it. Alfano's contribution to the score is a clever and a conscientious piece of work; but it has all the honest, earnest, eager crudity, not of youth (for Alfano was fifty when he completed 'Turandot') but of a mind that has not undergone the subtle spiritual chemistry that we can perceive to have been proceeding in Puccini during his last years.

Even in 'Gianni Schicchi' it was evident that Puccini had purged himself of his cruder Italianism—more thoroughly, I venture to say, than the seventy-four year old Verdi had been able to do in 'Otello'. There are several melodies in this that seem to be drawn in the traditional Italian fashion with the thick of the thumb in 'Gianni Schicchi' the bulk of the music is sketched with the tip of the finger, while even when Puccini seems to lapse into the conventional idiom for a time it is more probable that he is deliberately, smilingly, sporting with his own past. With what a charming grace, for instance, he hands to us Lauretta's 'O mio babbino caro', or the 'Addio, speranza bella'! It is as if he were saying to us, 'This that you and I used to take so seriously was after all only a game we put the whole of ourselves into when we were young and a little foolish; but if you would like, for the fun of the thing, to play it again, what about this for a move?' and he pushes a pawn across the board with such an air that it counts as a bishop at the least.

And in 'Turandot', whenever he uses the former apparatus it is to other ends than of old and with another grace and power. That he is still dogged by his past, as every artist is, goes without saying; and in addition he has certain peculiarly difficult problems of expression to solve. He had already had to struggle with them in 'Madame Butterfly'. In the greater part of that work he maintains quite easily the exotic atmosphere; but when he comes to write the love duet at the end of the first act, his little Japanese lady becomes the ordinary amoureuse of Italian opera; and in 'Turandot' also we feel that when he has to express one of the stronger primary emotions he has to revert to the traditional idiom of his own country and period. But even here, as I have said, the expression is subtilised in comparison with the old Puccini, while the great bulk of the score is a marvel of new ideas and new technique. It is useless to try to get any real idea of the opera from the piano arrangement, so organically is the harmonic tissue interwrought with the orchestral colour: things that are meaningless or repellent on the piano are found to be perfectly right when we hear them in the theatre.

I should say that the first and second acts of 'Turandot' are the very finest Puccini—even more his 'Falstaff' than his 'Otello'. Over the first act there broods a peculiar fatefulness: we shall have to hear it a good many times to get to the technical secret of this miracle of homogeneity. In certain passages, such as the writing in general for Ping, Pang and Pong, the three Court functionaries, the technical advance upon the earlier Puccini must be obvious to the most casual listener; but there are numberless things below the surface here that intrigue the sensitive musician.

SÉVÉRAC:

THE AMATEUR COMPOSER

I

10th April 1921

Déodat de Sévérac, whose death was announced a few days ago, is practically unknown in this country, apart from the 'Musical Box' that forms one of the movements of his pianoforte suite 'En Vacances' and his 'Baigneuses au Soleil', which has a certain technical attraction for pianists. My own acquaintance with de Sévérac's music began some years ago as a result of reading one or two French articles on him in which he was hailed as one of the most significant representatives of what is more or less vaguely known as the French spirit. I myself could see little in him that was representative of anything but the type of amateur composer that is as plentiful as berries in every country, but I was prepared to believe that this view of him came from some defect in myself and that the true light would dawn on me later.

In the ensuing years I read other articles on him, in which he was again treated as a French composer of distinction; and as some of the French writers who saw talent in him saw nothing in such people as Brahms and Hugo Wolf, I became still more puzzled. Since his death I have read again through all the music of his that I possess. I can again see nothing more in him than the honest amateur. I do not know all his work, and it may be that I have not met with the best of it. I see from the catalogues and the obituary notices that he wrote two operas and various symphonic works; but whether these are accessible or not I cannot say.

Anyhow, in all the articles on him that I have seen he has always been treated as a minor master in virtue of his piano works. I know, I think, all of these that have been published, including the 'Sous les lauriers roses' that was issued only last year, and I know also most of his songs. His was seemingly a small output for a man of forty-eight. That of itself is significant.

You can tell the big man, as Tennyson used to say, not only by the quality but by the quantity of his work.

The only conclusion I can come to, when I read the French eulogies upon de Sévérac, is that it is easier to be a composer in France at present than in any other country in the world. No matter how small your work, in size, in scope, or in importance, you will be welcomed and fêted by some circle or other. French music has become very conscious of itself during the last generation, largely as a process of reaction against the domination of German music. The natural corollary to the proposition that no good French composer would write like a German was that any Frenchman who did not write like a German was a good composer.

On the strength of this, a number of composers who have really no claim whatever to distinction have been treated by some critics with excessive consideration. Some French musical criticism has a curious way of ceasing to be critical when the products of its own nation are concerned. I can recall articles in which de Sévérac was discussed at great length, and in a very flowery style, as the composer of Languedoc.

One of the most amusing features of the theory of a 'national' spirit in music is that it always splits up, in practice, into the doctrine of a number of regional spirits. In one breath we are told that certain Russian composers are 'nationalistic'; in the next, that there is as much difference between the Little Russian and the Great Russian as between the Cockney and the Tyke. Albeniz and Granados are both 'national' Spanish composers; and then we learn that they represent two different physiological and psychological and cultural Spanish types.

We have not got as far as this in England yet. We do not ask of a composer that he shall express in his songs the soul of the Five Towns in which he was brought up, nor of another that the authentic voice of the Glasgow shipyards shall be heard in his chamber music. But in France the distinctions between the various regions of the country, and the way in which these distinctions are expressed in the art of this or that composer who first saw the light in one or other of these regions, are insisted upon with much gravity by some critics. Languedoc obviously had to have a composer of its own; and as de Sévérac was born there, his music must obviously be full of a spirit to be found in Languedoc and nowhere else.

Add to this fact the further fact that one or two French critics have the enviable faculty of being immensely pleased with very little, and you have all the ingredients for making a significant composer out of an insignificant one. These critics—we have one or two of the same sort among our own countrymen, by the way—find what is to most of us a daily trudge a delightful pilgrimage among masterpieces. A new talent flowers on every bush; every shilling they pick up has, for them, the gilding of the sovereign; and they see one of the supreme masters of Gothic in the designer of the parish pump.

So it comes about that a mere amateur like de Sévérac becomes, for a moment, a representative French composer. What do I mean by an amateur? Not necessarily one who has had no technical training. De Sévérac went through the mill, I believe, as thoroughly as any other young man. But there are people who are born amateurs, and no amount of training can make anything else of them. Glinka was of this type. De Sévérac was another; and he is representative of thousands of people of today who insist on composing. They mistake an aspiration towards composition for a gift for it and a call to it. A musical technique is not something that can be acquired in schools or out of a book—a sort of costume for the better display of an idea. It must be inherent in the ideas themselves, or it is nothing at all. A really vital idea makes its own technique. The free working of the technique in turn stimulates and liberates ideas. We might as well try to make an Italian poet of a non-poetically minded man by teaching him Italian as to make a musical technician of a man who was never meant by nature to be a composer by teaching him harmony and counterpoint and form and all the rest of it.

We can always tell the born amateur, no matter how much academic tuition he has had. His ideas, in the first place, lack vitality. 'Ideas' in themselves are next to nothing. Any man of ordinary artistic feeling, in the course of an hour's walk, may get 'ideas' enough for half-a-dozen sonnets or symphonies or novels or pictures or articles. What really matters is the indefinable thing we call 'treatment', 'handling', 'style'.

I do not mean that there are not degrees of excellence even among ideas. Obviously, the idea of the first phrase of Schubert's 'Serenade' is better than the idea of the first phrase of Ethelbert Nevin's 'The Rosary'. But many amateurs are visited by ideas that are excellent in themselves, but that come to nothing, like a rare bird's egg laid in a dustbin; while an idea that may seem at first sight to be utterly insignificant like that of the first theme of the 'Eroica' symphony, may become the foundation-stone of an edifice that is one of the world's wonders. 'Vitality', in regard to musical ideas, is a very complex concept.

II

24th April 1921

I SAID in my previous articles that there are some composers who are born amateurs, and amateurs they will remain to the end of their days, no matter how much practice they may get in their art. They may write a fair amount of quite good music; but the distinction between them and the real composers will always be unmistakable. It is the eternal distinction between even the very best of amateurs and the less than very best of professionals. The amateur champions among the billiard players and boxers, for instance, are not quite in the class of the second string of the professional practitioners of those sports. Amongst the amateurs in music I should class Glinka, de Sévérac, Meyerbeer, and Leoncavallo. There are degrees, of course, among amateurs; and now and then the best work of the amateur may come up to professional quality. But always the amateurishness keeps betraying itself.

In which way? the reader may ask. In various ways. One sign of the born amateur is that he cannot sustain his thinking at its best for very long. He can write a fine page; but he cannot write a fine work—at least, not one of any length. Nor can he write many really fine works in the smallest forms. I would instance, as a typical amateur, one Fritz Koegel, an unknown German whose songs came into my hands a few years ago when I was making a systematic study of the German song. Three or four of Koegel's songs are both beautiful in idea and admirably worked out; but in the majority of them the often excellent ideas come to much less than they ought to have done, simply because the technique is inadequate.

By technique, needless to say, I do not mean the formulae of composition taught in the schools and the text-books, but that way of working that every composer has to discover for himself —a facility of expression that not only allows him to say all he wants to say, but is itself a perpetual stimulus to the imagination. It is in this constant action and interaction of imagination and technique that the amateur composer fails; the result is invariably an impression of helplessness somewhere or other. Everyone knows Meyerbeer's difficulty in ending a phrase as finely as he began it; one illustration of this has become classic —the baritone aria in 'Dinorah', with its excellent first and third lines and its lamentable second and quite abject fourth. Leoncavallo had something of the same difficulty in finishing well; plenty of instances could be quoted from 'I Pagliacci'.

De Sévérac exhibits all the marks of the amateur. He invariably does his best work (it is never of much account, I think) in the small forms in which all he has to do is to fill a conventional mould with a standardised paste, to which he gives just a touch of colouring of his own. To this order belong the quite likable little pieces of 'En vacances'. He says nothing that has not been said a hundred thousand times before, but the voice has its own timbre. To a certain extent, again, he can exploit the standardised formulae of realistic imitation (horses galloping, etc.) or of subjective expression (religious feeling, and so on); but invariably the amateur is betrayed before he has got past the first page or two. A correspondent who, while not ranking de Sévérac's music as a whole very high, thinks more of it than I do, and demurs to my general characterisation of him, tells me he regards the 'Coin de cimitière au printemps' and 'Sur l'étang, le soir' (from the suite 'En Languedoc') as 'two of the most poetic works of modern piano music'. I am sorry I cannot agree. They are poetic enough in intention, but the intentions are mostly not realised.

As I pointed out before, good ideas are as common as blackberries: any of us can turn them out by the dozen as we sit at the piano. The test comes when the ideas have to be developed. Again let me explain that by 'development' I do not mean the formal procedure taught in the books and the conservatoires under that rubric; I mean the process by which the idea opens out and moves along, impelled by an inner, inexplicable, irresistible logic of its own. It is here that the amateur fails. He will often hit upon something that might not have occurred to a much greater composer; perhaps the first example of the use of the whole-tone scale is that curious passage in Glinka's 'Russlan and Ludmilla'.

But the amateur's imagination lacks the driving logic essential to the expansion of the idea. We may call it a failure of technique if we like; but the root of the trouble is in the quality and vitality of the imagination. I myself would cite 'Coin de cimitière, au printemps', as a typical example of de Sévérac's amateurishness. He does, at the beginning, just what any of us can do at the piano—beats out a phrase that suggests a mood or an atmosphere. But he can get no further with it; for all practical purposes, he has said all he has to say in the first twelve bars. In the remainder I can see nothing but the helplessness of the amateur.

He has no device, in fact, for lengthening a work except repetition. There is no evolution of an idea—merely repetitions of it with new piano figuration, generally of the most infantine kind. If I were teaching composition I should hold up page after page of de Sévérac to the student as a warning. He rarely gets beyond the exercise stage. If some of these works were shown me as extracts from the exercise book of a conservatoire student, I should regard them as fairly promising studies in the rudiments of composition technique. But, if, several years later, a new set of books were shown me, containing nothing but the same conventional formulae, handled in the same inelastic way, I should be compelled to say that such a student would never become a technician.

I say that of de Sévérac after studying piano works of his extending over some twenty years. His technique was as rudimentary at the end as at the beginning. He never even added to his original slender stock of devices. Of anything like a sense of design he was utterly innocent. He can build up a long work only by piecing together and repeating a number of fragments having no more connection with each other than the patches in a crazy quilt have. One of his latest works, 'Sous les lauriers roses' (1920), that runs to twenty-seven pages, is perfectly childish in its scrappiness.

He would hardly be worth considering in and by himself, but some of the French eulogies upon him do at least help us to take our bearings in modern music and modern criticism. When we see mighty architects and builders like Brahms and Beethoven being gibed at, and then see the sort of music that satisfies their detractors—well, we begin to put two and two together. We reflect that, after all, it is impossible to get a quart into a pint pot. What is the use of our talking about St. Paul's or Chartres to the little fellow over there with the tiny spade and bucket who is admiring the sand castle he has just managed to construct? We must wait till he grows up before we begin to discuss architecture with him.

THE SCHÖNBERG CASE

25th November 1923

Thanks to the admirable Federation of Music Clubs, London music lovers have had, during the week, three opportunities of hearing Schönberg's 'Pierrot Lunaire'—so long a bone of contention on the Continent—on Monday evening at Kensington, on Tuesday afternoon at Westminster, and on Wednesday at Chelsea. I do not know whether any one took all three chances —or shall I say risks? Some of my colleagues were content with one performance. A few of the Dreadnoughts among us braved two; but when we asked each other whether we were going to the third, we all with one accord began to make excuse, saying, 'I am engaged at the Queen's Hall tomorrow', or 'Tomorrow I shall be too unwell to listen to any music, especially Schönberg's.' This latter was no idle fear, it seems, for one colleague whom I saw on Wednesday assured me that after attending Monday's performance he had suffered all Tuesday from a distressing, though fortunately not dangerous, internal complaint that confined him to the house. He could not attribute this positively to 'Pierrot Lunaire', but he thought the sequence of events not without significance.

The reader who does not know the work may like to know that it is a setting of twenty-one short poems (translated from the French of Albert Giraud) for a solo voice and a small chamber orchestra consisting of piano, flute (interchanging with piccolo), clarinet (interchanging with bass clarinet), violin (interchanging with viola), and 'cello. The players at these performances (Jean Wiéner, Louis Fleury, H. Delacroix, H. Denayer, and Paul Mas) were said to have rehearsed the work 110 times, but I think the figure must be exaggerated, as they all looked in quite good health. Darius Milhaud conducted, with a touching blend of solemnity and anxiety. The poems were spoken (in French, much to the annoyance of those of us who had learned them in the German, so as to have every ounce of our cerebral energy free to follow the music), by Madame Marya Freund.

Schönberg writes definite notes for the voice in his score, but he specifies for the vocalist a method of delivery half-way between song and speech. I found this method not merely an annoyance but a strain. It is bad enough, we all know, to have to take in instrumental music and pure speech simultaneously; but that is a simple proposition compared with the one Schönberg sets for our ear and our brain. I thought Madame Freund often got, in spite of herself, much nearer to pure singing than Schönberg would have approved of: but I cannot dogmatise on that point. What is certain is that of all the forms of torture devised for the musical ear, this new style of 'Sprechgesang' is the cruellest; to myself, at any rate, it was a perpetual misery to be unable to fix the voice as either a pure singing or a pure speaking instrument. The method, too, becomes unbearably monotonous after a while.

The performance was a triumph for Madame Freund, who sang from memory. I shudder at the work it must have cost her to attain such accuracy of pitch and time. At the first performance I followed with the score. The singer and the players were not invariably on the same beat at the same moment, but the divergences were few; the marvel was that the timing should have been so generally accurate, considering the zig-zag nature of the writing.

I cannot imagine anyone who has heard the work two or three times ever wanting to hear it again; I certainly do not. Nothing more needlessly ugly and at the same time so pointless has ever been heard in London; and I doubt whether, on this occasion, we shall be solemnly warned, as we have been once or twice in the past, of the danger of hastily despising a work that may be acclaimed as a masterpiece by the next generation. We are all quite willing to run that risk. In the first place, there has never yet, in the whole history of music, been a composer of any value who was not recognised as such by his own generation; and it is hardly likely that Nature has gone out of her way to make an exception in the case of the later Schönberg. (The earlier Schönberg really could write music.) In the second place, this is not a case of our being bowled over by a startlingly new style. Schönberg's scores have been published long enough for us to get to know them as well as we know Franck's or

Strauss's. I myself have read through the 'Pierrot Lunaire' many times; indeed, to be able to submit it to *the* great test of music—running it through one's mind on one's walks—I went to the extent of committing a couple of the songs to memory. After all this trouble the music seems to me as ugly and empty as it did at first. However the Schönbergian *pur sang* may try to account for our poor opinion of the 'Pierrot Lunaire', he cannot do so by charging us with lack of familiarity with it.

The Schönbergians, indeed, are hard put to it to justify their own mild enthusiasm for the work. Singularly few of them will commit themselves to a point-blank declaration that they think it good music; and the one or two who do cannot tell us precisely why they think so. What they have to say in praise of it is mostly irrelevant; they tell us not what the music does, but what it sets out to do—which is quite a different matter. We are told that it is meant to be a satire on the romantic spirit. If so, the satire is a very poor one. If you want to kill a thing by laughing at it, your laugh must show a quicker intelligence than the thing itself; you will not do it merely by taking your own super-dullness with preposterous seriousness. Not only is the derision of Giraud and Schönberg a trifle dull-witted—especially Schönberg's—but it is hopelessly stale and conventional. For the true antique commend me to your up-to-date young man: there is not a slogan in his repertory that has not been staled by centuries of use by his innocent like. In one of these Giraud poems Pierrot shows his fine contempt for the romantic by turning a skull into a pipe-bowl and smoking through it. A very dashing little fellow, evidently; but how unoriginal! To go no further back than a century ago, the young Romantics (see, especially, the letters of Berlioz and a picture by Delacroix in the Louvre) were showing their contempt for bourgeois notions of life by treating the human skull with a familiarity bordering on disrespect. And it is the dabblers in these weary old clichés who ask us to take them as the last word in cynical satire!

Nor is it any use telling us that Schönberg's harmony and his general procedure are new. Nothing is easier than to do something new in music; the difficulty is to be at once new and interesting. Write, if you like—as in the seventh of these songs—

for a voice accompanied by a flute alone; but at least write a better line for the flute than Schönberg does. Do not imagine, again, that if only you use harmonies that have never been used before you are absolved from the old necessity of making your harmonies talk sense. You may say, of course, that your harmonic thinking is so far in advance of ours that our poor intelligences cannot follow you. The proper recipients for that story are the marines: there has never yet been a composer whose harmonic sense was so far in advance of his time that only two or three people in Europe in his own day could see what he was driving at; and, as I have hinted, it is hardly likely that Nature has conferred that unprecedented distinction on you.

Let me risk being called an ignoramus by the next generation, or the one after that, by saying outright that 'Pierrot Lunaire' is the music not of a genius but of a brain that has lost every vestige of the musical faculty it once had except the power to put notes together without the smallest concern for whether they mean anything or not.

SCHUBERT:

A POINT IN THE 'UNFINISHED'

2nd February 1941

I SEE a number of performances of Schubert's 'Unfinished' announced in various parts of the country; and I have no doubt that wherever the work is given enthusiasts are still discussing the old question of the switch-over from the first-subject matter to the second in the opening movement. The reader who has not a score handy may like to be reminded that Schubert's exposition of his first theme, or congeries of themes, is in B minor, and occupies thirty-eight bars. By the forty-second bar he is right into his second subject, the cantabile melody in the 'cellos in G major. That is to say, he takes us out of one world into another in four bars; and of these four, three consist of a single long-held note, so that the actual change-over is effected in one bar of modulation from the old key to the new:

There is a school of thought that regards this as an evasion of the symphonist's crucial problem of how to move convincingly from one main section of his structure to another. These changes, it is contended, ought to be more gradual, not a mere matter, as is alleged to be the case in this instance, of two sharply contrasted themes being hitched up together by hook or by crook.

I have never been able to agree with this point of view regarding the join in the Unfinished. It has its origin, I think, in a tenet of the nineteenth century to which Wagner gave expression in a letter *à propos* of the second act of 'Tristan', in which he says that the art of composition is really the art of imperceptible transition. The eighteenth century bothered little about this; broadly speaking, when Mozart has handed us the whole of his first-subject matter on one plate he calmly turns round and reaches out to the sideboard for the plate containing the second theme, keeping our attention occupied, during the few seconds the substitution of the one for the other takes him, with a conventional chord or two that have no other purpose than to inform the diners that the first course is over and the second will follow immediately. Beethoven took his transitions more seriously. So did Brahms, though his joins are often no more than skilled padding without any true organic life in it.

Is there any reason, we may surely ask, why a mind that does not work at all like Beethoven's should try to reproduce the Beethovenian manner of transition? Schubert's genius was far more naïve than reflective. He seems to have racked his brains hardly at all over problems of structure, trusting to his inexhaustible invention to see him through anything. Now and then, as in the slap-dash first movements of some of his feebler piano sonatas, he lands himself in real difficulties through this habit of his of plunging into a large-scale composition without having first of all thought out the connection of the parts to the very end. In his chamber music, as a rule, he makes no attempt at all to link up one thematic group with another by means of 'development': he just goes straight on, achieving, however, in his own peculiar way an inner logic that is perfectly convincing.

It is when he is in a more or less dramatic mood that he feels the necessity for building some sort of bridge that will at once mark off from each other and connect two contrasting emotional worlds. He does this in the most obviously purposeful and pointed fashion in the transition from the first to the second subject of the 'Rosamund' overture. But always on occasions of this kind his procedure is essentially the same—not to fumble about in the Brahmsian manner but to go straight to the point, poising the music for a while on a note or chord that is related to both the old key and the new, and then making a swift modulation into the new matter in the contrasting key. If the reader will compare the musical example already quoted with the join of the two main subjects in the 'Rosamund', or again with the corresponding transitional passage in the great C major symphony:

he will see at a glance that the procedure is basically the same in all three cases; and I, for my part, can conceive no possible criticism of the transition in the Unfinished that would not apply in precisely the same degree to that in the C major.

This, in fact, was Schubert's way of going about things, and it was the way most organically related to the nature of the characteristically Schubertian ideas. In the first movement of the Unfinished the determining factor at the critical point we are considering is not the melody of the first subject *per se*, but the sombre mood generated by a succession of dissonances of this type:

It is these that create that feeling of increasing tension in the exposition of the first subject, and the desire for relief from this tension, that make a complete change of mood at this point not a mere compositorial device but an irresistible necessity. It is this inevitableness in the spiritual sequences of the movement that make it the great thing it is; and I personally could wish for no better transition to the lovely second theme than the temporary poise, followed by the simple modulation, shown in No. 1. Both emotionally and structurally Schubert's join does all that is required of it, and does it in the minimum of time and without a trace of bookishness or self-consciousness.

SIBELIUS:

TWO SYMPHONIES

28th March 1920

At a rehearsal of Sibelius's Fourth Symphony some years ago I was approached by a man who asked if he might look over my score. Of course I was delighted. After a few minutes of the music, the man turned to me and remarked tentatively: 'Queer stoof, eh?' I replied that perhaps it was not easy to take in music of this sort at a first hearing—that it came from a different civilisation from ours, and that without a little imaginative insight into the history and the mental and physical environment of a nation it was hardly possible to understand all that a typical representative of that nation was driving at in his art. As my visitor still seemed a little puzzled I added: 'You see, this music comes from Finland.' His face brightened at once; he had the key to the enigma. 'Ah!' he said, 'that's it; aw coom from Halifax.' I remarked that Halifax was a very long way from Finland, and we left it at that.

I was reminded of this experience the other afternoon at the Queen's Hall. Sir Henry Wood and I seemed to be a minority of two in the voting upon the Fourth Symphony. It appears to have bored everyone else with whom I have discussed it. I console myself with the reflection that they all probably come from Halifax, either by train or by ancestry. Whether I *like* the work in the sense that I like the 'Boutique Fantasque', or the 'Siegfried Idyll', or tobacco, I cannot say; but I know it fascinates me. There is no arguing about taste, so I will not try to convince people to whom the characteristic gloom of Sibelius is temperamentally abhorrent. I can only say that this particular brand of gloom appeals to me. Sibelius's spectacles are not mine, any more than Tchaikovsky's are; but I have no objection to looking through them now and then for half-an-hour. The pessimist has as much right to exist and express himself as the cheerful idiot has. The only thing we in our turn have a right to ask of him is that he shall talk so persuasively that for the moment he really convinces us that the world is going to the demnition bowwows; and Sibelius, for me at any rate, does this. I greatly prefer his black-browed snubbing of Ormuzd to Tchaikovsky's hysterical appeal to Ahriman not to hurt him so much. But if other people are merely bored by the gloom of dense sunless forests I cannot say them nay. I would ask them, however, to take a little interest in Sibelius's Fourth Symphony on other grounds.

We often say of a work of art that we admire that it does not contain a superfluous note, or word, or line, as the case may be. This symphony of Sibelius's is one of the few works on a large scale of which that is literally true. He has left out more notes than most other composers would have put in; the symphony has always reminded me of one of those drawings in which every line, or every portion of a line, that was not absolutely essential to the suggestion of a form has been rubbed out. The eye easily accommodates itself to this economy in the plastic arts, for there is the memory of the thing seen to help out the artist's curt suggestion of it.

A non-representative art like music, however, adopts this method of compression at its peril. Yet a moment's reflection will show that music, like drawing and like literature, can, in the hands of a composer who knows what he is about, with impunity cut out everything that is not absolutely vital to the idea. Harmony, let us remember, has progressed by composers telescoping chordal progressions, as it were—that is to say, by anticipating part of the coming chord in the present one, thus making new harmonies. One reason of the obscurity of the later Schönberg is that he telescopes too swiftly, too drastically for us: *he* may see the logical connection between two adjacent chords, but we cannot; he has cut out too many of the transitions that make things easy for us. People who are used to travelling comfortably, even if a little roundabout, by the high roads are apt to get lost when they have to make their way straight across country.

Nevertheless, the original harmonists are always taking us by shorter and shorter paths; and there are minds here and there that are similarly bent on telescoping the forms of music. Sibelius is one of them; and the new method has never been so successfully followed as in this Fourth Symphony. He disdains transition for transition's sake: he lays theme endways to theme as the builders of some prehistoric walls or buildings may have laid stone upon stone, without mortar between them. But we have grown so used to mortar in music that without it the structure makes too many demands upon the speed of accommodation of the average ear. Music like this seems to have no softening atmosphere about it, no aerial perspective; every theme springs abruptly out of the earth and challenges the ear to take it in at once and adjust it to its fellows; and everything seems to be in the foreground, all in the one plane. For my part I like the stark strength and prehistoric roughness of the style; but it will evidently take some time for the general music-lover to feel at home in it.

The other extreme of style may be seen in the great Second Symphony of Elgar, of which Mr. Adrian Boult gave so fine a performance on Tuesday; in all Elgar's later music on the big scale, indeed—the two symphonies, the quartet, and the quintet. We are so used to using the one term, 'symphonic', to cover every kind of work for several instruments that lasts for half-an-hour or so that we are apt to forget the many differences of species there may be and are within the same genus. The text-books still go on with their innocent prattle about 'sonata form', and the guileless student imagines that it is in this ancient form that all symphonies are written. Elgar's symphonies, however, have about as much to do with sonata form in the Conservatoire sense of the term as the nervous system of a highly organised human being has with the skeleton of the chimpanzee. But this point cannot be adequately elaborated here. I must reserve it for another article.

SIBELIUS:

MOST PERSONAL OF GREAT COMPOSERS

1st October 1933

We need not be surprised that Sibelius, at the age of sixty-eight, and with considerably more than a hundred opus numbers to his credit, is still comparatively little known. In matters of this kind we must learn to think not in years but in generations, our public musical life being what it is. How much does the average man know, for instance, of the work of Berlioz, who died sixty-four years ago? I happened the other day to come across a complaint by a German writer that singers seemed to know next to nothing of Hugo Wolf's songs but 'Verborgenheit' and 'Gesang Weylas'. That was in 1909; and in 1933 things are not very much better in this respect.

If people would only learn to read music for themselves, whether they can play an instrument or not, there would be a different story to tell. As it is, they are dependent for their knowledge of music upon performers; and the average performer is considerably less of an artist than of a business man who wants to make the maximum of money with the minimum of trouble. Only the other day I heard of a star violinist who positively refused to learn either the Sibelius or the Elgar violin concerto; why, indeed, from his point of view, should he trouble to do so, when he knows he can go on to the end of his days extracting money from the pockets of the gullible public by means of the Mendelssohn, Brahms, Bruch, and Tchaikovsky concertos, plus a score or so of favourite trifles? And even when conductors, fiddlers, pianists, singers, and so on do take courage and now and then bring forward an unfamiliar work, the result, as often as not, is to make those who already know the work wish they had kept their hands off it, a subject upon which I shall have something to say in another article.

Even supposing that all performances of Sibelius were ideal, so that our audiences really heard what they thought they were hearing, and liked the works and encouraged concert promoters to give them again, it would still, at our past and present rate of progress, take something like three hundred years for the public to become acquainted with the whole Sibelius. Few people realise how many different aspects his work presents. The 'Finnish' Sibelius, the exploiter of an idiom that is vaguely supposed to be 'national', is actually only a small part of the total Sibelius, as anyone will discover if he takes up a few representative works in certain of the other genres cultivated by the composer—the songs, the chamber music, the concerted music, the choral music, the incidental music to plays, and so on. The string quartet, for instance, or the violin concerto that was given at the Promenades this week, presents us with a Sibelius very different from the Sibelius of the popular conception, derived mainly as this is from 'Finlandia', the 'Valse Triste', 'En Saga', 'The Swan of Tuonela', the 'Karelia Suite', and works of that kind.

Little that is written upon composers by their contemporaries turns out to be of any ultimate value—a sobering reflection for us critics, but one from which a study of the musical criticism of the past leaves us no escape, for even the contemporary critics who were best-disposed towards a Wagner or a Berlioz or a Brahms, for example, have really contributed very little towards our present understanding of these composers. We of today are much too close to Sibelius, and have had too little time to let the bulk of his music settle deep within us and throw out its own basic lines of contact with our conception of the main stream of musical history, for us to be able to attempt anything like a picture of him as the generation of 1960 or that of 2000 will see him.

His many-sidedness is of itself a little puzzling to us; we find it far from easy to bring into the one focus works so disparate as the 'national' pieces, the earlier symphonic poems, the string quartet, and the violin concerto on the one hand, and the later symphonies and 'Tapiola' on the other. The violin concerto, for instance, contains a great deal that, if the work stood alone, would prompt us to rank the composer of it among the epigones of German romanticism. The lovely slow movement in particular carries a step further the kind of expression we get in the greater Schumann—the Schumann of the song 'Requiem', the 'Genoveva', the 'Manfred', and the 'Faust'; while one of the themes in the finale, oddly enough, is not only almost note for note identical with the main theme of Wagner's 'Faust Overture', but suggests a good deal of the type of mid-nineteenth century romanticism of which this overture and the 'Faust Symphony' of Liszt are the finest expressions.

Many another work of Sibelius besides the concerto gives us the feeling that with the slightest of turns of fortune's wheel he might have pursued quite another development than the one we have come to associate with him. For it must be remembered that the concerto and the string quartet are not early works, representing a mental phase, derived from the music of his predecessors, that Sibelius was soon to abandon for the role of a 'national' composer, but works of his middle period, that follow upon works in what we would now call the more definitely Sibelian style. The concerto (1903), for instance, is later than the first two symphonies (1899 and 1902), 'En Saga' (1892), 'Karelia' (1893), and 'Finlandia' (1899), while the quartet (1909) follows upon these works, 'Pohjola's Daughter', and the third symphony (1908). Many of the songs of this middle period, too, are in a vein that it is quite impossible to associate with the 'Finnish' Sibelius.

But there seems to have been an instinct in him that drove him imperiously before it into a field that is wholly his own, bringing him to a music that is neither romantic, nor 'national', nor anything else to which one of the conventional labels can be attached, but purely and simply Sibelius. From the first, even when he was working in an idiom that others had cultivated before him, he had a note decidedly his own; and in the great works of his maturity he reveals himself as the most personal, the least derivative, of all the great composers.

The only one he can be compared to in this respect is Berlioz, who, like himself, appears to be without ancestors and without posterity. But we are discovering now that Berlioz owed more to some of his predecessors than was at one time thought: the line of connection has been obscured because, while Beethoven, Brahms, Wagner, Strauss and others derived from composers whose works are familiar to everyone, the composers to whom

Berlioz was in some degree indebted are now completely unknown except to a few students of the byways of musical history. Sibelius, in his latest and greatest works, reminds us of nobody. Gradually, out of the mixture of influences to which he was subject in his earlier and middle years, there emerged a musical personality that is completely and solely itself both as a whole and in detail. An urgent instinct to economy in him first of all drove him to dispense with the formal beginnings and endings upon which most composers have had to rely. A study of his songs is very instructive in this respect; they plunge into their subject without preamble, and having said what they have to say they cease abruptly, trailing no conventional fringe behind them as they leave the stage.

The dividing line in his career—a line none the less definite because of an occasional dip to this side or that of it—is the remarkable fourth symphony, a work of a laconicism that is at first disconcerting. No other music that has ever been written is so spare of build as this: it is an athlete's body, without an ounce of superfluous flesh upon it, with most of the weight in the bones and with the muscles all tension and power. From that point onwards his best musical thinking has tended more and more towards drastic concision: the culmination of it all has been 'Tapiola', in which a work lasting some fifteen minutes has been constructed virtually from first to last out of a single germ-idea, and the seventh symphony, in which the music follows a logical development of its own without the smallest reliance on the standardised structural devices of the ordinary symphony: we do not know why this or that thematic fragment should suddenly emerge at this point or that—all we know at the finish is that it could not have been otherwise, that the work is not only extraordinarily expressive but formally one and indivisible. And the peculiar thematic weaving is matched with a style of orchestration that complies with the definition of the highest style in any field of literature or art—it is not something applied from the outside, but something pertaining only to those particular ideas, so that it is impossible to say which is the idea and which its clothing.

I remember Sibelius astonishing me, some thirty years ago, by saying that a certain composer who is rightly regarded as, in the current phrase, 'a master of instrumentation', was really only a thinker in terms of the piano. I found it difficult to agree with him then; but after 'Tapiola' and the seventh symphony I see better what he meant. He himself is the pure type of the composer who does not simply 'orchestrate' but thinks in terms of the orchestra as a natural language of its own. A 'piano arrangement' of either of these two works of his would be a pure absurdity.

SIBELIUS ON COMPOSITION:

THE FALLACY OF 'PURE' MUSIC

30th December 1934

IN an interesting article in the *Daily Telegraph* the other day, Mr. Walter Legge gave us the substance of some recent conversations he has had with Sibelius. According to the latter, 'since Beethoven's time all the so-called symphonies, except Brahms's, have been symphonic poems. In many cases the composers have told us, or at least indicated, the programmes they had in mind; in others it is plain that there has been some story or landscape or set of images that the composer has set himself to illustrate. That is not my idea of a symphony. My symphonies are music conceived and worked out in terms of music and with no literary basis. I am not a literary musician; for me music begins where words cease. . . . A symphony should be first and last music. Of course it has happened that, quite unbidden, some mental image has established itself in my mind in connection with a movement I have been writing, but the germ and the fertilisation of my symphonies have been solely musical. When I set out to write symphonic poems it is a different matter. "Tapiola", "Pohjola's Daughter", "Lemminkaïnen", "The Swan of Tuonela", are suggested to me by our national poetry, but I do not pretend that they are symphonies.'

All this, admirable as it is in some ways, seems to me to be based on an aesthetic misconception that is so common that it is worth while examining it for a moment.

Amateurs in musical aesthetic are fond of talking about what they call 'pure' music, by which they mean, if they mean anything at all, music that simply weaves notes into patterns for the notes' sake and the pattern's sake. The other kind of music is motived by, or in some way associated with, ideas and emotions derived from the outer world—from poetry, scenery, stories, characters, and so on. Now since the antithesis of pure is impure, this other kind of music must be impure music: and that being so, we reach the saddening conclusion that all the greatest composers the world has ever known have been monsters of artistic impurity. For without exception they have not only dipped their hands in these unclean waters but bathed, nay wallowed, in them: Monteverdi when he sets the story of Orpheus to music, Mozart when he lets the shape, the colour, the expression of his music be determined by the literary image he had formed of a Don Giovanni or an Osmin, Beethoven when he takes as his musical starting-point a Florestan, a Pizarro, or the verbal images suggested by the words of the Mass, Brahms when he sets out to find a musical equivalent for the words of his German Requiem, are as guilty of the same supposed descent into the unclean as Liszt when he writes an 'Orpheus', Strauss when he writes a 'Till Eulenspiegel', Elgar when he writes a 'Falstaff', Debussy when he sets the sea at different times of the day to music, or Holst when he 'paints' for us the planets.

To be strictly logical, we ought to write off nineteen-twentieths of the best music in the world as impure, for it is literary or pictorial music. The amount of 'pure' music in the world is extremely small. Music of this kind is typified by the first of Bach's 'Twelve Little Preludes', or, on a larger scale, by one of the rapid movements of a Brandenburg Concerto. Our delight here is purely and simply in the way the notes go and the symmetrical patterns they weave. Music of this kind resembles a kitten chasing its own tail—a charming spectacle, but not the conceivably highest of intellectual functions.

If we are going to frown upon the symphonic poem and the programme symphony, we must also frown upon the opera, the oratorio, the cantata, and the song, for the difference between these and the other two are superficial, not basic. 'Ein Heldenleben' and 'Don Juan' are operas without words: the 'Ring' is a symphonic poem with visible instead of imagined characters: 'Pelléas and Mélisande' becomes an opera in the hands of Debussy and a symphonic poem in the hands of Schönberg: and so *ad infinitum*. It will be said, however, that in the case of a symphony pure and simple the composer, as Sibelius implies, lets his musical faculty function in a different way from what it does in the symphonic poem. To some extent that is true; but even that proposition is not quite so simple as it looks.

On the one hand, only a bad composer makes his symphonic poem (or his song) a mere point-to-point illustration of episodes or verbal ideas. When Sibelius says that his symphonies are music conceived and worked out in terms of music, he forgets, if I may say so, that even in a symphonic poem or a song of the best kind the composer's mind functions in much the same way.

A genuine musician's nature is too musical for him to think organically in any other terms but those of music, no matter on what 'literary' subject his eyes may appear to be turned. Very often the subject is something added later, some external irritant, as it were, that merely crystallises an emotion that is already at work inside the composer. Strauss has told us, *à propos* of his own songs, that 'one evening he will be turning the leaves of a volume of poetry: a poem will strike his eye, he reads it through, and at once the appropriate music is instinctively fitted to it. He is in a musical frame of mind, and all he wants is the right poetic vessel into which to pour his ideas. If good luck throws this in his way, a satisfactory song results. But often the poem that presents itself is not the right one; then he has to bend his musical mood to fit it the best way it can; he works laboriously and without the right kind of enthusiasm at it. The song, in fact, is made, not born.' In other words, a good song is not the mere pointing of the words, but a *piece of music* that exists in virtue of its own nature, the poet's idea being caught up into the very being of music and reconstituted *as* music.

Wagner, who was the clearest thinker among all the great composers on the subject of musical aesthetic, has expressly laid it down that a composer must *not* rush to set his ideas down on paper the moment he has been stirred by some experience, whether from books or from actual life. He must wait until the germ thus sown has had time to develop within him according to the unconscious laws of music; and then, when he sits down to compose his work, though it may bear a literary title such as 'Faust' or 'Hamlet', it will be *music* shaping itself and evolving not as literature or a picture but as music. The man who imagines that Wagner first of all wrote texts and then set himself to find equivalents in sound for them merely exhibits the grossest ignorance of his subject: Wagner himself tells us, more than once, that the poetic and the musical impulses always functioned simultaneously within him; in the very act of conceiving the words of an opera he was also conceiving, in essence, the music, and a subconscious musical plan was all the time dictating to him the substance and the form of his poem. We thus arrive at the very position Sibelius takes up in defence of his own symphonies.

It will be objected, no doubt, that I am not doing justice to his distinction between his symphonic poems, in which, as he admits, his imagination works simultaneously along the poetic and the musical line, and his symphonies, in which, he contends, he is 'first and last' writing just 'music'. But the fallacy here is that unless a composer is writing out-and-out 'pure' music, music of the simple pattern-for-its-own-sake order, music that just delights, like the kitten, in the game it is playing with its own tail, he must be making his music express, in all its phases, some strong emotion that has taken possession of him; and as soon as he begins to do this, his imagination will take a course subconsciously dictated to him by that emotion.

Now the musical faculty does not exist in a watertight compartment, shut off from the rest of the mind and the nature and the experience of the man. As George Henry Lewes put it, 'the whole man thinks'—not this or that convolution of his brain, functioning in a sealed recess of its own. And so, even though the composer is not specifically working to a programme, none the less, if he is expressing himself and his experience of life in the music he has in hand, he is letting the substance and the pattern of his music take on the nature and the contour of something that is not, in the strict sense of the term, 'pure' music.

Sibelius himself gives up his own case when he admits that 'of course it has happened that, quite unbidden, some mental image has established itself in my mind in connection with a [symphonic] movement that I have written,' 'the germ and the fertilisation' of the work, however, having been 'solely musical'. Precisely: his seventh symphony, though 'purely musical' in the sense that it has no programme that could be put into words, is all the same controlled by 'mental images' that are, in essence, poetic or pictorial or experiential. That is to say, the notes go this way or that, a theme is silent for a long time and then suddenly recurs, not because Sibelius is working, in the style of 'abstract' music, to a preconceived decorative pattern, but because the vicissitudes of his emotions, of his 'mental images', control the nature and the course of the music.

Why, for instance, should that impressive trombone call occur twice just when and where it does, if not for the reason that it *had* to come then and there and nowhere else and at no other times, because it answers to some controlling 'mental image' that has its organic part to play in the evolution of the total musical idea? The seventh symphony is 'purely musical' in the sense that, unlike 'Tapiola', it has no extra-musical basis that could be put into words, but it is none the less 'poetic' music as well as being 'just music'. It is a symphony, not a symphonic poem; but the distinction is one less of kind than of degree.

It is not generally recognised that externally-derived 'mental images' often play a considerable part in the tissue of a musical work that is held to be 'just music'. Composers are rightly reticent about these matters, for they do not want absurd 'programmes' to be read into their music, which would be sure to happen if they gave their listeners the clue to this or that 'image'. Nevertheless, these 'mental images' come and go in their imagination in the act of composition to an extent that would surprise us did the composers take us into their confidence. It is only through a chance remark of Brahms that we discover that the horn call in the preamble to the finale of his first symphony was associated in his mind with a shepherd and a pastoral scene. There is a passage in 'Gerontius' that was always associated in Elgar's mind with the impressions he used to receive, as a tiny boy, of the swaying of the tops of the noble trees in a private park which I also know well. The reader can amuse himself, if he likes, by trying to locate the passage in the score; but I can assure him in advance that he has not the ghost of a chance of finding it, for there is nothing whatever either in the words or in the shape of the music to give him the clue; the 'mental image', visual in origin, has been transmuted into music pure and simple.

A composer's imagination functions not as a self-contained faculty on a sort of a desert island of its own, but as a whole—

the whole man thinks. It is inevitable, therefore, that his music, whether he knows it or not (and often he is unaware of it himself), shall be the expression of images from life and from books that have sunk deep within him and become part of the tissue of his brain and being. If, then, we are going to call his music 'pure' music because it has no formal programme or is not a setting of words, it is evident that we must give a special meaning to the word 'pure'; the music is certainly not 'pure' in the sense that the first movement of a Brandenburg Concerto is.

When we thus get to the back of the beyond of the composer's mentality we find that many a procedure on his part that seems, on the face of it, to be dictated by words, or episodes, or some other external prompting, is in reality merely the spontaneous musical expression of a mood that pre-existed in him already; that is to say, it is not determined by the words or the situation, but merely seizes upon these in order to realise itself.

THE INDEPENDENCE OF SIBELIUS:

AN OBITUARY NOTICE

2nd September 1957

Sibelius had become almost a legendary musical figure even during his lifetime, so long ago was it that he produced his last major works. His Seventh Symphony seems almost as remote in time from us as the Fourth of Brahms or the Sixth of Tchaikovsky or the Ninth of Mahler.

Whether he actually completed an eighth or not we do not as yet know for certain, or if he did, what his reasons were for withholding it from publication or performance.

In no country, with the exception of his own, will the news of his death have been received with such regret as in ours. His first vogue in England was primarily due to the insight and the zeal of Henry Wood and Granville Bantock in the Concert hall, and Mrs. Rosa Newmarch in the Press. Those beginnings were so long ago that comparatively few of Sibelius's English admirers of today can have taken part in them: my own acquaintance with him, personal and artistic, dates from over half a century ago.

* * *

Until he came upon the scene, Finland had not been musically 'on the map', and none of us knew in those days quite how to 'place' him. Obviously he owed next to nothing to Germany or France, nor, when one really got down to thinking about it, to the geographically adjacent Scandinavia or Russia, each of which had already by that time staked out a claim to a musical idiom and a musical field of thought of its own.

The talk current at that time about performances of the nationalistic 'Finlandia' being frowned upon by the Russian authorities seemed to suggest that this young Northerner's affiliations were not precisely Muscovite, though I still have the clearest recollection of his being placed somehow or other, on the strength of his First Symphony, in the Tchaikovsky succession.

It was not long, however, before he came into full clear definition as just Jean Sibelius, the most individual composer, perhaps, the most purely self-forming and self-maintaining, the world has ever seen. He seems to have inhabited a mental world entirely his own.

To what extent that world can be regarded basically as a Finnish world only a Finn can say. For the rest of us it is a case not of seeing Sibelius through Finnish eyes but of seeing Finland through the eyes of Sibelius. By 'individual' I mean simply that he talks, in his minor as well as his major works, in an idiom melodically, harmonically, rhythmically and orchestrally his own. The tracts of thought he opened out to us are purely his own: no one could ever imagine any other signature, personal or racial, upon any page of his music than that of Jean Sibelius.

*   *   *

The intriguing thing about it all is that he achieved this individualism without resort to any factitious doctrinaire nonsense about 're-creating himself', or 'making a new language for himself'. In one work after another, the musical language he speaks is the ordinary one, but he manages to say entirely different things in each work according to the mood or the vision of the moment.

It may turn out that this curious independence of mind and of speech will operate in Sibelius's favour as one generation succeeds another. It not infrequently happens that a composer falls somewhat out of fashion, at any rate for a while, because of his association in the public mind with some 'ism' or other—romanticism, neo-classicism, realism, impressionism, etc.—that happens to have got out of fashion; but it is impossible to pin any 'ism' label at all on Sibelius's music. Acceptance of it depends on nothing but itself, what it says and how it says it.

STRAUSS:

DE SENECTUTE

18th April 1948

A SENSITIVE performance of Strauss's 'Metamorphosen' by Dr. Boyd Neel and his orchestra the other evening set me thinking afresh not only about the work itself but about the perpetually fascinating question of old men's music.

There have not been very many opportunities of hearing the 'Metamorphosen', but latterly we have been able to study it intensively, the full score having been published by Boosey and Hawkes a little while ago. Strauss describes his work as a Study for twenty-three solo strings. It appears to have been written in 1945, when he was eighty-one. The title is intriguing. A 'study' in what, and to what end? 'Metamorphoses' of what, and why? He introduces at the ninth bar a fragment from the Funeral March of the Eroica; he makes liberal use of it in the course of the work, and towards the end the main theme of the March appears in rather fuller form with a footnote, 'In memoriam!' This Beethoven reference can hardly escape any listener; but there are others, less immediately obvious, to the theme of King Marke's lament in the second act of 'Tristan' and to certain passages in the 'Rosenkavalier'. It does not matter whether all these references are willed or unconscious on Strauss's part; they are unmistakably there, and they play as important a part in the building up of the overriding mood of the work as the Eroica theme does.

The publication of the score has enabled us to get a much better idea of the 'Metamorphosen' than was possible a couple of years or so ago. On those occasions it was inevitable that what should engage our attention most was the reminiscences: now we can take these in our stride and concentrate on Strauss's contribution to the matter. The result is that now, for myself at any rate, the 'Metamorphosen' reveals itself as one of his major orchestral works. It shows a remarkable command of a way of working new to him. The distant beginning of that way is found in the sonatas and quartets of Beethoven's last period. The old attempts to expound these in terms of sonata form, variation form and all the rest of the old classroom terminology have visibly ended in futility. The error of the analysts has been the one bequeathed to us by the nineteenth century pedagogues—to approach music through the medium of 'forms' instead of through the mental complex of which a form is merely the envelope.

Beethoven's mind had undergone a profound transformation in his final phase, and the last works are the outcome of that change, not of an impulse to 'extend', to 'modify', certain 'forms'. 'Sonata form' and all the rest of it had by that time gone by the board so far as he was concerned, because the conditions that had brought that form into being had served their historic turn and passed away. Beethoven now constructs in a new way because he is thinking in a new way; he no longer creates by means of parallel and converging lines—'subjects'—but from a centre outwards; everything that happens in the music of a movement is the proliferation of a single cell.

Nineteenth-century instrumental composers, Brahms included, did not, because they could not, follow Beethoven in his last period; their model was the Beethoven of the second. But with the final liquidation of sonata form—which, as I have said, accomplished its historic mission long ago—the concentric way of thinking and building has become more and more attractive to the greater composers; and I find it fascinatingly employed in the 'Metamorphosen'.

My object today, however, is not to discuss third-period Beethoven but to touch on Strauss's work as a sample of old men's music. The great composers have finished in various ways. Beethoven fled to the mystic heights with Pater Seraphicus. So did Wagner, in a different fashion and by a different route. Bach put the whole weight of his great brain into the task—even though he did not consciously see that as his task—of demonstrating by means of a fugue subject certain cosmic laws of growth and form. The gloomy Verdi became a prism of pure light in 'Falstaff'. Strauss, in the 'Metamorphosen' and the lovely oboe concerto, turns with a smile from the ugly and stupid and vulgar world that is now ours and finds a way of his own to a Xanadu of his own.

One question I often ask myself is what the music of certain geniuses would have been like had they attained to old age; and that question confronts us in its most intriguing form in Schubert. His dates make us think of him as a little later than Mozart and a contemporary of Beethoven; it is not generally realised that had the ordinary span of years been allotted to him he would have ended his days in a world more different from that of his youth than has been the case with any other composer. He could have heard every one of Berlioz's works and seen Berlioz himself into his grave, and still have been only seventy-two. He could have heard 'Aida' at seventy-four and still been nearly ten years younger than Strauss is now. At sixty-three he could have studied the published score of 'Tristan'; he could have heard that work in the theatre at sixty-eight and the 'Meistersinger' at seventy-one—five years younger than the still-growing Vaughan Williams is now. What, we ask ourselves, would have been the effect on his unique genius of the impact of all these and other experiences?

RICHARD STRAUSS:

AN OBITUARY NOTICE

I

18th September 1949

Bülow said of Mendelssohn that he began as a genius and ended as a talent. Would he say the same if he were living today, of the Richard Strauss whose early promise he was one of the first to perceive? (Bülow died in 1894, after having lived to hear the 'Aus Italien' and 'Macbeth' of 1886–7, the 'Don Juan' of 1888, and the 'Tod und Verklärung' of 1889.) Perhaps not, having regard to the Oboe Concerto and the 'Metamorphosen' of the composer's last years; but he would still have maintained regretfully, I think, that the worst enemy of the genius in Strauss was the talent that dogged its footsteps from first to last. The trouble with Strauss was not, as with Mendelssohn, that the talent succeeded the genius in time and dissipated the rich heritage, but that the two walked and worked hand in hand throughout the greater part of his career.

It is a significant fact in this connection that the majority of the works of Strauss that will endure were written between the twenty-third and forty-eighth of his eighty-five years—between, that is, the 'Macbeth' of 1887 and the first 'Ariadne auf Naxos' of 1912. The notable works fall also into two ten-year periods, each of intensive exploration and creation in a particular sphere. Between 1888 and 1898 he produced the remarkable series of orchestral works of which the world is now familiar—'Don Juan', 'Tod und Verklärung', 'Till Eulenspiegel', 'Also sprach Zarathustra', 'Don Quixote', and 'Ein Heldenleben'.

Half-way through this brilliant decade he made his first excursion in opera with 'Guntram' (1894). The great operatic period began tentatively in 1901 with 'Feuersnot', a work of mixed quality; then, after an interval of four years, during which the only big orchestral work that came from his pen was the inflated and mostly abortive 'Symphonia Domestica' (1903) —which gave many of us at that time the uncomfortable feeling that he had written himself out at thirty-nine—came, like a bolt from the blue, the challenging 'Salome' of 1905, which, defective as it was in parts, was manifestly the sign of a growth in both imaginative range and technical mastery to which the only parallel in the history of opera is Wagner's development from 'Tannhäuser' and 'Lohengrin' to 'The Rhinegold'.

Three years later came the still more astonishing 'Elektra', and two years after that again the incomparable 'Rosenkavalier', which played with equal ease and certainty of touch over the most varied psychological fields.

After that came, in 1912, the first version of 'Ariadne auf Naxos', in which, side by side with miniature masterpieces such as the quintet of the comedians ('Es gilt, ob Tanzen, ob Singen, tauge'), there were indications that the great sea of his inspiration was setting to an ebb-tide. After that he made only one big attempt at purely orchestral writing in the 'Alpine Symphony' of 1915, a work which, for all its occasional flashes of pictorial ingenuity, was and remains a failure.

He now devoted himself for many years almost entirely to works for the stage—two ballets: 'The Legend of Joseph' (1914) and 'Schlagobers' (1924), and the operas 'Die Frau ohe Schatten' (1919), 'Intermezzo' (1925), 'Die aegyptische Helena' (1928), 'Arabella' (1933), 'Die schweigsame Frau' (1935, based on Ben Jonson's racy *Epicoene*), 'Der Friedenstag' (1938), 'Daphne' (1938) and 'Die Liebe der Danae' (1944). There is some first-rate Strauss in most of these; but it is significant that none of them has won a footing in the world repertory. (The only one of them that has been given in England is 'Arabella'.) In all of them the talent bulks larger than the genius.

A fascinating subject for the study of Strauss as man and artist is the youthful opera 'Guntram'. It attacts us in the first place by a peculiar spiritual highmindedness; Guntram is a sort of latter-day Parsifal. The spiritual, the ethical, seems however to have faded out of Strauss's make-up in later life. The opera, for all its unevenness of texture, is a work that still commands the respect of the Strauss student of today. It contains in embryo practically all the later operatic Strauss except, of course, the humorist, for whom there was no place in such a subject.

Most interesting of all, perhaps, to us as we look back upon it in the light of the entire Strauss are the first, unmistakable hints here and there of the weakness so characteristic of him in the after years, the talent in him masquerading for long stretches as genius, speaking with the same voice, wearing the same clothes, adopting the same postures, making the same gestures as its counterpart, and saying what appear on the surface to be the same vital things but are only the simulacra of them.

Long ago I tried to characterise this aspect of him in the simile of a great windmill beating the air majestically with its arms but grinding out no corn. I will have more to say on this subject in a following article before embarking on a discussion of Strauss's real qualities as an artist.

II

25th September 1949

STRAUSS, of course, was not the only composer to call occasionally upon almost-as-good talent to carry on glibly with the job of music-making while his genius took a day off. Eighteenth-century music provides us with examples of this kind of thing by the thousand.

Handel is particularly given to it. There is no outward difference between one of the very best and one of the least best of the opening movements, let us say, of his concerti grossi. The difference is internal; one movement is the real thing, the other, going about the same business in precisely the same way, is only good-quality make-believe. We have no complaint against procedures of this kind in music, such as a great deal of that of the eighteenth century, that makes no bones about complacently working in certain accepted patterns; we cheerfully admit that in the nature of the case there must be times when the pattern is less vitalised from within than at others.

But we are not tolerant of it in modern music, where the first thing we demand of a composer is that the form and the substance of a work, or of a long stretch of a work, shall be the natural and specific outward manifestation of the ideas, not a mould into which ideas can be poured by any capable journeyman.

Our grievance against Strauss is that when at less than his best he drops lazily into formulae, moulds, patterns of his own. Mechanics of that sort, on any but the smallest scale, are unacceptable today because, the composer's train of thought being largely psychological, we expect both the matter and the manner of the expression to be organically germane to the psychology or the situation of the moment, not simply a reach-me-down garment thrown hastily about it. Strauss's worst incursions into the hocus-pocus occur in moments when a big gathering up of all the threads is called for. His method at times like this is to play off concurrent or imitative orchestral strands against each other in great surging and receding waves of tone. We see the real thing in the orchestral postlude to the great trio in the 'Rosenkavalier'. Of the make-believe thing I could cite examples by the hundred from his less distinguished operas and the 'Symphonia Domestica' had I the space to do so.

But this distressing bluff of posing in the full majestic panoply of great Mars just when the warrior's arm is secretly most weak and tired is seldom resorted to in the two ten-year periods in which his genius burned most brightly.

In these he did enough to ensure him a permanent high place in musical history. He left music a different thing in many ways from what he found it. He diverted the great main stream of German music into several new channels, each time with conspicuous success. He enlarged enormously the scope of psychological and characteristic expression, not only in his best operas but in his concert music; his Don Juan, Don Quixote, Till Eulenspiegel, Macbeth, Baron Ochs, Octavian, Marschallin, Sophie, Salome, Elektra, Orestes and Clytemnestra are as alive as any characters in music.

Certain types evaded him, of course. He himself gave comic expression to his lack of imaginative sympathy with the Joseph of his ballet: the simplemindedness of Chrysothemis baffled him. (See how, on the other hand, Wagner has limned his simple Gutrune in a couple of immortal bars that go to the very root of the psychological matter.) Still, the portrait gallery of Strauss is extensive enough and varied enough and vital enough to make an occasional failure pardonable.

He laid the foundations, in the great sweeping melodies of his youthful 'Don Juan'—which were something without a parallel at that time in German or any other music—for a new melodic style, that of musical prose, which at its best can be as wonderful as the finest musical metric, surpassing this, indeed, in sweep of line, variety of phrase-articulation, and the shifting of the accentual footfall. (In this respect he was the heir not of Wagner but of Berlioz, whose achievements in this field have not yet received the consideration they deserve.) In 'Salome' and 'Elektra' in particular he proved that tonal harmony is still capable of new subtilisations: 'Why do you trouble to write atonally,' he remarked ironically to a leading young member of the atonal school, 'when you have talent?'

Finally, in each of his best orchestral works he cast his structures unerringly in a form appropriate to the subject; witness, for example, his choice of the variation form for 'Don Quixote', the rondo form for 'Till Eulenspiegel', and the vast reconstruction and rehabilitation of the classical sonata form in 'Ein Heldenleben'. His virtuosity was at times amazing; there is nothing in all instrumental music like the section in the latter work ('The Hero's Works of Peace') in which he quoted theme after theme from his own earlier works. The mere fusion of them all into an organic musical whole would of itself have been a technical feat of the first order; but more astonishing even than that is the imaginative power that somehow made a psychological unity of it all, a poignant expression of resignation and nostalgia.

Yes, he was of the royal line, even if some queer kink of indolence and cynicism in him made him too often content to play the part of the Old Pretender.

VERDI AND 'DON CARLO'

4th June 1933

We hear a great deal in these days about Verdi overhauling Wagner in the matter of popularity in Germany; but when we also read of the 'adaptations' to which the Verdi operas of the late middle period have to be subjected to make working modern propositions of them, we find it difficult to repress a smile. Wagner may sometimes have to be cut, but that is purely and simply to suit the exigencies of normal theatre hours. We have not yet arrived at the stage when a whole scene of 'Tristan', let us say, can be sacrificed without the audience feeling that the work has not been at all damaged, but, if anything, improved: still less the stage at which this page or that can be taken bodily out of, say, the 'Götterdämmerung' and a page or two out of the 'Meistersinger' or 'Parsifal' advantageously substituted for it. And the fact that this kind of thing can, roughly speaking, be done with certain works of Verdi, and occasionally, indeed, has to be done, is hardly calculated to make us believe that in Verdi we have a musical dramatist of the thoroughbred kind. This week, at Covent Garden, we have seen 'Don Carlo' put on the stage in a form that represents the co-operation of more than one hand besides Verdi's, a fact which of itself makes us approach both 'Don Carlo' in particular and Verdi in general with mixed feelings. I am not, be it understood, quarrelling with this drastic adaptation: on the contrary, I thoroughly approve of it, for it is only on some such terms as these that 'Don Carlo' becomes possible at all in these days.

It is generally urged, as an excuse for so much in the work that is feeble and clumsy, that it was written for the Paris Opéra, an alien institution in which Verdi never felt altogether at home. But that really will not do. When 'Don Carlo' was first produced, in 1867, Verdi was a man of fifty-four, with the experience behind him of more than twenty operas. He was not bound to accept a badly constructed drama from anyone, still less to write so much bad music for it. The simple truth seems to be that he knew neither how bad the libretto was nor how bad most of his music to it was. Later reflection brought him a certain amount of wisdom on these points; hence the later revisions of the opera. But the mere fact that a writer of his age and experience could turn out such a work as the original 'Don Carlo' justifies a doubt not merely as to his being fundamentally a front-rank musician—which few thinking people would claim for him today—but as to whether he was the consummate dramatist he is popularly supposed to have been. A real dramatist would have seen at a glance that the first libretto of 'Don Carlo' was third-rate stuff, and, holding the position of power that Verdi then did in the European operatic world, would have refused point-blank to have anything to do with it.

Verdi seems to me to have had comparatively little of the genuine dramatist in him. He was something superficially similar but not quite the same: he was a good man of the theatre—but, I make bold to say, not even in the first rank of that category, otherwise he would not so often have accepted a poor libretto and so often have been content to repeat the same wretched formula in one work after another. We might define the difference between the real dramatist and the skilled man of the theatre as being very much the difference between the statesman and the politician: the latter knows all the tricks of the trade, but he has neither the brains, the cultural background, nor the vision of the former. Verdi has created very few real characters in music; all he has done, for the most part, is to ring the changes on a certain number of formulae that do indeed take on a slightly different aspect in this opera or that, but remain basically the same. And it was because at bottom he had so little of the genuine dramatist, the genuine psychologist in him that his music remains, underneath all its surface changes, so astonishingly the same through all his periods; he was by nature incapable of that growth in the understanding of human nature that gave a new turn and a new tissue and complexion not only to each of Wagner's dramas but to the music of each of them. It is a far cry from 'Rienzi' or even the 'Flying Dutchman' to 'Parsifal'; but in 'Aida' and 'Otello' we remain in very much the same house as that of 'Rigoletto', 'Il Trovatore', 'La Traviata', and 'Ernani', even though the structure of the old house be strengthened later at this point or that, the walls hung with a better paper, the furniture better carved and more tastefully upholstered.

It is astonishing, when one comes to study Verdi's music critically, how little he really changed from first to last; time after time, in his latest works, we discover that a really fine piece of expression is actually nothing more than an old formula with a better face on it. Unfortunately the reverse is also true; as likely as not, a later work will show us not an improved but a degraded version of the formula. His inventive powers as a musician were singularly restricted. His works are a series of palimpsests; scratch away the upper writing from this or that scene or number in a later work, and you will generally discover, underneath it, an inferior version of the same thing that has figured in some earlier work. But frequently, as I have said, the later version of the stereotyped formula is not better, but worse. Scratch out, for instance, the wretched mandoline chorus in 'Otello' and you find beneath it on the parchment two of the choruses from 'Don Carlo'. And the trouble is that, paltry as these two 'Don Carlo' choruses are, that in 'Otello' is paltrier still in itself, and, in addition, so foolish in respect to that opera as a whole that it is really difficult to give the title of a great dramatist to the man who could deface such a work as 'Otello' with so stupid an excrescence.

There are ensembles in 'Don Carlo' in which Verdi exploits the formula for conflicting or dovetailing personalities of which he makes use in the celebrated quartet in 'Rigoletto'; but unfortunately what is genius in the specimen of it in the earlier work degenerates into mere talent in the later. Each of the operas of his later period keeps alternately harking backward and looking forward: in one case he will do rather better, in another case rather worse, what he has already done more than once before. 'Don Carlo', for instance, is often interesting because it reads like a sketch for something that Verdi was to do better in 'Aida' or 'Otello'.

He developed, of course, as he went on, but in a way of his own that was consistent with the stubborn nature of his whole being, both as man and as artist. He could hardly enlarge his first range very much; but he could give a new intensity or a new beauty or a new distinction to something he had already hammered away at a hundred times. The final truth seems to be that Verdi was just beginning to be a great composer when he died; paradoxically enough, this man of over eighty was one of the composers who can be said to have died too young. I find the first really great upward swing not in the 'Aida' of 1871 (when Verdi was fifty-eight), but in the Requiem of 1874. There are inspirations of a rare order in 'Aida', but there are also lapses into the old Verdian vulgarity and inanity of a kind and of a frequency that would astonish us in the case of any other composer. His progress in 'Aida' and the great 'Otello' has three aspects. He generally subtilises and refines his old formulae to such an extent that to the ordinary listener the affiliation of the new music with the old is not apparent. He develops an extraordinary beauty of orchestral tone-combination, and a new art of getting dramatic atmosphere by this means—witness the Nile scene and the temple scene in 'Aida'. And, to the limited extent that was possible to any Italian composer of that epoch, he unconsciously obeys the law that makes every practised opera composer become more symphonic as he gets older.

This development was very striking in Wagner, though criticism has not yet dealt with it adequately. Verdi, in his smaller way, and lacking, of course, the great symphonic tradition that was at the back of the big German writers, also reaches out, latterly, into the symphonic, that is to say, into the working-out of a figure for its own intrinsic musical possibilities, at the same time that he makes this purely orchestral evolution of it serve the dramatic intention. From the first he had been given to deciding upon a certain accompaniment figure and repeating it throughout a number. But in his earlier works not only is the figure itself often banal or downright ludicrous, but his handling of it is amateurish. Compare with any of these earlier efforts his fine treatment of the iterative ascending figure in one of Amonasro's phrases in the Nile scene, or the magnificent evolution of the writhing orchestral figure that accompanies Otello's 'Dio, mi potevi scagliar' (in the third act), and you will realise the extent to which, in his later years, Verdi was developing as a musician pure and simple.

Yet, still obeying that curious law in him that made his

evolution not the consistent thing it has been in the case of certain other composers who have lived long, but a series of leaps forward and slippings back, he was capable of the strangest lapses almost to the end. His string quartet of 1873 (i.e., two years after 'Aida') is a dilettantish piece of work. Make what allowances we will for the fact that this was his first effort (or at all events his first public effort) in symphonic form, still one expects something better than this from a man who had been writing music for more than half a century. It has been said, somewhat unthinkingly, that his greatness, as compared with Wagner, is shown by his ending his days with a comedy rather than with a work of brooding seriousness. But it was really much easier for him to write a 'Falstaff' than it would have been to go on, from 'Otello', to a work that should be to the whole of his previous life's-work what 'Parsifal' was to Wagner's. For in 'Falstaff' he had a comparatively easy task. A composer of declining powers can somewhat easily achieve a masterpiece, or something near a masterpiece, in a genre that gives him the support of a great tradition, as Strauss has proved with the 'Rosenkavalier'. At that stage of his career Strauss had virtually written himself out as an original and significant thinker in music; yet out of the formulae transmitted to him by Johann Strauss and others he could still weave new shapes of the greatest beauty.

In 'Falstaff', Verdi had the great tradition of Italian comic opera to fall back upon; he had not much more to do than follow in the steps of masterpieces like 'Il Barbiere' and 'Il Matrimonio Segreto' and 'Don Pasquale', and, with his now refined sensibility and his skilled old hand, give a fresh turn of his own to the old methods. He did it, of course, superbly; but who can deny that his task was relatively easy, in the way that Strauss's was in the 'Rosenkavalier', and that he would have found it as much harder to write a new serious drama that would go as far beyond 'Otello' and 'Aida' as these are beyond 'Il Trovatore' and 'Rigoletto' and 'Don Carlo', as it evidently was for Strauss to do, in 'The Egyptian Helen', anything better than, or even as good as, the orchestral works of his prime?

One of the very worst things in 'Don Carlo' is the 'marziale' episode in the last act; even the most fanatical Verdians have nothing but an amused contempt for it. We could have understood, and might have forgiven, this appalling lapse had it been in the original version of 1867. But when we discover that this passage is one of those added to the work when Verdi revised it in 1884—only three years before 'Otello'!—we are faced once more with the fact that he developed along a curiously zigzag line, the downward curves of which were liable to dip so low as occasionally to drag him practically back to the point from which he had started.

PART III

GENERAL ARTICLES

FIRST AID FOR CRITICS

14th November 1920

I SEE from the November Bulletin of the British Music Society that 'among the subjects suggested for the morning debates' at the Society's next Congress is, 'What is wrong with musical criticism in England?'

They've evidently noticed it!

* * *

Well, what *is* wrong with musical criticism in England? Some people, of course, will answer, 'The musical critics'; but that is only a fragment of the correct answer. Something will have to be said on the economic side of the matter; something, also, on the strange conditions under which the critics mostly have to work. There will be no difficulty in coming to the conclusion that musical criticism as a whole, in this country, does not play its part in musical culture as it might do. The trouble is to get the editors on the one side, and the public and the performers on the other, to see that a change is desirable; and a still further trouble is to decide what form that change should take. We want to get the best brains possible into the business, and to give them the scope that the best brains get in every other department of art or science or literature where it is recognised that the only people who have a right to talk on a specialised subject are the specialists.

We must first of all get rid of the idea that it is the business of the musical critic to be always right about everything. An American musical journal used to amuse us by printing in parallel columns all the passages in which the New York critics had contradicted each other over this or that work of the week, or this or that person's singing or playing. But whoever expects everyone to think alike, on music or any other subject? If they did, one newspaper would suffice for a whole country. We expect a given score of people to take as many views of the value of a piece of music or a performance as they would of the motives of a politician or the evidence in a trial.

All we ask, in either case, is that a man shall not express an opinion, especially in public, till he has the knowledge of the subject and the cultivated reasoning faculty that alone would entitle him to do so; or, failing that, that he shall at least be a personality and a stylist, so that even his wrong-headedness (if he be wrong) may have some sort of interest for us. Which of us, in the old days, would not have preferred to read John F. Runciman when he was hopelessly wrong than Joseph Bennett when he was hopelessly right? The great thing is that the public shall be taught to think for itself; and the dull writer or the conventional thinker will never make it do that.

But getting the best brains in England into the business will not be much use unless they are employed on the newspapers. The specialist musical journals of the better class are, of course, indispensable; they can print articles that would either be too long for a daily newspaper or would be out of place there. But human nature being what it is, and the Press being as dependent as it is upon advertisements of hair-restorers and safety razors and ladies' *lingerie*, no specialist journal can hope to have anything like the circulation of a big newspaper.

It is strange that the Potterite press has not already seen that a large new public that is keenly interested in music has sprung up in recent years, and that it would not be uneconomic idealism but sound business to cater intelligently for it. The criticism in the specialised journals is sound enough. It is in the daily Press that the weakness lies—partly because, even when the paper has an able man for its musical critic, it often will not allow him to show his best; and until the daily newspaper realises that its musical readers expect the same level of intelligence in those who write for it as the business man expects in the business columns, or the political man in the political columns, we shall never get any further.

The suggestion was made to me a year or so ago by a correspondent that, instead of writing about the music of the past week, the critic would be more generally interesting if he were to write on the music of the coming week, separating the good from the bad, and telling the intending concert-goer why he ought to go to hear this work rather than that, and what he ought to listen specially for in it. That plan bristles with difficulties; but part of it may be practicable some day. A better plan for the immediate present, I think, would be to administer first-aid not only to the audiences but to the critics. It is becoming increasingly difficult to take in new works at a mere first hearing. I do not mean the tiny new works of the type of those of the French and Russian schools that we have been hearing lately; *they* present no more difficulty than a child's box of toys. But occasionally we meet with a longer work, to the making of which some hard thinking has gone, and that shows some complexity of design. The best musician living cannot grasp it all as it passes swiftly by him in performance. Sometimes a programme note will help him, especially if the leading themes are quoted. But often there is no programme note, particularly in the case of new Chamber music.

Would it not be to everyone's advantage if someone—preferably the composer—would give us ten minutes' preliminary talk about it at the piano, playing us the chief themes two or three times, so as to fix them in our memory, sketching the sort of development they receive, drawing our attention to points that we particularly ought to observe, and so on? It would be better for the audience, because under the present system the ordinary non-practising music-lover must often lose himself in the course of a complicated work. It would be better for the critics, because, once familiar with the thematic skeleton of the work, they need waste none of their time or energy in trying to pick this out and memorise it, but could give all their attention to the imaginative use the composer was making of his material. It would be better for the composer, because the next day's criticisms of his music would be at any rate a stage further from evasive guesswork than they usually are at present. And if it were better for all these people, it would necessarily be better for the reader of the criticism. Something of this sort, I feel, will have to be done some day in the case of new works of any scope.

READING AND HEARING

I

23rd September 1923

A COUPLE of weeks ago Mr. Kalisch told us a story which, he seemed to think, settled finally those of us who, on the average of cases, prefer our music at home to going to the concert room or the opera house for it. Weingartner, it appears, has told how Wagner once stopped a rehearsal of one of his own operas and said 'Cut out the trombones; they are too loud', or words to that effect. (I have lost the cutting, and can quote only from memory.) Mr. Kalisch's argument, if I remember it rightly, was this—how can any of us pretend to get from the reading of a score the picture the composer had in his mind when he wrote it, seeing that the composer himself, no matter how skilled in orchestration he may be, sometimes miscalculates an effect? Do we profess to know more about orchestration than a Wagner or an Elgar, to have a finer ear than he has?

That would be a crushing argument if it were relevant: the only objection to it is that it is quite irrelevant. In the first place, perhaps I may be permitted to remind Mr. Kalisch that complicated orchestral music constitutes a very small proportion of the music that a musician is interested in. I cheerfully concede that it is often difficult—sometimes even impossible—to imagine precisely what the effect will be of a certain combination of instruments. But though none of us can work out complicated mathematical problems with the celerity and certainty of the freaks who now and then astonish the scientific world, we can all of us do ordinary little sums quite rapidly, and, with a little figuring, sums of a more advanced nature. If the man I am sitting next to at Queen's Hall tells me he can realise a page of Schönberg's 'Pelleas and Melisande' after one reading of the full score, I shall regard him as either a unique genius or a good fellow with a prodigious gift for fiction; but I shall look upon him as a very poor musician if he tells me that he cannot read with perfect understanding the score of any song, any piano piece, any violin piece, any quartet, any madrigal or part-song, or the vocal score of any opera. Further he needs only to be a passable musician to be able to read any full score, a few of the more complicated modern scores excepted.

Any one who contends that only the physical ear is to be trusted as the judge of music declares, by implication, that the history and the criticism of music are impossible: for the historian and the critic have to rely wholly and solely upon their reading in the case of nine hundred and ninety-nine out of a thousand works about which they write. Not one of us has *heard* a hundredth part of one per cent of the polyphonic music of the fifteenth and sixteenth and seventeenth centuries that we discuss so freely: our knowledge of it is derived entirely from the printed page. No opera is now regularly performed of earlier date than Gluck's 'Orfeo' (1762); yet historians pass judgement confidently on a hundred operas earlier than that. No writer upon Bach or Mozart or Haydn has *heard* more than a very small proportion of the works of these men: he bases his judgement on the other works upon his reading of the scores. Even in the case of modern works it is upon the score rather than a performance that a careful critic relies: a page of 'Le Sacre du Printemps' may puzzle him in performance, but it will hold no puzzle for him after half a dozen readings of it.

The mere reading of music is, then, a necessity to the student of musical history. But it is more than a necessity: it is a keen pleasure, and, for me, a keener pleasure, in nine cases out of ten, than that of concert-going. I have never committed myself to what would be the nonsensical statement that the eye can do the work of the ear so well that there is no need ever to *hear* music. All I have claimed is that—for me, at least—a reading of a piece of music gives me so much more pleasure than the average performance that I would not go to more than ten or twenty concerts in the year of my own free choice. The performances that give me the greatest pleasure do not throw the slightest new light *on the work* for me: it is the performer who thrills me. I see no more in a Schubert song after Elena Gerhardt has sung it than I did before: what has made the experience worth having is the beauty of her voice and the perfection of her style. Perfection in performance is indeed worth leaving one's fireside for on a winter's night: but in how many cases are we fortunate enough to get it?

Further, there are some modern orchestral works that it would be an impertinence to judge finally from a reading alone, though the reading—or, rather, many readings—may be as necessary as the performance. I make no extreme claims for the pleasure of score-reading: I contend only that more reading and less hearing of music would be better for every music lover. It would spare him a good deal of physical exhaustion: it would prevent many a masterpiece becoming staled by excessive repetition; it would ensure a great widening of his musical culture. He would get to know his favourite works better, and so enjoy them more when a perfect performance of one of them was given. There are many other benefits that he will discover for himself when he has practised score-reading for a year or two. He will then see that it is as ridiculous for him to be dependent on other people for his music as it would be for him to be dependent upon public readers for his knowledge of poetry or fiction. He would be ashamed of himself if he could not read Swinburne or Hardy for himself: he apparently feels no shame in the illiteracy that renders him unable to read Sibelius or Mahler for himself.

Let us return to Mr. Kalisch, Weingartner, and Wagner. If I had wanted to invent a story that would have been all to the advantage of score-reading I could not have hit upon a more serviceable one than this. Let us suppose that Wagner had in this case miscalculated. I am not wholly convinced, let me say in parentheses, that he had. The acoustics of theatres vary greatly: what may sound too strident in one may be mellow enough in another. And needless to say, there are trombone players *and* trombone players. If a composer began cutting out effects that did not 'come off' at this or that rehearsal or performance, there would soon be precious little of his score left. Let me match Weingartner's story with another.

In 1881, Lilli Lehmann was entrusted by Wagner with the selection and training of the 'Parsifal' Flower Maidens. In her reminiscences she quotes a letter of his in which he insists that each of the sopranos shall be able to take the high B flat 'easily and pleasingly'; 'a single shrill organ', he adds, 'would spoil everything for me'. At Bayreuth in 1882, presumably, he got what he wanted; but had he been at some rehearsals or performances of 'Parsifal' that I have heard he would probably have said to the conductor, 'Cut out the B flat: the effect is too painful.'

He would, of course, have been wrong to have done so: whether this soprano or that can sing the high B flat purely and easily or not, the B flat is the right thing. I do not know the trombone passage to which Weingartner refers, so I cannot say whether it is one that has been deleted from the score as we now have it. But this much is certain—that Wagner *wanted* the trombone colour there. He would not have put it in unless it had been vital to his conception of the emotion of the scene. He imagined, that is to say, an ideal trombone tone and an ideal trombone player.

Why then should the passage be cut out merely because some trombone tone and some trombone players are anything but ideal? If we were *reading* this page of the score, we would do exactly what Wagner did when he wrote it—mix up with the other timbres just as much trombone tone as was required for a perfect blend, and no more. Let us grant that the trombone tone is too much in the theatre, and has to be cut out. Then what happens is simply this—that we are hearing something different from what Wagner desired, and that only some defect in the instrument or the player prevents him from conveying to the physical ear of the listener.

So far from being an argument against score-reading as against score-hearing, it seems to me that is a convincing argument for it. I am pretty sure that even after that rehearsal, whenever Wagner let that page run through his mind, it was with the trombone colour, not without it; and if the trombone part is in our present scores, I am sure he would be glad to think that we, as we read the page, hear it mentally as he conceived it. In fact, the story sets me dreaming of the possibility of a new kind of music, meant entirely for the inner ear, through the eye, and quite impossible of performance.

II

30th September 1923

I THREATENED in last week's article to outline a new kind of music, addressed in the main, to the eye rather than the ear, or, perhaps I ought to say, to the inward ear through the eye —in a word, composers' music rather than performers' music.

It may astonish the reader to learn that he rarely gets what I call composers' music, but it is true. What we get is generally a rough compromise between composers' music and performers' music, between what the composer imagined and what the instrument, whether vocal or instrumental, can do. Dramatists would feel it very awkward if actors were incapable, under certain circumstances, of pronouncing certain letters or combinations of letters. Suppose, for instance that *l* and *v* could be sounded together pleasingly only at a pitch very much above the ordinary pitch of the speaking voice. The result of this would be that the hero could only say to the heroine 'I love you' by raising his voice to an unholy screech on the vital word of the sentence; and the result of *that* would be that the word 'love' would be barred from the stage. What, under these circumstances, would the dramatist do? Being unable to refrain from the use of such words as these merely because actors found it difficult or impossible to pronounce them without becoming raucous or ridiculous, he would write two kinds of plays, one to be spoken, the other to be read.

Now this is what my prophetic eye tells me will be done in music some day. The instruments through which the composer has to express himself are lamentably imperfect. It is not merely that the performers sometimes fail to reach the ideal: a much more serious trouble is that the instruments, purely *qua* instruments, are full of limitations and imperfections. They are limited in range; they are often dumb when we would like them to speak, or (which is worse) speak when we would prefer them to be dumb; they get tired, and refuse to go on with their phrase just when it is becoming most interesting; they are touchy, and, if you do not understand them or humour them, will indeed play the phrase for you since you insist on it, but will make it sound hideous, and then tell you it doesn't suit them—that you have put in an A flat, let us say, and they have a constitutional objection to A flat.

The wood-wind, in particular, are extraordinarily touchy. They have their good registers and their bad; they change their colour and their substances as they traverse their scales; they petulantly refuse to play this note or that, alleging that 'it isn't on the instrument', and insist on the composer handing it over to one of their colleagues; they warn him not to write for them in this key or that fashion, because the fingering is difficult; he must not write shakes or tremolos for them on certain notes; and so on.

I often wonder why composers stand it. One of these days, I am sure, they will rebel and write not for the clumsy instruments of the orchestra but for the ideal instruments, that can do anything, go anywhere, give forth any height or depth or quality of tone that he may desire. No longer will he have to spend anxious hours peering over treatises on orchestration. I was once with a composer when he was correcting the proofs of an overture. To his amusement he found that in a moment of abstractedness he had asked the violins to play a note lower than the lowest note on the instrument. Of course he had to modify the passage. But he would not have written that low A for the violins unless he had wanted the A in just that colour and no other.

Think what a boon it would be to all orchestral composers to be set free from these irritating restrictions, to be able, at last, to put down on paper precisely what they wanted, not what the instruments will allow them to put down, and be sure that the reader will hear the tone-complex internally just as he, the composer, heard it! No longer would he have to submit to the clarionet throwing up the sponge when it reaches the lowest note of its compass and handing over the continuation of the theme downwards to the bassoon. No longer would he have to take the theme out of the hands of one instrument at a certain point and give it to another, merely because at that point the first instrument, though it may have the notes, enters with them, upon its 'ineffective' patch. No longer would he have to endure the ignominy of being told by the experts that one of his favourite passages has been partly spoiled by his doggedly insisting on a certain instrument having it—the lovely clarionet tune in the 'Oberon' overture, for instance, which has the misfortune to circulate round the three or four notes that are weakest on the clarionet.

When I am told that we must wait until we have not only read but can hear a composer's work before we judge it I cannot repress a sad smile. For not in one case in a thousand, perhaps, do we hear the music as the composer dreamed it. There is no means by which he can convey his dream to us in all its purity. He has to tell it to us through instruments of all kinds, the imperfections of which make his music, in its practical form, a series of fakes and compromises. Sometimes he has to choose between a method of performance that deliberately makes nonsense of his conception, and one that, doing its best to realise his conception, ends in a catastrophe for the instruments. Which of us has ever heard the last fifteen bars of 'Also sprach Zarathustra' made to sound as Strauss intended them to sound? If the flutes and piccolos play softly, their tone is thin, tremulous, ragged, uncertain: if they play loudly, Strauss's idea is blown to the winds. If we really want to hear this passage as Strauss conceived it we must rely on the score and our imagination. In 'Lohengrin', Wagner writes a low B natural that is not on this modern flute.

If I can imagine the effect of this, why should we not be allowed to imagine the effect of many another note that is not on a given instrument, or is 'ineffective' on it? Why should not composers be allowed to suggest to me, on paper, ideal combinations that are impossible or dangerous in performance? The overtones of the double basses make it risky to combine these instruments with the lower notes of the flute. But these notes are very lovely, and it is sad to be deprived of them merely because the basses are apt to muddle them up. I can imagine all sorts of ideal blends of these two instruments; why should the composer be barred from at any rate giving me these blends on paper?

In his 'Requiem' (the last few bars of the 'Hostias'), Berlioz narrows his orchestra down to a few notes from the three flutes over some deep notes in eight tenor trombones. 'It probably sounds very nasty', says Mr. Cecil Forsyth, who quotes the passage in his admirable book on orchestration. Perhaps it does to the physical ear, and on flutes and trombones as they are now. But it certainly did not sound nasty to the mental ear of Berlioz, nor does it to mine; I can perhaps imagine the ideal effect that Berlioz desired from the strange mixture of these two contrasted colours at that distance, with the ebbs and flows of the diminuendi and crescendi. I have never yet heard a performance of 'Sea Drift' that did not sound more or less nasty (generally more, sometimes much more), because of the difficulty the soloist has in singing Delius's chromatic music dead in tune with the orchestra; but that is not a reproach against Delius. Thank Heaven we have eyes as well as ears, and a spiritual as well as a fleshly ear. And I fervently hope that one of these days some composer will give me a work intended solely for my spiritual ear.

While I am in this generous mood perhaps I may give composers the benefit of another suggestion. While I was listening to Miss Rosina Buckman singing an aria from 'Fidelio' the other evening I was reminded of an article I wrote a dozen years or so ago, suggesting a new art-form—concertos for singers. All other soloists have concertos specially written for their instruments, if a pianist wants to play with the orchestra, he does not have to cut a fragment out of a symphony and present its bleeding flesh and severed nerves to the audience. But the singer who wants to sing with the orchestra has little choice but to tear a fragment out of some opera, bad for the singer, and bad for us, for it is as difficult for her as it is for us to plunge into the psychology of the part at a moment's notice. 'One fine day' is effective enough in the second act of 'Madame Butterfly' after all the emotional tension that finds its natural easing in the aria; but neither the singer nor we can be expected to summon up two hours' dramatic emotions in a twinkling of an eye.

Why then does not some composer write a vocal concerto on the lines of the instrumental concerto—a work that shall give the singer all possible opportunities, traverse a wide field of expression, and yet be an organic whole? We have a hint of such a work in Beethoven's 'Ah perfido'—a little concert-room drama in itself. Singers, I am sure, would welcome a development of this kind. Audiences certainly would. And it would give immense scope to the many composers who have the dramatic instinct without the faculty for full-scale opera.

THE ARTIST AND HIS VITALITY

15th January 1922

Watching the Carpentier-Cook fight the other evening, I could not help reflecting, as I had often done before, how much nicer it is to be an artist of some sort or other and improve as you get older, than to be an athlete or a sportsman or a game-player or something of that kind, and become a back number in your youth. Nature has really been very generous to the artist, when we come to think of it. Carpentier is still a miracle: the difference between his boxing and that of the ordinary heavy-weight is the difference between Chopin as played by Pachmann and the 'Meistersinger' overture thumped out on the piano-player by the man next door. But in my humble non-professional way I venture to think that though Carpentier can still beat any ordinary heavy-weight, he is not quite the old Carpentier. Some of his blows in the first two rounds were misjudged in a way that would have been impossible to him a couple of years ago. Something of the old perfect adjustment of all the faculties and nerves and muscles is beginning to fail, I imagine—at the age of twenty-seven. It is the same story in almost every sport; the younger players make players very little older than themselves look like men of a past generation, and in a short time will themselves be edged out of the limelight by some fresh infant.

Now see what happens to the artist of corresponding genius—the composer, let us say, since this is a musical column. We speak condescendingly of these people's 'early works'—works written at an age when the boxer or the billiard player would be winning championships: many of the art-works that really matter have hardly begun to be thought of until an age at which the boxer has either discreetly given up the game or is attempting the pathetic process known as 'coming back'. I need hardly recall the standard instances of the vitality of the middle-aged or old musician—Gluck commencing the reform of the opera at forty-eight; Rameau beginning his long series of operas at fifty; Beethoven writing his last great works in his fifties; Wagner writing the 'Meistersinger' at fifty-four or so, the 'Götterdämmerung' at fifty-eight, and 'Parsifal' at sixty-five; Verdi beginning a new period with 'Aida' at fifty-eight, then producing 'Otello' at seventy-five and 'Falstaff' at eighty; and so on. My point is that it is upon people like these, not upon the Carpentiers and Dempseys, that Nature has poured out her vitality with both hands.

We think it wonderful that a boxer should be so strong. But given a good physique to begin with, what is there so wonderful in a man being strong when the whole of his daily life is devoted to the task of conserving his natural strength? For a bit of a fight that at the most can run only to an hour or so, a boxer has to prepare intensively for weeks, on top of his ordinary regimen of care and commonsense. He grabs and hoards every possible particle of strength, and wastes himself in no way. He denies himself most of the ordinary pleasures of normal man; his whole energy is devoted to the attainment of one end. And with all this, he is out of the running long before he is forty.

Look now at the life of a Wagner—using himself up in every imaginable way for something like fifty years, always doing three men's work, writing great works at a cerebral white heat that lasts for months at a time, simultaneously interesting himself in almost everything else under the sun, thinking about it, talking about it, writing about it, carrying on an enormous correspondence by hand, travelling, conducting, undergoing all sorts of strains of body and spirit, pulling wires in a score of towns for the realisation of his one great desire for a theatre of his own—and with it all, in spite of what he imagined to be constant ill-health, always lively in body and vigorous in mind, larking about among friends like a schoolboy, and running up trees for the pure boyish fun of the thing at sixty.

Read the volume of *Bayreuth Letters*—those dealing with the founding of Bayreuth and the arrangements for the first festival—and you will be astounded at the energy and the competence of the man who, in addition to all the purely musical duties he had to attend to at the time, calmly works out, with the cold persistence and thoroughness of a general or the manager of a multiple store, every detail, down to food and lodging, of the problem of the influx of some hundreds of strangers into the little backwater of a town.

Who can doubt that, all in all, Nature has put into a seemingly frail little body like this fifty times the vitality that she has put into the frame of any boxer? The material must be wonderful to bear so much for so many years. And the question arises, if men like this do so much being what they are, what could they accomplish if they never wasted themselves? Suppose a Wagner or a Beethoven (whose natural strength was enormous) had been taken in hand very young, and trained, as the boxer is trained, to live rationally and husband every ounce of his vitality, keeping always in view the one end of getting the best out of himself that Nature had made possible for him, to what age might he not have lived and what work might he not have done?

It is impossible to doubt that Wagner's constant satisfying of an insatiable appetite for all the good things of this world drained him of a good deal of vitality. Without his malady Beethoven would probably never have become deaf, and certainly would never have developed that group of ignoble internal troubles that ultimately wore down even his iron frame at fifty-seven. Hugo Wolf, after some days and nights of incredibly intense cerebration, would disappear for days at a time, and then emerge from the lower haunts of Vienna as broken and bedraggled as a cat after a week's absence from home: there would follow a few days' rest—or rather complete exhaustion—and then another spell of white hot creation. (It was on one of these absences that he contracted the dire disease that first made him mad and then slew him in his prime.) No athlete who ever lived could go through what these and other artists went through and do anything like the same fine work in his own line that the artists did in theirs. Is not the conclusion irresistible that the artist's brain and body are the greatest storehouses of energy that Nature has ever hit upon?

There is another side to the question, of course. Without his indulgence—even his vices—would the artist do as good work? Would Montaigne ever have written the beautiful essay on Prayer had he not been the very human Montaigne revealed in some of the other essays? Would Wagner ever have written

'Parsifal' had he lived the life of a saint? How much of an artist's vision into the world beyond this one comes as the result of a reaction from the over-enjoyment of this? These are questions which I leave the psychologist to thrash out with the moralist.

THE VIRTUOUS AND THE VIRTUOSO

21st June 1925

'What *are we?' said Mr. Pecksniff, 'but coaches? Some of us are slow coaches——.'*

'Goodness, Pa!' cried Charity.

'Some of us, I say', resumed her parent with increased emphasis, 'are slow coaches; some of us are fast coaches. Our passions are the horses; and rampant animals, too!——'

'Really, Pa!' cried both daughters at once. 'How very unpleasant.'

'And rampant animals, too!' repeated Mr. Pecksniff, with so much determination that he may be said to have exhibited, at the moment, a sort of moral rampancy himself; 'and Virtue is the drag. We start from The Mother's Arms and we run to The Dust Shovel.'

When he had said this, Mr. Pecksniff, being exhausted, took some further refreshment. When he had done that, he corked the bottle tight, with the air of a man who had effectually corked the subject also; and went to sleep for three stages.

* * *

In all ages there has been an inability on the part of the Aristotelian and the Platonian, the cat and the dog, the Brahmsian and the Wagnerian, the slow coach and the fast coach, to see things from the other's point of view. Recently we have seen the two eternal opposites at warfare over the 'virtuoso' conductor. The virtuoso has once more been cold-shouldered by the virtuous.

There is a certain type of mind that looks with suspicion on brilliance, even on speed. This type found its most characteristic expression in the Victorian epoch, but representatives of it still survive. It regards art as a branch of morals, frowns on anything in art that does not seem to tend to virtue, and, of course, is as sure of its own virtue as it is doubtful of that of the people in the other camp. Mercy and Charity Pecksniff thought it shocking that any portion of mankind should be like a fast coach, drawn by those rampant animals, the passions; but if such people there were in this wicked world, Virtue, in the person of the slow coach, felt called upon to supply the drag. In the circles of the virtuous, speed is looked upon as something, if not positively immoral in itself, at any rate highly suspicious. When the Victorian female wanted to express reprobation of another female, she described the latter as 'fast'; while a man who was not of the company of the virtuous would be described as 'going the pace'. That was condemnation enough; celerity was something in itself reprehensible in the eyes of the slow.

A good deal of the Victorian young person has survived in our musical criticism. When one of the virtuous wants to be especially severe on a conductor, he tells us that he 'took liberties with the tempo'. 'Took liberties with!' The dear old Victorian phrase! The implication of it is that music is a sort of unprotected female who is never safe when a 'fast' man is about—particularly at night, which, as we all know, is when the virtuoso conductor is given to prowling about, seeking music that he may deflower. And in spite of myself I cannot help feeling shocked when I read that a conductor 'took liberties' with a symphony: I feel the same horror as when I read, in the police-court evidence, that the body of the murdered girl was found with its clothing disarranged. I am not surprised that the virtuous cry out against the 'fast' conductors who 'take liberties' with music. And in public, too! With the virtuous looking at them!

To the outsider, this eternal conflict between the virtuous and the virtuosi is very diverting. The latter have a predilection for regarding art as a personal expression; the former look upon it as a religion, of which they are the only true high priests. The slow coach holds up his hands in pious horror at the fast coach; the fast coach has an amused contempt for the slow coach. The musical history of the Wagner-Brahms epoch might almost be written as a conflict of opinion between the virtuous and the virtuoso.

That dear old prig in petticoats, Clara Schumann, may almost stand as the supreme type of the musical virtuous. She and her associates honestly thought that they were the last bulwarks of the virtuous in art against the inroads of the immoral virtuosi; Codlin felt called upon to warn the public against the demoralisation that would be certain to follow in the wake of Short. When Brahms and Joachim made their famous 'Declaration' against the Wagner-Liszt party in 1860, they were anxious to make it clear that musical virtue was with their party alone: 'they can only bewail or condemn, as against the inmost and essential nature of music, the production of the leaders and pupils of the so-called "New German" school.'

Clara Schumann lamented in her diary (1872) that 'this enthusiasm for Wagner seems to me a kind of disease which sweeps across a country and carries away the very best people.' 'Tristan,' she thought 'the most repulsive thing I ever saw or heard in my life. . . . Every feeling of decency was outraged. . . . It is not emotion, it is a disease, and they tear their hearts out of their bodies, while the music expresses it all in the most repulsive manner.' We might almost be reading a criticism of Koussevitzky conducting the 'Poem of Ecstasy'! Joachim, for Clara, was 'a brilliant example of how all that is beautiful and noble in music should be expressed'—so different from those immoral fellows at Bayreuth, who merely exercised an 'intoxicating influence'. Still, Providence—whom the virtuous are always magnanimous enough to regard as one of themselves—deserved credit for having sent 'so strong and healthy a genius [as Brahms] into the world in the midst of the Wagner mania.' Liszt, of course, being a virtuoso, could not be, artistically speaking, virtuous. Clara could not deny him merit as a pianist, but 'it is a pity that one can get so little calm enjoyment out of it; it is always a demoniac force that sweeps one along.' There we have the eternal complaint of the slow coach against the fast, of the penny plain against the twopenny coloured. For Clara, 'demoniac' was a self-evident term of reproach, just as 'brilliant' is for some people today; as if a man could not be both brilliant and sound, swift and yet steady on his feet.

So much for the slow coach's point of view. What was the point of view of the fast coaches? Walter Bache, irritated by the claim of the virtuous to be the only authorised custodians of the 'classics', described somebody or other as 'a refined classical player—*Angelicé*, a wooden-headed brute'. Schumann did not like Wagner's performance of the Ninth Symphony: 'he almost invariably takes the tempi wrong and very often mistakes the feeling.' But Wagner and Liszt thought as little of the virtuous as the virtuous thought of them. 'If you want to hear Schumann's works played as they should *not* be played,' said Liszt, 'listen to Clara.' The virtuous regarded Beethoven—as indeed they still do—as their own special preserve; what right has a virtuoso like Wagner or Liszt or Koussevitzky to intrude into the temple? But read Wagner on the subject: 'I ask all who have heard, for instance, the opus 106 or 111 of Beethoven played by Liszt in a private circle, what they previously knew of these creations and what they then discovered in them'; and he follows this up with a veiled sneer at the pretensions of Brahms and his school. In his essay 'On Conducting' he resents as an impertinence the Brahmsians' patronage of Liszt as a mere technician, and says how much he was 'distressed' by 'the woodenness and primness of Brahms's playing'; and he concludes with words that the virtuous perhaps might bear in mind when next they feel their classic purity assailed by the virtuoso: 'We ought to defend ourselves against having our great living Beethoven clothed for us in the garment of this Sanctity . . . as though, where *they* could make no difference [between Beethoven and Schumann] there really were no difference to make.'

Apparently the final word is not with the 'refined classical players'. Those rampant animals the passions object to the drag of Virtue.

A FINGERPOST FOR CRITICISM

29th January 1922

THE problem before all of us musicians just now is to take our bearings in the sea of controversy. There is a certain amount of dissatisfaction not only with the music of the past but with the music of the present that confesses the past to be its parent. Some of our younger men feel, more or less dimly, that music can express many things that have hitherto not found expression in it, and are working out, more or less successfully, the new forms and the new technique for this expression. The critics on either side keep up a pretty tumult and shouting: the public feels vaguely that while the old kings have departed the new captains are not quite equal to their job. It hears the great composers—or what it takes to be the great composers—of the past and the present scolded and sneered at by this critic or that as dullards or mummies.

It is true that the spectacle, to the normal music lover's eye, is very much like that of an office boy at the War Office calling Earl Haig over the coals: but the rating is done so confidently, and with a flow of language that, if it is not always intelligible, is assuredly copious, that the listener can hardly help saying to himself now and then, 'What, after all, if there's something in all this? What if Haig really is wrong and the office boy right?' None of us can be quite sure of anything in art. In a world the very law of which is change, it cannot be pronounced an utter impossibility that the B minor Mass will some day be thought very small beer in comparison with that of 'The Nothing-Doing Bar' of Milhaud: even 'Chout' may be to the next century what 'Tristan' is to this. But most of us cannot wait that long. If only we could find some sure touchstone that would help us to distinguish between the false metal and the true in the music of today!

We all want, so to speak, to be always backing winners: we should like to turn to these our articles twenty years hence and see that Time has proved us right in the controversies of today. As it is, we can only gamble on it, giving our fancy such backing of stable information, such knowledge of weights and courses and jockeys, as we can. But it will certainly help us a little to delve into the past occasionally and see what has happened in circumstances that, in essentials, resembled our own. By a curious chance, I came this week, in less than five minutes, upon a couple of pieces of writing that between them present us with a problem worth pondering upon.

The first is Mr. E. J. Dent's account in the *Nation* of the local criticisms of the concert of English music at Prague. Quoting, apparently, from one of these notices (or perhaps summarising several of them), he writes: 'The three English composers represented three tendencies which were little different from those of Central Europe—Butterworth ("The Shropshire Lad") making a conscious return to the simplicity of folk-song, Bliss (the "Mêlée Fantasque", I think) the modernist and "masterly blender of musical colour", and Elgar (one of the symphonies) the Pope of music, the man of ripe experience, the conservative who has gone through the school of Liszt's technique, and there fixes, more or less, the boundaries of music.'

This last sentence is a gem, but we must not linger too long over it: this tracing of Elgar to Liszt is as rich in its way as M. Diaghileff's filiation of him to Brahms. They cannot, of course, both be right; but both can be, and are, ludicrously wrong. The main point of the passage is clear: Elgar represents the ripe conservative in music, Arthur Bliss the 'modernist'. Which is a perfectly sound discrimination. What we have to guard against is the hasty assumption that it is the 'modernist', not the conservative, to whom people will be listening a couple of generations hence.

Let us turn now to the article on 'A Forgotten Master' in M. Romain Rolland's book *A Musical Tour through the Land of the Past*, which has just been issued in an English translation. The very title is both ominous and paradoxical. A master—but forgotten! *Does* the world forget its masters so easily—even its little masters? And what shall it avail a man if his own contemporaries and a future historian or two acclaim him as a master if his work does not survive for the public?

This forgotten master, according to M. Rolland's sub-title, was 'Telemann, the successful rival of J. S. Bach'. Again our eyebrows lift. Successful? Do we usually call the boxer successful who has been counted out, the football team successful over whom their despised opponents have trampled backwards and forwards for ninety muddy minutes? We all know where Bach is today. Where is the 'successful' Telemann? Vere is dot barty now? How many people outside the ranks of the historians have even heard his name?

The 'success', it seems, was in Telemann's own day, and in the eyes of people of his own way of thinking. He had a long run: born in 1681, four years before Bach, he died seventeen years after him, in 1767. For something like seventy years he poured out a never-ending stream of music: between 1720 and 1740 alone he produced some scores of works for the church, nineteen 'Passions', twenty operas, twenty oratorios, forty serenades, many clavier pieces, trios, concertos, etc., six hundred overtures, seven hundred airs, and a variety of other works which the exhausted biographer contents himself with summarising as etc., etc.

He was the darling of the German public of his day—a very long day, as we have seen. One coveted post after another fell into his hands: church and town authorities and private magnificos tumbled over each other in their haste to provide him with commissions: wherever he appeared, older musicians (some of them, such as Kuhnau, still famous) were slighted and embittered.

The particulars of his career have a curious touch of today about them. He good-humouredly despised the solid polyphonic style and the out-of-date technique of such old fogies as Bach: even as a boy he recognised that his teachers could teach him nothing. He made himself as a musician. Not for him were the stick-in-the-mud methods of the ordinary German *kapellmeister*: he assimilated all the newest methods of France and Italy, and refreshed the stagnant German waters with currents from Poland and Moravia. He was, in fact, the modernist of his time and place. Then, as now, the younger men, and perhaps the largest section of the German public, were weary and a little contemptuous of the conservatives—Bach, for instance. There was a new spirit in the air, new things to be said in music, new ways to be found of saying them. The modernists were as active with words as with notes. The opera drew people away from the church—especially the young people, to the great scandal of the elders.

Of these modernists Telemann was the recognised leader. Bach had little reputation, except as an organist and clavier player: to the great majority of people he was merely a capable church employee, turning out the expected works in the accepted style. Burney's History shows how slight was his reputation as a composer forty years after his death: even his musical sons spoke patronisingly of him as 'the old perruque'. But Telemann always had an enthusiastic public and an excellent Press. His music, as M. Rolland says, 'was admired in every country in Europe, from France to Russia'. Schubart (not Schubert!) called him 'the peerless master'. Mattheson, the most eminent musicologue of the day, hailed him, after a passing glance at Lully and Corelli, as 'the only musician above all praise'. He made no secret of his contempt for the 'fossils' who stuck to the contrapuntal style. He was an innovator in several fields: as M. Rolland puts it, 'This audacious innovator amazed even his fellow-innovators, such as Scheibe' (the young man, it will be remembered, who 'went for' Bach).

We may be sure that to his ardent contemporaries he seemed what M. Rolland declares him to have been—the man who let 'great draughts of fresh air' into the 'musty' German music of the day. Let M. Rolland sum him up once more: 'He is a modern, in the great quarrel between the ancients and the moderns; and he believes in progress.' 'One must never say to art,' we read in one of his letters, ' "Thou shalt go no further". One is always going further. . . . If there is no longer anything new to be found in melody, it must be sought in harmony.'

Substitute other names for those of Telemann and Bach, and who would not think we were reading an account of the controversies of our own time?

And yet this audacious innovator, this peerless master, this unflinching modernist, is today completely forgotten except by a student or two! And the moral is, let us keep our heads. Telemann, could he return to earth today, would be painfully astonished to find that the old fossil of a Bach was the most admired musician of the whole world, while he himself is a person of so small account that ninety-nine out of a hundred readers of this article will now be hearing his name for the first time.

All this does not mean that we should give up trying to progress in music. There is room for the modernist as well as for the conservative: it would be as great folly for Mr. Bliss to try to write in Elgar's style as for Elgar to try to write in Mr. Bliss's. But the conscious innovator must not count too positively on immortality. His function, as a rule, is not to create masterpieces himself, but to help to make a new language and new forms in which some later man of genius—of rather conservative tendencies, on the whole—can create masterpieces. Telemann undoubtedly helped to prepare the way for Mozart, Haydn, Beethoven, Weber, and others; but he himself does not survive. He was just one of the busy insects that help to make a coral reef for higher organisms to disport themselves upon; a worthy insect, but still—an insect.

THE ABSURDITY OF THE LABEL

12th October 1924

A WRITER in one of the morning papers the other day chanted yet another dirge over musical romanticism. The theme was the old one that 'amongst the younger generation . . . the classical masters are those of the eighteenth century, who were the children of an aristocratic society and worked within the conventions that such a culture demands. Bach, whom Parry, true to his age, tried to label as a romantic, and Mozart and Haydn, these are the chosen spirits of this year's Promenade concerts. And if Wagner still holds our audiences under his magnetic spell, our composers, who have travelled still further away from the old landmarks, have with few exceptions eliminated him from their works.' Beethoven's stock, the writer thinks, is low just now; Mendelssohn counts for little; Schumann has lost ground; and of the romantics only Chopin, 'temperamentally the product of an earlier epoch, holds his sway with undiminished lustre'.

That a change is coming over music is unquestionable. But is the change quite so great and so consistent as the writer of the article would suggest? A picture is being painted of a world from which the romantics are being banished in order to make way for the eighteenth century classics. But, in sober truth, were the classics ever ousted by the romantics? I doubt it. We have only to turn up the programmes of any orchestral concert society from, say, 1840 to the end of the nineteenth century to find that Mozart and Haydn and certain smaller eighteenth century composers more than held their own in the public favour against the romantics. And what precisely *is* a romantic? What *is* a classic? Under which category does Brahms come? Does he not defy all attempts to put him definitely in either? Bach, again, was both classic and romantic; the romantic Bach may be found in plenty in the Matthew Passion; and in some of the church cantatas his romanticism even tends to become decadence. And how are we going to apportion Beethoven's work between the romantic and the classic?

In fact, do these and other labels matter in the least? Cannot they be safely left to the type of critic who can think only in formulae? *His* psychological processes are very simple. He dislikes a certain kind of art for temperamental—perhaps even physiological—reasons, just as some people dislike cats and others apples. He looks round for a reason that, he thinks, will justify his oddity in other people's eyes and his own. The man who does not care for apples merely because Providence has built him like that will not admit that this is the real reason; to do so would be to brand himself as an oddity, or a person of weak digestion. So he persuades himself, and tries to persuade others, that his reaction against apples is due to a well-founded scientific distrust of malic acid. The type of critic to which I have referred is merely a man of limited musical sensibilities, in whom certain kinds of musical expression arouse no imaginative reactions. So he calls himself a 'romantic', or an 'anti-romantic', as the case may be, and thinks that he has established a valuable artistic principle when all that has happened is that he has gummed a label on himself.

The plain, sensible man—who, I think, forms the vast majority of the public—does not bother his head about labels. He knows that you have not made a dull piece of music into a good one by calling it classical, or destroyed the flavour of a Schumann song by sneering at it as romantic. I have known critics to praise a work simply because it was 'anti-romantic' —as if there were a magic in the mere label! The plain man is above this intellectual childishness. He knows that a label, in art as in commerce, is not necessarily a guarantee of the goods; and in any case he is, thank Heaven, too simple-minded to go by labels. He knows what he likes, and that is enough for him. If he likes a piece of music, the fact that some critic has pasted an uncomplimentary label on it will not prevent him still enjoying it; and if he does not like it naturally, he will not be persuaded to do so because some critic or some school has placed the seal of his or its approbation on it.

What we are witnessing today is, in small part, a real reaction against romanticism *per se*, due to our having been rather overdosed with it. A short period of abstention from the abused diet is all that one needs to go back to it with a new appetite. But the bulk of the present reaction is not against romantic music *per se*, but only against inferior romantic music. Chopin and Wagner, as we have seen, hold their own, in spite of their romanticism. The explanation is that they happen to be composers of the front rank. In the other cases also it is only the composers' inferior work that is being shelved. 'The Hymn of Praise' and 'Elijah' have worn thin; but the 'Hebrides' and the 'Midsummer Night's Dream' overtures have not lost a grain of their vitality. Schumann's weaker romantic works are losing ground, not because they are romantic, but because they are weak; but the 'Carnaval', though romanticism incarnate, is as popular as ever. Beethoven is no longer the impeccable god that some of his worshippers once thought him to be. But the truth is simply that Beethoven, like every other artist, did a fair quantity of work that was below his own best, and this inferior work is at last being found out. The reaction against him is in no sense whatever a reaction against romanticism or classicism or any other ism; it is merely the healthy reaction against boredom, whether inflicted on us by a Titan or a pigmy.

People are always reluctant to seem ungrateful to a great artist, to say to him, 'Thank you, master, for this jewel; but the thing next to it is only paste, which you will forgive me for refusing.' Beethoven is sometimes very dull and unbearably long-winded; and I am wholly at one with the listener who rejects the dull Beethoven, so long as he will kneel with me before the mighty master of the other works. Frankness in matters of art is most desirable; but let us be consistently frank. The people who estimate artistic values by labels are inclined to be as uncritical in their admiration of goods that bear their own labels as in their denigration of the goods that do not. The *mot d'ordre* has gone round that the thing now is to leap over the romantic period and drink of the fountain of eighteenth century music. But did the eighteenth century composers never write below their best? Is Mozart never dull and feebly repetitive, especially in his symphonic slow movements? I cannot understand the mentality of the classicist or neo-classicist who objects to Wagner's occasional slow-footedness yet has not a word of criticism of Mozart's dilly-dallying in the slow movement of the G minor symphony.

Let us throw all labels into the waste-paper basket, and judge a musical work simply by the music in it, whoever wrote it or to whatever period it may belong. To swear by names or periods or 'movements' is simply to delude ourselves into many a false admiration. There is just now a reviving interest in sixteenth century music; and one result of it is a frequent failure to discriminate between good sixteenth century music and bad. The Elizabethan madrigalists and lutenists and virginalists very often turned out mediocre work; but I have seen audiences professing, over some dull piece of music of the time, a rapture they certainly would not feel if it bore the name of some composer now living. The clan spirit is fatal to judgement. There are only two kinds of music, the good and the bad; and the good of any one period has no quarrel with the good of any other.

THOUGHTS ON THE PRESENT DISCONTENTS

I

1st December 1929

I PROPOSE to devote this and the next article or two to an examination of the fundamentals of a question that is evidently still disturbing large numbers of thoughtful music-lovers—the question of what is implied by, and what will be involved in, the change that has come over the face of music during the last twenty years. Having had to touch incidentally upon the subject in some wireless talks during the past twelve months, I have been deluged with letters that have shown me how the mass of the public feels about it all. But these letters have shown me also that the problem is not quite so simple as it appears to be on the surface.

The wireless has brought a new element into the world's musical culture. In the old days the infiltration of new ideas in music was relatively slow; a Berlioz, for instance, might be setting all Paris by the ears for a couple of decades without Bremen or Toulouse or Bradford knowing a note of his music at first hand. Even ten years ago it was still possible for a few enthusiastic partisans to tell fairy tales in the Press about the 'revolution' effected in music by this or that work of Stravinsky or Schönberg or some other of the heaven-sent geniuses in whom our fortunate generation was alleged to be so rich; and the plain man, never having heard a bar of the music that was so extravagantly praised, could not say the enthusiasts nay.

But all that has been changed by the radio and the gramophone, especially the radio. Thanks to this, the propagandist musical journalist no longer has the gay, irresponsible run he used to have. It is one thing to laud a new work as a revelation from on high to people who have never heard it and are never likely to hear it: it is quite another thing when about a million people have heard it for themselves. For the first time in musical history, the plain man all over the country now hears for himself and judges for himself the very latest music. And this plain man is manifestly disinclined to sit dumbly at the feet of any journalist. He is no longer the talked-to; he is the talker. He tells us bluntly that he does not like, and is sure he never will like, most of what is called 'modern music'; and any critic who has a good word to say for it is promptly challenged to give a reason for the faith that is in him—a challenge which he is generally unable to meet.

My correspondence, as might have been expected, has disclosed the existence of all varieties of taste and all degrees of knowledge among listeners. For some of them, everything is 'modern', and therefore incomprehensible or detestable, that has been written since Wagner; in a letter I received the other day, Strauss, Debussy, Bax, Lambert, Delius and Elgar were mentioned as specimen objects of the writer's particular abhorrence. Evidently nothing can be done for people of this kind but to ask them to enlarge their experience by constant listening to music of a later date than about 1880.

Our real problem is the large number of intelligent and eager music-lovers who, do what they will, are unable to persuade themselves that 'modern' music, in the broad sense which musicians give to that term, gives them any pleasure or, as a rule, conveys to them any meaning. I cannot help feeling that the B.B.C. has so far not quite realised its responsibilities towards this vast mass of ordinarily intelligent music-lovers, no doubt because it had no suspicion of their difficulties. Through the medium of Sir Walford Davies, the B.B.C. has catered excellently for the needs of listeners in the more elementary stages of musical appreciation; but, paradoxically, no provision has been made for the large number of listeners who stand in much greater need of instruction on a much more perplexing subject. It is good to have the reasons for the excellence of Bach and Handel clearly set forth, especially when this is done in Sir Walford Davies's agreeable style. But after all, Bach and Handel and Mozart and the rest of that family are intelligible to the plain man without any explanation; the explanation is only an extra flavour in the cup of his delight. The trouble at the other end of the scale is that the B.B.C. has been flinging a huge mass of modern music at the head of the plain man without making the slightest systematic attempt to help him to the appreciation or even the comprehension of it. It has told him a thousand times the fundamental principles in virtue of which a melody or a work of Handel is good and the superficially similar melody or work of an inferior composer of the same genre is bad. But it has not told him in virtue of what fundamental principle Schönberg's third quartet, let us say, is good or bad, or even whether any fundamental principle has yet been formulated that would authorise us to declare such a work good or bad. Sir Walford Davies, in a recent talk to which I listened, was once more expatiating on the virtues of the common chord—God's chord, I think he called it. But if it takes all these years to bring the musical community to a sense of the true inwardness of God's chord, how many years will be necessary for the explanation of the devil's chords? The plain man has a suspicion that 'modern' music is largely made up of these; yet he had had no explanation of what their devilry consists in, or how to tell the handiwork of Beelzebub from that of Jahveh.

It is impossible to over-estimate the service the B.B.C has done the musical community by broadcasting, during the last few years, so enormous an amount of the most recent music. Its musical policy has been thoroughly enlightened; thanks to it, the ordinary music-lover in the remotest part of the country is in a position to exercise his own judgement upon a number of composers and works that would otherwise have been no more than names to him. But he has as good as been told that if he wants to learn how to swim in this boiling sea he must adopt the drastic course of plunging in and taking his chance of drowning. It is hardly to be wondered at that thousands of his kind have already been drowned, while other thousands have resolved not to risk their lives again. I submit, then, that the time has come when the B.B.C. might consider the advisability of doing for the man who is curious about modern music, and utterly unable to find his way about in it, something of what has been done for the lover of the older music at the skilled hands of Sir Walford Davies—something on the lines of Dr. George Dyson's masterly book on 'The New Music', but with a special eye to the necessities of the ordinary man who, though interested in music, has little or no technical training in it.

For we are plainly in the thick, if not of a revolution in music, at any rate of a rising, or at least a conspiracy. The older vocabulary of the art, the older grammar, the older forms, the older principles, the older purposes, are all being vigorously called in question. What amount of justification is there in the audacious challenge of the new music? How much of it is the instinctive striving of the spirit of the new age towards a genuine expression of itself, how much of it is mere scientific experiment, how much of it the purest bluff? So far, 'criticism' has failed to help us very much. If anything, indeed, were necessary finally to discredit musical criticism as it is generally practised, it would be a survey of its record during the last ten or fifteen years. Faced with a definite problem—the calm appraising of the meaning of the change that had been coming over music from about the turn of the century—it failed abjectly to apply even the rudiments of a scientific method to it. All that criticism could do was to divide itself into two camps, equally vociferous and equally unintelligent. One camp, if anything the more naïve of the two, was anxious to pose as the discoverer and sponsor of new genius; and so many new geniuses were discovered each month that today we can hardly recall the names of most of them. The other camp simply declared *tout court* that it thought the new music horrible, which gave the other camp the obvious opportunity to say that so the story had run in every age, the advocacy of the new spirit being always left to the 'progressives'—modestly meaning themselves. It never occurred to any of them to ask what is the meaning of 'progress' in music, or whether the word has any real meaning at all. The 'progressivists' were fond of showing, or imagining they were showing, that history was now repeating itself, the geniuses of today being left, as those of the past were alleged to have been, to the discovery of a few rare souls such as themselves. In their pathetic innocence it never occurred to them to examine history to see if such phenomena as themselves had perhaps existed in the past, and if so, what had happened to them. They appealed to history only so far as they thought history could be pressed into their own service. Yet the clue to the present situation was plainly to be sought, if anywhere, in the past; for Nature never does a thing merely once. There are laws in musical as in other history. We may not be able fully to understand the present even in the light of the past; but without the past, even a beginning at an understanding of the present is impossible. In my next article I will discuss a recent remarkable attempt to trace the operation of law in musical history.

II

8th December 1929

It is not much use trying to write musical history without some sort of a philosophy of history. Without something of that kind you are not a historian but only a chronicler. Your philosophy of history may, indeed is bound to be, an imperfect one; but it is at any rate a stone contributed to a building that may one day be completed. And a philosophy of history of some kind or other is a necessity if we are to try to estimate the trend and the potency of the forces at work in the world that lies around us. We may not be able to understand these fully even with the aid of the past; but without the aid of the past there cannot be even the beginning of an understanding. Let us accordingly approach the problem of present-day 'modernism' in what may seem, at first sight, a roundabout way.

Today I want to introduce my readers to a notable book, on which I have been intending to write for some time past, on the operation of law in musical history. Its author is Alfred Lorenz, and its title *Musikgeschichte im Rhythmus der Generationen*, the literal translation of which is 'Musical History in the Rhythm of the Generations'. Alfred Lorenz first came into general notice about five years ago with a remarkable book dealing at great length with the form of the 'Ring'—*Der musikalische Aufbau des Bühnenfestspieles Der Ring des Nibelungen*. This he followed up with an equally remarkable study of *Tristan*; the two books are intended as contributions to the study of 'Das Geheimnis der Form bei Richard Wagner' ('The Secret of Wagner's Form'). Lorenz, who is now a man of about sixty, had had a long experience in German opera houses as repetitor and conductor before he became, in 1923, 'Lector für Musiktheorie' at the University of Munich. He has composed a fair quantity of music of his own. He is, in short, unusually well-equipped for writing upon the art.

Alfred Lorenz is a son of the historian Ottokar Lorenz, whose writings will be familiar to students of general history. Ottokar Lorenz developed systematically a theory of a 'rhythm of the generations' that had been faintly hinted at by Ranke. This theory has been carried further by other modern German historians, notably by Wilhelm Pinder, some of whose conclusions with regard to general history have been utilised by Alfred Lorenz for the purposes of musical history.

I can summarise here only the broadest of his conclusions. He begins with the demonstration that, in history, what the century is to the generation, three centuries are to the century. A generation is usually accepted as implying about thirty-three years. A man of any particular generation forms a nodal point between his father and his own children; the active portion of his own life is a solid mass, as it were, midway between the old age of his father and the adolescence of his son, and touching upon each of them. With each generation, roughly speaking, there comes an orientation towards the world that is different from that of the generation preceding; and the culture-form or culture-force that makes a tentative appearance in one generation gathers strength in the second, while in the third it reaches a maturity that is the prelude to decay. Three of these generation-groups constitute a century; and the general change of orientation from century to century needs no demonstration. But as the century is to the generation, so is the three-century period to the century; and it is to the three-century period that we have to look for changes that are even more positive, as being on a large scale, than the normal century-change.

All this may look, at a first glance, like mere word-spinning and theory-building. For the full justification of the generations theory I must refer the reader to Lorenz and Pinder. In this latest book of his, Lorenz deals briefly with some of the objections that are so superficially obvious that I am confident the reader of this article has already made them—that there is no such thing as a 'generation', since people are being born every year, so that there are always a number of generations within any arbitrarily selected generation; that no generation and no century is all of the one way of thinking and acting; and so on. This is all quite true; but it does not affect the theory in the broad. As regards the latter objection, for instance, there has never been, as Lorenz says, an epoch in which all men shared the same view of either the theory or the practice of government; yet there have been epochs that were as predominantly aristocratic in this respect as other epochs were democratic. To give a more specialised illustration from musical history, the turn of the sixteenth-seventeenth centuries witnessed a *general* change-over from polyphonic to monodic and harmonic methods, in spite of the fact that certain composers still cultivated the older polyphonic style for some years after 1600.

Leaving the detailed justification of the theory of rhythm-by-generations to its sponsors, let us see how, according to Lorenz, it works out in musical history. His special thesis is that a radical change occurs about every three centuries.

That a drastic change in the technical methods and the orientation of music set in about the turn of the present century is obvious to any observer; and it is one of the common-places of musical history that there was a radical change about 1600. According to the three-century theory, then, there should have been another about 1300. The reader who relies for his knowledge of musical history upon the older historians and their present-day copyists will say that no such turnover took place in 1300 as admittedly took place in 1600 and 1900. (I use these round numbers for convenience' sake; they must not, of course, be taken with absolute literalness.) But what has recently taken place in musical historiography is rather like what once took place in astronomy. When Bode worked out his law of the planetary distances, it seemed to break down at two points, because no planets were then known to exist at those theoretic distances from the earth. The essential truth of Bode's law was demonstrated, however, by the discovery of Uranus in 1781 and of Ceres in 1801. Something of the same kind has lately happened in musical historiography—the justification of a theory by the discovery of facts unknown to earlier students.

The dividing line between the older music and the new was formerly held to be about 1450. It was on the basis of this traditional conception that Hugo Riemann planned his great history of music. The first volume, published in 1904, dealt with the music of the ancient world. The second volume (1905) bears the sub-title 'The Music of the Middle Ages (to 1450)'. In the preface to his third volume (1907), however, Riemann offers 'an apology for an error in form'. 'Our increasing certainty of knowledge with regard to the epoch-making significance of the trecento Florentine art,' he says, 'has made it an imperative necessity to regard not 1450 but 1300 as the close of the Middle Ages in music'; and he admits that a new 'periodisation' of musical history is now necessary. I need not pause to explain to the non-professional reader what this 'ars nova' of the Florentine school was. The essential point for our present purpose is that about 1300, as again about 1600 (and once more 1900), musicians were confident that a 'new art', as they expressly called it, had come into being and superseded the 'ars antiqua'; the reader will remember that the proud term 'Nuove musiche' was given to *their* innovations by the men of 1600. It will be seen that Lorenz's theory that 'the more significant changes in the style-intentions of musicians have taken place every three hundred years' has so far been vindicated; the year 1300 has acquired, in the light of the most recent research, a significance in musical history that was formerly attributed erroneously to 1450. In a following article we will see how the theory works out in other respects; and later, if the long-suffering reader's patience endures till then, I shall try to show how all this bears on the 'revolution' of our own day.

III

15th December 1929

In last week's article I showed how Lorenz found rather unexpected support for his theory of a three-centuries rhythm in the fact that historians now regard 1300, instead of, as was formerly the case, 1450, as marking the close of the Middle Ages in music. (Perhaps I may again remind the reader that all these round numbers are used for mere convenience' sake; they do not imply that a drastic change in the orientation of music always occurred precisely at the turn of a given century.) Let us now see how the theory works out in connection with earlier periods.

First of all, however, we must beware, as Lorenz does well to point out, of viewing the last nineteen centuries or so in a wrong perspective. Our material for the last couple of hundred years is so copious, and that for the first thousand years so scanty, that we are apt to suppose that radical changes have been more frequent in the later period; with Carl Philipp Emanuel Bach, Haydn, Mozart, Beethoven and Wagner, for instance, music moves so visibly on from point to point that a quasi-revolution seems to have been taking place every thirty or forty years, whereas the period from 700 to 1000, let us say, or from 1000 to 1300, seems to present a uniform aspect. This is only a kind of historical optical illusion, however: we distinguish the separate hills in the later epoch because we are so close to them, while our distance from the earlier epochs causes the individual hills to blend into an apparent mass. It is all a matter of the profusion or the scantiness of records. The changes from generation to generation in the earlier periods must have been wrought by one mind or one tendency piling itself upon or reacting against another, just as in the period from the death of Sebastian Bach to the present day; but in the later period we clearly see each successive individual at work, whereas in the earlier we see only the broad course of evolution over a long period. And it is only with the broad course of evolution that we must concern ourselves in modern as in primitive times if we wish to test the validity of the generations theory.

Let us divide musical history into five periods of three hundred years each—I, from 400 A.D. to 700; II, from 700 to 1000; III, from 1000 to 1300; IV, from 1300 to 1600; V, from 1600 to 1900. Lorenz's thesis is that the musical impulses and desires of men move in a rhythm that swings them for about three centuries in one direction and then for three centuries in an opposite one, a reversion then coming to an older ideal under a new form. He begins with a classification of music that is not so blankly metaphysical as may appear at first sight. There is the time-conception and the space-conception. The former results in homophony, the latter in polyphony; the controlling impulse in the one case is towards melody that moves along freely in time, in the other case towards the coalescence of simultaneous melodies into a mass that has a sort of spatial existence. As with all attempts to elucidate the essence of music, this suffers from our inability to express the intangible—and perhaps in the last resort incomprehensible—in words; but, as every musical reader will recognise, the verbal distinction corresponds to a reality of which we are all conscious, phrase it how we will.

Lorenz argues, then, that the course of musical evolution is a see-saw between the time-conception and the space-conception —or, to put it in terms in more common use, between the monodic ideal and the polyphonic. He brings out, in a series of chapters dealing with the five periods in turn, the basic tendency of each of them; and he appends to his book a graph in which the curve of the line shows clearly the rhythmic swing of musical evolution. The first period covers the great creative period of monodic plain-song. In the second period the unconscious impulse is towards the polyphonic. No instructed person now believes that organum—the supposedly first clumsy attempt to make two lines of tone go in harness—was a novelty when Hucbald began theorising about it at the end of the ninth century. Theory, as usual, came after practice; Hucbald was merely aiming at a rationale of what had long been in the air. Polyphony of some sort or other was far older than our historians used to think; and Lorenz is right in looking upon the second period as one in which there was going on a steady orientation of music towards the polyphonic space-conception.

In the third period, the monodic reasserts itself; this is the epoch of the great outpouring of lyrical sentiment which we associate with the Troubadours and the Minnesingers. The fourth period begins with that Florentine 'ars nova' of which I have already spoken, and polyphony now moves on from Dunstable and Dufay to the great Netherlands school and its climax in Lassus and Palestrina and others. The close of the sixteenth century brings with it a sharp revulsion against the polyphonic; and the fifth period, like the third and the first, takes monody as its ideal; the time-conception once more becomes predominant.

I have given only the barest outline of Lorenz's thesis; his book, indeed, is itself only an outline, the details of which will be filled in a later and larger work. But even on his present small scale of treatment he must be held to have proved the essential workableness of his theory. Objections to it here and there will no doubt have occurred by now to more than one of my readers; but I can assure him, I think, that these have been anticipated and answered by Lorenz. It will probably leap to everyone's mind, for instance, that in the fifth period, which is claimed to be predominantly monodic, there comes the great master of polyphony, Sebastian Bach. But Lorenz has no difficulty in showing that counterpoint in connection with Bach means a rather different thing from counterpoint as the Netherlanders conceived it. Counterpoint was, so to speak, simply a habit with Bach, a bias partly natural, partly acquired. But his music has its roots not in the space-conception but in the time-conception; the free onward sweep of his melody, the symmetry of his rhythm, and his feeling for form (which is in essence lyrical) are characteristic not of a truly polyphonic but of a homophonic orientation.

Leaving the reader to pursue Lorenz's fascinating thesis further on his own account, I now propose to examine the present situation in music in the light of the past.

IV

22nd December 1929

It has occurred to me that before we proceed to attempt to see the present situation in music in the light of the past, the student and the general reader may be interested in some of the curious results yielded by a re-examination of musical history on the lines suggested by Lorenz's thesis. If that thesis was merely a general one of recurrence and reversion in history it would not call for much attention. The theory of a cycle in the cosmos is as old as philosophy itself, and modern political and culture historians have done a good deal of speculation on these lines. Rhythm being at the root of things, it would indeed be surprising if occasionally the swing of the pendulum did not bring us back to a point very close to one that humanity has occupied before. The virtue of Lorenz's book is the detailed illustration of the operation of rhythm in musical evolution over a period of nearly two thousand years—an illustration only made possible by his wide and deep knowledge of musical history and by his unusual powers of correlation. The larger book he promises us, in which the details of the present broad outline will be filled in, should be exceptionally interesting.

It is certainly curious how, as he points out, 'humanity has had to re-discover eurhythmy three times in the course of a thousand years'. The distinction he has in mind is the one I mentioned in my third article, between time-music, of which the very essence is a delight in eurhythmy for its own sake—monodic or homophonic music—and contrapuntal music, in which the space-element of the mass is more prominent than the time-element of the line.

It is not implied that the older contrapuntal music was devoid of rhythm; indeed, one of the complaints of the Florentine reformers of 1600 was that in a complicated polyphonic piece every part followed a rhythm of its own, to the great confusion of the listener. But broadly speaking these counter-rhythms, interesting as they are in themselves, tend to cancel each other out in the work as a whole, which does not move forward with the same regular, definite beats as those of a song or an instrumental melody. We shall probably never know precisely how plain-song was phrased in the earlier periods; but the latest authorities agree that it was much more rhythmical than was at one time thought. This eurhythmic ideal of the first of Lorenz's periods (400 to 700) revives in the third period (that of the Troubadours and Minnesingers, 1000–1300), and again in the fifth period (from 1600). Something of the rhythmical sense is lost or undervalued in the intervening periods, which concentrate on another ideal—that of a polyphonic space-mass instead of a time-flow. Musical humanity, like political humanity, seems to be unable to cultivate all the theoretically possible forms simultaneously. It can proceed only by action and reaction, can create a more or less stable equilibrium only by rejecting certain unassimilable elements, with the inevitable result that in the process of time these elements creep back, causing a dis-harmony that leads in turn to an attempt at equilibrium along new lines, and so *ad infinitum.* Unceasing war between rival and irreconcilable egoisms is the law of music as it is of life. There is no stability and no 'progress'; there is only change, only rhythmic ebb and flow.

How the same tendency recurs, of course under different forms, in one period after another is shown again by the history of coloratura, which is the result of the natural impulse to indulge one's delight in the free melodic line to the point of wild excess of ornamentation. The rich melismata of the earlier plain-song may serve as an illustration from the first period. The coloratura virtuoso of the sixth century returns in the twelfth: a treatise of that epoch censures the singers for trying to dazzle the congregation with their 'ornaments'. 'These are not human melodies', we read, 'but those of the sirens; and although we must admire this agility of the larnyx (which the nightingale himself could not excel), this skill in running up and down, in the binding together of tones, their rapid reiteration or their welding together, yet is the sense confused, the mind befooled, and a right judgement of the value of what is being sung is made impossible.' As Lorenz says, we might be listening to the polemic of a Gluckist of the eighteenth century against the coloratura excesses of the prima donna or the castrato of that day! And the case for the rhythmic swing of the pendulum in these matters every three centuries or so is even stronger than Lorenz has noted; for this 'embellishment' of solo song was a characteristic not only of the twelfth and the eighteenth centuries but of the fifteenth. Max Kuhn has collected a wealth of evidence on this point in his book *Die Verzierungs-Kunst in der Gesangs-Musik des 16 und 17 Jahrhunderts*; it appears that it was the practice in the fifteenth century to 'ornament' even the madrigals.

Historians who have followed Kiesewetter too blindly have assumed that coloratura was applied only to the soprano part when the madrigal was sung as a solo, with instruments playing the remaining parts; the supposed explanation being that, as the single vocal part was ineffective as it stood, it was 'embellished' in order to make it more interesting. But that *all* the parts of a four or five part madrigal could be tricked out with coloratura at the sweet will of the singers is shown by the following passage from Hermann Finck (not, by the way, the living master of that name, but a sixteenth-century predecessor):—

> 'The method of employing coloratura depends entirely on the dexterity, the natural talent, and the originality of the individual singer. Each has his own way. Many are of the opinion that the bass should be "coloured"; others say the discant. My own view, however, is that *all* the voices can and must be provided with coloratura; but not from beginning to end, and not in all the voices at the same time, but at suitable places, so that one coloratura may be clearly distinguished from another, the composition being thus left intact and underanged' (*sic*).

It is difficult for us of the present day either to understand the mentality that could indulge in these escapades or to imagine the practical result in performance; though we should be equally amazed and baffled if we could hear the 'Messiah' sung as it must have been in Handel's day.

Lorenz, I gather from his final chapter, rather shrinks from examining the practice of our own music in the light of the past. Yet it is already obvious that some quite piquant analogies exist between the two. I will cite one that may interest and amuse the reader. He will be familiar with that device of jazz that consists of the breaking of the melody and the rhythm at an unexpected point, either by syncopation or by the insertion of a rest. The effect is that of a hiccup. The jazz illiterates and mechanicians have probably never suspected that this little dodge, which they think so new and so clever, is quite six hundred years old. It even bore the name of Hocket (Hocquet, Hoquet, Ochetus, Ochetto)—the hiccup. If the reader will turn to his 'Grove' he will find this definition of the hocket: 'A naïve device of the early mediaeval contrapuntists, by which the notes of a melody are interspersed with rests, and that with little or no regard to the chopping up of words or syllables in the process'—a definition that can be transferred without the slightest change to the similar trick in jazz. 'Grove' gives the following passage from a motet by Guillaume de Machaut (1364) as an illustration of the practice:

(To save space I have cut out the two lower voice parts; my purpose is only to show the working of the hocket.)

Listening the other evening in Queen's Hall to the fine 'Rio Grande' of Mr. Constant Lambert, I was amused to find him hocketing away with all the simple gusto of a primitive of six hundred years ago. More than once he separates the syllables of a word by means of a hiccup rest—for example:—

'like a bitter [*hic!*] wind calling':

and again—

'the plectrum and the kettle- [*hic!*] drum':

and once more—

'they dance no sara- [*hic!*] band.'

There is nothing new under the sun; and the admirers of jazz—if there are any left—will be gratified to learn that it can lay claim to so respectable an ecclesiastical ancestry. In his excellent programme note on the 'Rio Grande', Mr. Foss told us that 'the words are not "set to music" in the sense that is applicable to most choral works.' They 'are used as a background of atmosphere, they are something for the chorus to sing. . . .' Precisely: as Grove says *à propos* of the hocket, 'the notes of a melody are interspersed with rests, and that with little or no regard to the chopping up of words or syllables in the process': the notes are just 'something for the chorus to sing'. Thus does musical history repeat itself: to employ the intrepid figure of a recent writer, the pendulum has come full circle.

V

5th January 1930

THE Habas and the Hauers may or may not be minds so far in advance of ours that it will be centuries before we can catch up with them; but they are certainly minds so different from ours that there can be few points of contact between them and the present generation. Their speculations are theoretically very interesting; but there is no earthly possibility of the general musical consciousness veering round in their direction within our lifetime.

Here, indeed, we come upon the main difficulty the 'new music' has to face—the awkward, stubborn, inescapable fact that it does not make much of an appeal to the plain musical man; and how it is to establish itself without *his* co-operation I confess I do not see. No one can deny that a change was due to come over the face of music—the language and the forms that it took three hundred years to perfect having approached the end of their resources about 1900—and that a change is in fact now taking place. But the weak point of the present 'revolution' is that it seems to have no backing from the ordinary musical man, whereas previous revolutions have owed their instantaneous success to their being merely the conscious expression, on the part of some artist or group of artists, of impulses and desires that were already latent in the subconsciousness of the musical world as a whole. The change-over of 1600 was not something forced upon an uncomprehending and reluctant world by the Florentine Camerata; it was simply the coming to the surface of streams of tendency that had long been running underground. The new melodic and harmonic art was so rapturously acclaimed by the multitude because it answered, in a way that the older polyphonic modal art did not, to the inmost desires of the multitude. The trouble today is that the new music rarely gets beyond the conclave of a limited intelligentsia; that it answers to no deep-seated desire of the plain man is shown by his stout refusal to have anything to do with it. He may be right or he may be wrong; but the fact of his hostility is beyond dispute.

There is no case in history of any drastic change occurring

in the orientation of music without a predisposition on the part of the general musical public towards such a change. Any opinion to the contrary is based on a misreading of the plain facts of history, or of an ignorance of the facts. In a recent thoughtful article, Mr. Fox-Strangways rather gave his readers the impression that some sixty years ago the plain man had the same difficulty with Wagner that his successor of today has with Schönberg and Hindemith and Webern and the rest of them. He cites 'a prominent musician', who said of 'Tannhäuser' in 1867, 'I didn't know whether to laugh or cry, but when I came out of the theatre I wept, for, said I, this is the downfall of German music'; and he tells us how Hubert Parry, then aged nineteen, could do no more than find 'some of the overture very fine', and how nine years later, having 'absorbed the "Ring" by dint of much score-reading and with the help of a dictionary', Parry came to the conclusion that 'we had lost the art of saying something spontaneously because we have exhausted the present resources of music'.

The only comment I can make upon all this is that Parry and the 'prominent musician' and the others of that type must have been people of singularly slow apprehension. Round about 1867 Wagner was thrilling thousands of quite ordinary music lovers not with 'Tannhäuser', but with 'Tristan' and the 'Meistersinger'. Twenty years or so before that, the multitude had welcomed in 'Tannhäuser' and the other operas of Wagner's first period a superior mind that was expressing all that they had longed to experience in music. Between about 1844 and 1864, in which latter year King Ludwig took the composer under his protection, Wagner had become the most talked-of musician in the whole world precisely in virtue of these early works; if the world quarrelled as it did over him, it was for the simple reason that a large section of the general public showed a liking for his music that the professors and the critics and the other members of the ignorentsia found very disturbing. The point needs insisting upon again and again that there is nothing whatever corresponding to this in the present situation. Quite the reverse, in fact; it is mostly the theoreticians alone who hail this or that 'modernist' as a master, while the world at large remains stonily indifferent to his music, if not in actual revolt against it. The only possible inference is that the present 'revolution', unlike its predecessors, has not its roots in the general musical consciousness, the general musical instincts of mankind.

At any rate not in its present form. It seems probable that at first theory outran practice, that the reformers tried to get along faster than the rest of the world could follow. It rather looks as if the period of meiosis—that 'stage in a malady when the symptoms tend to abate', as the dictionaries define it—has already set in. We are now in the second stage of the revolution, and already the distance between the leaders and the followers (or at any rate spectators) is lessening. One of the reasons for the comparative popularity of Hindemith, whose brain is obviously not a first-rate one judged by our normal standards, is that in comparison with, say, Schönberg he is easily intelligible. Dr. Hans Mersmann, in his admirable little book on *Die Tonsprache der neuen Musik*, has to admit that the beginners of the 'revolution' have lived to see something of the first arrogance of their theory watered down by their successors. He quotes four passages from works by Hindemith, Jarnach, Schönberg and Webern respectively. I reproduce the last of these: it is a song by Webern which I think I have already quoted in another connection:—

As Dr. Mersmann hints, the course of evolution indicated by these four citations is the opposite of what the superficial believer in continuous 'progress' would imagine. The more extravagant of the four passages—the lunatic outburst of Webern—is the earliest in time, and the one that has the most affinity with music as we have been in the habit of conceiving it—that of Hindemith—is the latest. The pioneers pitched their claims too high; they were impracticable idealists, and their successors have had to be more accommodating. The 'revolution', in fact, has followed the usual course. The inaugurators of all these little diversions, political as well as musical, inhabit a Cloud-Cuckoo-Town of their own. An organised society could be run on their fantastic lines only on the condition that the rest of humanity shed all its old habits and its old mentality and achieved the impossible feat of commencing the world afresh. Failing that, there is nothing for it but for the revolutionaries to come to terms with the old Adam in man; and when the process of compromise between the new theory and the old practice is at last accomplished, there turns out to be astonishingly little difference, in essentials, between the new world and the old. All experience suggests that this is what will happen in modern music. The process of accommodation has already begun: the newest 'new' music is simpler, less purely speculative, than the older 'new' music. Revolutionaries, like other people, are subject, though they may be reluctant to admit it, to cosmic law. Upon this subject I shall have something to say in another and, the reader will be relieved to learn, a final article.

VI

12th January 1930

THE twentieth century 'revolution' is running true to form, so to speak; history is repeating itself just in the way that might be expected of so conventionally-minded a muse. Mr. Fox-Strangways is quite correct in saying, in the article from which I have already quoted, that we must each of us make our own account with the 'new system', 'for there is no going back. Works will continue to be written in classical tonality, just as through the seventeenth century works continued to be written in ecclesiastical polyphony; but they will have, as those had, no future.' The two cases, as I have already pointed out, are not precisely on all fours, inasmuch as the 'new system' of the seventeenth century was eagerly welcomed by the musical world in general, for it answered to something for which all had been longing and for which the plain man was fully ready, while the 'new system' of today is received with suspicion, if not actual hostility, by the plain musical man, the inference being that it does not, in its present form at any rate, answer to anything that is yearning for expression in the general musical consciousness, but is rather the creation of a few musicians who work by theory rather than by impulse and instinct. But taking the broad view Mr. Fox-Strangways is no doubt right. The language and the forms of 1600 to 1900 have seemingly exhausted their resources, the works that may still be written in that language and those forms must lack vitality.

The future, however, if the past can be taken as a guide, is not with the language and the forms of the last couple of decades. It is not the pioneers who will enter the Promised Land; and those who ultimately do will owe their success to their having effected a compromise with the art of the past. The next phase that is due is one in which some man or other of genius has an intuition of the necessity of some such compromise. The geniuses are always less inclined to speculation than the talents. It is probable that to the historian of a couple of centuries hence Schönberg and his followers will appear to be the eager semi-amateurs that Caccini and Peri are to us: the new Monteverdi will reach both far in advance of them and back over their heads.

Moreover, nothing very striking or durable will be achieved until the new language and the new forms have become flexible enough, and sufficiently a matter of instinct rather than of reflection, for genius to express itself through them without too much taking of thought as to means. It must be obvious to everyone that as yet the new language is not one that permits of the free and clearly-defined expression of artistic personality. Even the usual distinctions of racial culture and tradition are lost in it; not only is the atonal music of A very like that of B, but it is very much the same whether it happens to be written by a German, a Frenchman, a Russian or a Pole. The atonal composers, generally speaking, sound much alike for the same reason that Peri and Caccini do: the language is not yet plastic enough, the form not yet vital enough, for a personality out of the common to use it freely for the purpose of self-expression—even were such a personality anywhere visible at the moment.

Nor will the music of the future any more correspond to that envisaged by the present theorists, than the music of the later seventeenth century and the eighteenth did to that of the early seventeenth. Not only did the early opera take a direction utterly unforeseen by the Florentine Camerata, but a new art, of which they had no inkling whatever, sprang into being—the art of organic instrumental forms, an art that not only profited by the new ideas of symmetry brought into being by the development of the aria but actually reached back in the fullness of time, to that very polyphony that the Florentines hoped and believed they had banished. We can hardly doubt that within the next fifty years or so the 'new system' also will settle down into patterns of which the too self-conscious reformers of today have no conception.

For there are forces always at work that are stronger than the individual. The great historian Ambros, discussing the revolution of 1600 and its results, says truly and profoundly that the Spirit of Music knew what it wanted and in the process of time achieved it, taking over only so much of the new methods as would serve its purpose. It is impossible for a handful of speculative theorists to force the hand, so to speak, of the Spirit of Music. Things will happen at their due time and not before, and in a form that is the outcome of all the forces at work not merely in the consciousness of individuals but in the soul of history. The story of the whole-tone scale will serve to point this moral.

The whole-tone scale suggested itself as a new possibility to composers long before Debussy set himself to the systematic exploitation of it. Glinka had used it in the overture to 'Russlan and Ludmilla'. Some time later it evidently attracted the attention of a Russian composer of the name of Baron Vietinghoff, who wrote under the pseudonym of Boris Schell. An overture of his came into the hands of Liszt, who wrote thus to a correspondent concerning it:

> Give him [i.e., Vietinghoff] this little scale of chords. . . . It is nothing but a very simple development of the scale, *terrifying* for all the long and protruding ears—
>
> 
>
> that M. de Vietinghoff employs in the final presto of his overture. Tausig makes a pretty fair use of it in his 'Geisterschiff'; and in classes in the Conservatoire, in which the high art of the *mad dog* is duly taught, the existing elementary exercises of the piano method—
>
> 
>
> which are of a sonorousness as disagreeable as they are incomplete, ought to be replaced by this one—
>
> 
>
> which will thus form the unique basis of the method of harmony—all the other chords, in use or not, being unable to be employed except by the *arbitrary* curtailment of such and such an interval. In fact, it will soon be necessary to complete the system by the admission of quarter and half-quarter tones until something better turns up!

This was in 1860; evidently the theoretic possibilities of the whole-tone scale were already engaging the attention of thoughtful musicians. But no composer of the first rank attempted to exploit these possibilities. The time was not yet ripe; the ordinary scale sufficed for all practical purposes, and it would only have been a needless embarrassment then to try to incorporate an alien element with it. It was not till about a generation later that Debussy experimented systematically with the new theoretic scale. He in turn found that its possibilities, consistently with a free use of the scale that was still the main instrument of musical thought, were rather limited; and as time went on, the whole-tone system became more and more, in the hands not only of Debussy but of others, less a new scale than a new harmony. (Not so very new, however, for Chopin had used it as a harmony about half a century before.) Manifestly it was impossible to force upon the Spirit of Music, in the name of theory, something that it had only a limited use for in practice. It was willing to extend the resources of harmony by this new conception, but it stubbornly refused to abandon the historic tonality for it.

The whole-tone scale, with its abolition of the old dominant-tonic relationship and its division of the ordinary scale into six equal full-tone intervals (with sundry other relations of sectional equality upon which I cannot enlarge now) was obviously the father of the atonal twelve-tone scale, in which all the old distinctions between tonic, dominant and so on are completely abolished. And the question prompts itself, Will the twelve-tone scale be any more successful than the whole-tone scale was in its attempt to oust the scale that for so many centuries has been the very root of humanity's musical thinking? If the modest half-revolution of Debussy failed, is there any hope of success for a revolution that aims at a complete reversal of previous practice? Is it not *a priori* more probable that the Spirit of Music will once more take, with imperturbable blandness, just so much of the new system as it can comfortably incorporate into its own tissues and reject the rest, or at least postpone tackling it until it is in a better condition for the full digestion of it?

The future course of things it would be vain to try to forecast in detail. It is abundantly evident already, however, that the manipulation of the atonal system is much easier in the abstract than in the concrete. An essay like the now historic one of Erwin Stein on 'New Form-Principles' is flawless as a piece of constructive speculation; the only trouble is that these new principles have not yet resulted in a single work that can satisfy the aesthetic desires of musical humanity in general. Surely a compromise will have to be established sooner or later between the over-eager demands of the new theory and the stubborn *j'y suis, j'y reste* of the old practice? Some such compromise, indeed, seems to be already in the air. It will be a relief to everyone when the main terms of it have become matters of general agreement, so that composers will once more have at their disposal a language in which they can *think* without having, as at present, to keep thinking every moment of the mechanism of their thought. No poet can make vital poetry in a language that is not so natural, so instinctive within him that he has no need to consume half his energy in thinking out the vocabulary and the grammar of it as he goes along; no architect can construct a beautiful and durable building if he is perpetually preoccupied with the problems of a material whose inner laws he only half understands.

RUMMAGING IN THE LUMBER ROOM

19th April 1925

All of us who are given to the bad habit of book-collecting have a lumber room full of books that we cannot be sure we are ever likely to look at again, but that nothing in the world would induce us to sell. For one thing, there is always the possibility of our wanting them; for another, when we do happen to take one of these wastrels down we find that in its way it is as interesting as any of the pampered darlings we keep in the library. For there is a touch of the analyst and the coroner in all of us: it is pleasant now and then to turn from the still living in literature and art to what was once alive, and to try to find out what it died of. I have already thrown out the suggestion that a perfectly fascinating history might be written of bad music—a sort of guide to the chamber of horrors in the musical Tussaud's. I am sure that the average reader would be far more interested in such a volume than in the ordinary history of music, with its dreary conventionalities about a host of composers of whose works he will never hear a note, and most of whose music would give him no great pleasure could he hear it. What does it matter to him whether Buxtehude wrote five hundred or a thousand fugues? What's Hammerschmidt to him, or he to Hammerschmidt? But a searching, ironic study of the world's worst music for the last three hundred years, with copious illustration, would be as amusing and instructive as a history of the more absurd costumes of the same period. There must be hundreds of bad composers only waiting to be dug up and given, by the genius of the historian, a life they never had while they were alive. Every age must have had its Ethelbert Nevins, its Carrie Jacobs Bonds.

More pathetic than the really dead in music, however, are the many who are neither quite dead nor quite alive, and who are apparently destined to remain throughout the ages in a state of, at best, suspended animation. No one now listens to their music, or at any rate to more than the merest fragment of it; yet the works of some of them are published in complete editions, and historians write learnedly and at dutiful length about them. Will any audience from now until the end of time hear one of Rameau's twenty or thirty operas and ballets? Yet Rameau not only was, but still is, a great man—great not only in relation to his own time but judged by the standard of our time, as anyone may discover for himself by reading through the score of 'Castor et Pollux'. Is Rameau, then, alive or dead? At all events he kindles a glow in the heart of the historian. But there are others—hundreds of them—who were people of importance in their day, of whom, as of Rameau, the public knows nothing, or next to nothing, but who, though the historian feels it his duty to mention them, are fobbed off with a mere sentence or two of half-contemptuous wonder that the world should ever have taken them as seriously as it did. Are there ten people among all Europe's musical millions who could sing you, at a moment's notice, two consecutive bars of Telemann? Yet Telemann in his day enjoyed a reputation as great, for the area in which he was known, as either Strauss or Puccini today.

These are the truly pathetic figures in musical history. The really dead or the never alive may be taken as a joke, and treated humorously. But these poor fellows are no joke. They touch us to pity. Their life was once so abundant! They look at us from their shelves in the lumber room with a pathos in their eyes like that of the gazelle in the Arabian stories that is really a prince reduced by enchantment. They plead to us for release, for a chance to come out of their bondage and show what they really are and what they can do.

And the curious thing is that we have only to cut into them to see, by the blood they yield, that they are still alive. It is astonishing what prime cuts can still be had from some of these seeming carcases in cold storage. There comes in every man's life a time when he discards a hat because it has gone too shabby to wear. He takes to himself a new one, and goes about radiant. Then one day he looks at the hat and says, 'I really can't be seen out again in this awful old thing.' His eye lights on the hat he had discarded a few months before, and he finds to his astonishment and delight, that it is not nearly as shabby as the one to which he had transferred his affections has now become. He had thrown the other aside too soon, too thoughtlessly; he had built too great hopes on the new one, and persisted, from habit, in believing in it long after it had ceased to deserve his confidence. So it is with our music. We are proud, for a time, to be seen in the company of this or that composer of our own day: nothing can he do that is wrong. Suddenly we weary of him, we suspect his mortality, we smell the mould beneath the rose. And then we idly take down from our shelves a volume of Cimarosa or Krieger or some other long-forgotten worthy, and lo, struggling through the mould we find indubitable roses, still fair to the eye, still sweet to smell.

Here, then, is another subject for the historian—a history of music that shall leave out most of the things that are discussed at the greatest length in the present histories, and give us a detailed anatomy of the really good composers who once had a great vogue, but are now virtually forgotten. Interlocking with this history might be another that I have always wished some student with the necessary means and leisure would undertake—a history of musical opinion; not merely the opinion of the professional critics, but the opinion of music lovers in general. Such a history, if done in a thoroughly scientific way, would manifestly help us a good deal in our own criticism. In a book that will be published in a few days I have tried to work out some laws that may, I fancy, be seen to be operating in the music and the contemporary criticism of music of each age. All the diverse opinions as to the value of the music of this or that composer of our own day cannot possibly be right; and the best critic would be he who had the good luck to have the most of his judgements confirmed by posterity. We have only to look at any past age to see that it is all a question of relative values. History teaches us that in any country, in any generation, not more than three or four composers are produced whom the future regards as first-class. No first-class composer, I have tried to show, ever left his intelligent contemporaries in any doubt as to his being the biggest man of his day; but in every age there has been a number of composers who have had a vogue the extent of which surprises posterity. A phenomenon of this kind cannot be dismissed with a shrug of the shoulders. It is our business to try to understand it and explain it, not merely because it is of such psychological interest in itself, but because the explanation of it would give us, as it were, another sense by which to find our way about in the music of our own time, for we may be certain that in every age the phenomena and the problems of art are virtually the same, only the names of the protagonists and the surface look of things being different.

It is no use, for instance, scoring Meyerbeer off the slate in the slick way the modern historians do. They would show their fitness for their task more conclusively not by cursing Meyerbeer for a charlatan and sneering at his public for being taken in by him, but by finding out just what it was in him that gave him his extraordinary hold upon his public. This would mean not only the historian abandoning his conventional pose of the head thrown back and the nose wrinkled in scorn and distaste at the mere mention of Meyerbeer's name, but first of all a thorough absorption in Meyerbeer's music and then a thorough insight into the psychology of the operatic public of his day. There *must* have been something in the man's music, some peculiar flavour, some odour about his mentality, that made an irresistible appeal not only to the big public but to some of the best musical minds of the time. Let us call it a poison if we like, a subtle poison that corrupted men's sense of values as it stole through them. At any rate we shall never understand that chapter of the history of music until we have discovered what this poison was; and to do that we must get off our moral stilts and examine Meyerbeer and his public as a pathologist would the stomach of a man suspected to have been poisoned. Meyerbeer was a supreme specimen of his type, but only a specimen *of* a type. That type has probably existed in every age, and is no doubt to be found in the music of our own time. If we could understand through and through what the poison was, how it worked, whence came its attractiveness, and why the healthy musical mind gradually revolted against it and rid itself of it, should we not have in our hands a sort of chemical test that might help us to detect a similar poison in the music of some composer of today, to account for his vogue, and to prophesy men's ultimate reaction against it?

The history of critical opinion that I have suggested would

add many a new and fascinating chapter to musical history in general. For there are two sides always to art—the artist and the public; and the latter is as important a factor as the first. Could we really understand why Telemann's public, or Spohr's, worshipped him in the way it did, we should be the better able to understand the bigger forces that in the end swept men like these away. But for this understanding it is not enough for the historian to throw a contemptuous glance at the forgotten man from the superior height to which he has been lifted by three or four further generations of musical evolution. He must go down among these people and try to feel as they felt, to see things as they saw them. Holding the theory, as I do, that no man has ever had a big vogue in his own day without having done something to deserve it, I cannot but believe that there was something, for their time, unique about these composers who were once so popular. If the historian cannot see what this unique quality was, then he is not fit to be the historian of the man or his period. He may be an admirable grammarian, but he is a poor psychologist; and unfortunately, it is the grammarians, the formalists, not the psychologists, who have so far written most of our musical histories for us.

No anthropologist of any intelligence would think of writing about the religious beliefs and rituals of a savage tribe without trying to get inside the mentality of the savage, and see what the beliefs and the rituals meant to him; but where is the historian who, writing about an epoch of music the forms of which are now antiquated and the leaders of which are now forgotten except by name, tries to place himself at the point of view of the men who wrote the music and the people for whom it was the natural expression of what they felt and thought? The modern historian airily dismisses a Spohr in half a dozen lines. But when we discover that a Wagner could have a sincere admiration for a Spohr, is it not worth our while to try to find for ourselves not the stuffed figure that Spohr has become for us, but the real Spohr as he knew himself and as his contemporaries knew him? To be able to do this kind of thing in one case after another would perhaps necessitate a special training for the historian—a training of the need for which no one at present seems conscious.

Some recent reading of mine has made me anxious to find out, if possible, just what it was in Spohr that gave him his great contemporary popularity. During the last few days I have read through three of his operas, 'Jessonda', 'Faust', and 'Der Berggeist'. At first it all seemed hopelessly old-fashioned in form, faded in texture, and empty in expression. But as I read on, I began to have a curious sense of an odour emanating from it, faint but individual, and an odour that, in the language of today, one would call oddly intriguing. I began to realise, however dimly, what the people must have felt to whom this odour was both new and powerful—as new, say, and as powerful as Falla's is to us. I began to understand the attraction it must have had for them. A history of musical opinion would help us to get nearer to the secret of this attraction by showing us, from contemporary written records, precisely how the men of the day reacted to this music. And such a history, on a large scale, covering in detail the musical history of the last four hundred years, could not fail to provide us with valuable data for our own critical practice. I fancy we should find more of ourselves and our present music in the past than we now imagine.

'AND THERE WAS WAR IN HEAVEN'

26th April 1931

'ARE you coming to London? . . . The season does not promise to be brilliant. . . . There is nothing striking in the programme of the Italian Opera: political affairs are complicated, the income tax is an excellent excuse for the people with money to economise, while it presses terribly hard on the middle classes. Everything is in a state of depression and transition, which fact, however, will not prevent —— and —— and —— and many other [foreign] artists from directing their flight towards these shores.'

'—— wrote to me a little while ago, asking me for information about the English Opera. Well, there is every sort of opera here except English opera, and no one knows whether by any chance there will be one in the winter. The two opera houses are in competition with each other as usual. . . . Covent Garden has lately been in a very critical situation; it was whispered that it was on the point of collapsing. It seems, however, that it has found a means of keeping on its feet. . . . Spare me the recital of the names of all the artists who are here. . . .'

The reader may be forgiven if he assumes that these are extracts from letters written from some pessimistic music lover in London to a foreign friend during the last week or two. But he will be mistaken in that assumption. Both letters were addressed some time ago to Franz Liszt in Germany. The first one is from Sir Julius Benedict, and is dated from London, 12th February 1844: the second is from the violinist Ernst, and is dated from London, 7th June 1849. I have done nothing to the quotations except omit an irrelevant passage or two here and there, and substitute rules for the names of dead and forgotten foreign artists; the reader will be able to supply for himself the modern equivalents.

I give these extracts—I could easily add to their number, by the way—to show that nothing ever changes in musical London. There is not a sentence in these citations that might not have been written by any Londoner to any foreign friend in April, 1931. Until the other day the situation in London opera, the hopes and fears of London opera lovers, were precisely what they have been at any time during the last hundred years or more. I say until the other day, because obviously a new era has dawned for us all. I will not say that the fight for English opera and English artists has been won; but the battle has been opened, and there is a champion in the field under whose banner we should all be proud to fight. I refer, of course, to Mr. Szarvasy.

It seems that, incredible as it may appear, another Syndicate has had not merely the temerity but the indecency to announce a season of opera at the Lyceum during the very time when the doors of Covent Garden are open! Shameful as this is in itself, worse remains to be told. The persons responsible for this crime against England are actually bringing to the Lyceum a *Russian troupe performing nothing but Russian operas*. The outrage has wrung a spirited protest from the patriotic throat of Mr. Szarvasy. 'If Sir Thomas Beecham' (I ought, by the way, to have said that this gentleman, who has notoriously never done anything for the opera lovers of Britain, is connected with the nefarious Lyceum undertaking), 'if Sir Thomas Beecham', said Mr. Szarvasy in an interview the other day, 'wants to carry out the plans which he has advocated for so long—to support British art and British artists—I rather think that in depressed times like these it is hardly the right thing to bring Russians over to this country. I should have welcomed his plans and congratulated him if his artists were British.'

Every decent patriot will be wholly on Mr. Szarvasy's side in this matter. I personally think the conduct of Sir Thomas Beecham and his co-conspirators is disgraceful. To people so manifestly sunk in turpitude it is, I am afraid, useless to point out the crime they are committing against the country which, though, I am sure to its regret, must admit having given them birth. If they were not utterly lost to any sense of decency I would invite them to contrast with their own anti-British scheme the all-British scheme that Covent Garden is setting before us this summer.

As Mr. Szarvasy truly says, the only two things to be considered are British art and British artists. The Covent Garden prospectus is beyond reproach on both counts. The programme, so far as the operas to be given are concerned, is one hundred per cent British: among the works to be performed we may note the following:

'Tristan and Isolde' .... 'Lohengrin' .... 'Der Ring des Nibelungen' ..	By Ethel Smyth
'Der Rosenkavalier'	By Vaughan Williams
'Die Fledermaus'	By Rutland Boughton
'Rigoletto'	By Gustav Holst
'Francesca da Rimini'	By Armstrong Gibbs
'Fedra'	By Villiers Stanford

As for the all-British artists, for whose interests Mr. Szarvasy is so patriotically and so commendably solicitous, I cull the following names at random from the Covent Garden prospectus for the present season: Bruno Walter (Liverpool), Frida Leider (Bradford), Rosa Ponselle (Leeds), Soffi Schönning (Putney), Elvira Casazza (Ashby-de-la-Zouch), Maria Olczewska (Bristol), Gianna Pederzini (Galashiels), Dino Borgioli (Southend), Luigi Cilla (Bournemouth), Lauritz Melchior (Glasgow), Giuseppe Nessi (Newport), Aureliano Pertile (Whitechapel), Heinrich Tessmer (Hammersmith), Marcel Wittrisch (Manchester), Willi Wörle (Worlesden), Ivar Andresen (Andover), Ernesto Badini (Basingstoke), Aristide Baracchi (Burton), Eduard Habich (Harwich), Otto Helgers (Helsby), Gerhardt Hüsch (Hull), Michele Sampieri (Saltmarsh), Friedrich Schorr (Heckmondwike), Mariano Stabile (St. Annes-on-Sea), Waldemar Staegemann (St. Ives), Tullio Serafin (Solihull), and Beniamino Gigli (Soho).

As for the Lyceum troupe, I can see only one English name in the list, and that, I regret to say, the name of a renegade. I refer to Chaliapine. That this great artist is really—or was until recently—an Englishman is proved by the fact that last season—or was it the season before that?—he was engaged at Covent Garden. By allowing himself now to be engaged at the Lyceum he has obviously depatriated himself; one suspects that all the while the man has really been nothing but a Russian in disguise. Now he has thrown off the mask, and we shall know what to think of this one-time compatriot of ours.

But the Lyceum conspirators will not be allowed to get away with it so easily as they imagined. The lists are opened, the battle joined; and the country will look forward to seeing these Muscovite hordes driven with fearful slaughter down Wellington Street into the Thames: in the forefront of the British charge will be Mr. Szarvasy, making all London E.C.4 and W.C.2 ring with his clarion cry of 'Saint Ladislas for Merry England!'

Perhaps, however, in my enthusiasm, I am expecting too much from the majority of my degenerate countrymen. Among them, no doubt, will be beings so abandoned that they will shamelessly declare that they do not care two pins where their art and their artists come from so long as both are first-rate, and, failing to make the national distinction they ought to do, will profess themselves equally grateful to Covent Garden and to the Lyceum for providing them with the choice of two good things, and will listen this summer with equal pleasure to opera in both buildings. And, though I should not care to make the disgraceful confession publicly, I should have little hesitation in admitting privately that I myself am one of these reprobates who set artistic quality before nationality. I do not care a brass farthing whether a singer or a conductor or a dancer or a composer comes from Peckham, from Parma, from Petrograd, or from Potsdam, so long as he can really sing, or conduct, or dance, or compose. Mr. Szarvasy, I know, will not agree with me as to the morality of this point of view; but then I could no more rise to Mr. Szarvasy's patriotic level than he could sink to mine.

THE EUROPEAN MIND IN MUSIC

27th April 1924

The two anniversary celebrations of the last couple of weeks—the centenary of Byron and the eightieth birthday of Anatole France—may have set other people besides myself thinking about the question of nationalism and internationalism in art in general and in music in particular. Should we, we may ask ourselves, be troubling about either Byron or Anatole France today unless each of these men, in his own way, represented Europe at least as much as he represents his own country or himself? And are not all the great men in music during the last three hundred years not merely good Germans or good Frenchmen or good Italians or good Britons, but what Nietzsche would call good Europeans, and is it not in virtue of their Europeanism rather than their nationalism that they are really great? Is there any hope of immortality for any composer of today who is so intensely national that he fails to be European?

At present the enthusiasts for nationalism in music are very vociferous, though what precisely they mean by nationalism none of them has so far succeeded in making clear to us. It is a formula rather than a principle. When we find a little difficulty in seeing clearly a situation in any one sphere of human activity it is always helpful to look at a corresponding situation in some other sphere. Quite by chance I happened to take down from my shelves the other day the second series of Dean Inge's *Outspoken Essays*. Re-reading the masterly series of articles on 'The State, Visible and Invisible', I found a number of remarks that threw, for me, a good deal of light on our rather futile musical controversies.

In art, as in politics, we are always unconsciously striving towards a unity that has never yet been fully realised—though some State systems and some musical periods have come nearer to it than others—and which is, perhaps, for ever unrealisable. At present, in music as in politics, the concept of nationalism is almost sacred for some minds. As Dean Inge shows, nationalism in the political sense is mainly a nineteenth century growth:

'It was not a very strong sentiment in the eighteenth century, when culture was more European and less national than it is now.' That is true of music also. 'Personally', says Dean Inge, 'I think it is more superficial than we usually suppose, and a vast amount of deliberate nonsense has been talked about it since 1914.' That, too, is pathetically true of music. Nationalism, the Dean goes on to point out, cannot mean racialism, 'for the nations are all mixed in blood beyond the possibility of disentanglement'; moreover, the racial differences between men of the same nation are sometimes as great as those between men of different nations: 'Italy is indubitably a nation, though it is obvious to the most casual observer that the North and South Italians are racially quite different.' Nor can it have anything to do with language, 'for the Scots speak two languages, the Belgians and Swiss three each, and the Americans at least a dozen'.

'It is impossible', as Dean Inge rightly says, 'to define a nation except as a body of men who believe themselves to be one.' And this definition at once sets us right in the matter of music. For while this or that material pressure, internal or external, can for a time persuade the people of a nation that they are one, there is no force whatever that can make them feel that they are one in matters of emotion or of taste. I may have far less in common with the man next door than I have with Anatole France or Croce. The man next door, then, must not regard me as an enemy of my country because I do not share his enthusiasm for this British composer or that, or prefer some foreign composer to the whole lot of them. I have no objection to his saying that as we are both Britons we ought to be one on the point, so long as I am allowed to be the one. But as there is probably the same desire on his part to be the one, the only thing for us to do is to agree to differ.

It would save some of our younger composers from a good many displays of childish petulance if they would only recognise that there is no such thing as 'a nation' in the musical sense, and, further, that it is as impossible in music as in politics for any one party to claim that the sole truth and the whole truth is with it alone. Only a day or two ago one of the most gifted of our younger musicians was declaiming angrily against the people who, in his opinion, are holding back the wheels of progress in music. May I point out to him that exactly the same sort of declamation may be heard any Sunday in Hyde Park, or any evening from any soap-box where Socialists do congregate? No doubt it is difficult for honest enthusiasts of the latter type to understand that the smile on the face of one of his auditors does not mean that he is indifferent to the sufferings of the poor, but only that, being a political economist, he doubts the perfect wisdom of the scheme that has just been put forward from the soap-box for making all men rich. And no doubt it is difficult for the young composer who believes that *his* music is the music of 'progress' to understand that the critic's smile is prompted not by any lack of interest in new developments but by the knowledge that change and progress are not always and necessarily the same thing.

The critic's real business, as I have often said before, is simply to observe and estimate; and he cannot do either properly if he is mixed up as a partisan with any of the contending camps. His studies in the history of music have taught him that the one thing we can confidently predict will *not* come out of a certain movement in music is the thing that people inside the movement were sure would come out of it. Indeed, the very violence of the movement may, by stimulating antagonisms, that otherwise would have remained dormant, be its own undoing: as Dean Inge says, 'Some movements disintegrate so rapidly that they live only in the vigorous reactions which they produce. . . . Thus the Jacobinism of the French Revolution, which looked like mere anarchism and bloodthirstiness, inaugurated the bourgeois *régime* of the nineteenth century.' The revolutionary ideas of Caccini and his friends inaugurated not, as they imagined they would, a revival of the Greek drama, but a very different thing—the Italian opera. And the unrest of the last twenty years in music has brought the average man, not to a new freedom, but to a tighter riveting on him of the fetters of the past; in despair of finding anything in the new music that he can take close to his heart, he is going back to the classics, even those of the second rank.

We can foresee nothing certainly, in politics or in music. Men think they are creating, and it turns out they are only destroying; they think they are destroying, and they are giving a new life to the thing they wish to destroy. 'What the Babylonians, the Persians, and Greeks and Romans did for Judaism, by liberating the idea from the mould in which it had taken shape, and which prevented its expansion, that the Barbarians did for the Roman Empire. In both cases the idea triumphed. . . .' The phenomenon is not unknown in musical history. The Florentines thought they had smashed counterpoint for ever; in reality they only set it free for new and bigger purposes. The late eighteenth century thought it had buried Sebastian Bach; it could not foresee his resurrection in the nineteenth. Wagner thought he had slain the old-style Italian opera, both in argument, and by his practice; and lo, in Germany there is a revival now of Handel's operas, that the historians have all regarded as dead for ever. And we may be pretty sure that the musical history of 1930–40 will be something very different from what the little busybodies of 1914–24 thought they were going to make it. 'The ironies of history,' as Dean Inge sadly says, 'are on a colossal scale, and must, one is tempted to think, cause great amusement to a superhuman spectator.'

Of one thing, however, we may perhaps be certain—that when the next truly big figure comes, he will be not a nationalist but an internationalist. He will have, like Palestrina and Bach and Beethoven and Handel and Wagner, the European mind. The cause of Stravinsky's decline in the last few years is his inability to fertilise the purely Russian soil of his brain with European musical culture. His 'Noces' was recently described to me by an eminent Russian as the first genuinely Russian opera; in Moussorgsky, Borodine, Tchaikovsky, and all the other Russian composers of opera there were Western elements, but 'Les Noces' is purely Russian. That seems to me precisely its weakness. It suffers from what we may call, from the European point of view, provincialism—a provincialism of thought expressed in a local musical dialect. It is very interesting and often fascinating, but we of other nations cannot see ourselves in it as we can see ourselves, irrespective of our nationality, in Euripides, in Dante, in Shakespeare, in Goethe, in Bach, in Beethoven, in Cervantes. The Octavian and Marschallin in the final scene of the first act of the 'Rosenkavalier' are Everyman and Everywoman; but Le Marié and La Mariée in 'Les Noces' are not Everyman and Everywoman, but only Russian-man and Russian-woman. The local mind and the local dialect can give us very precious things at their best; but if we want music to take another real leap forward, let us pray for the return of the European mind, and some skull—it does not matter whether English, German, French, Italian, or Russian—big enough to hold it easily and unconsciously.

MR. BERNARD SHAW AS MUSICAL CRITIC

26th June 1932

I HAD no idea, until Messrs. Constable and Co. sent me the other day the first volume of Mr. Bernard Shaw's *Music in London, 1890–94* (a reprint of his *World* articles of that period, 6s.), what excellent work he was doing for music in England forty years or so ago. My own reading in criticism, in my first youth, was confined to writers like Saint-Beuve, Hennequin, Taine, Brunetière, Lessing, Matthew Arnold, Leslie Stephen, Walter Pater, and so on, none of whom, of course, ever specialised in music. I studied music, and read histories of music and other books on the subject; but of musical journalism I knew next to nothing until I was foolish enough to become a musical journalist myself. So all the time when Mr. Shaw was pouring out this brilliant stuff in the *World*, I, who was a young provincial at the time, was unaware of its existence. Every line in *Music in London* is therefore completely new to me. I do not know how these articles struck people at the time; but today they strike me as being by far the most brilliant things that musical journalism has ever produced in this country, or is ever likely to produce.

Mr. Shaw, I am sure, would be the last to claim for them that they were anything more than journalism, or that he himself was anything more than a cultivated dilettante. Perhaps I ought not to speak in this apparently slighting way of journalism, which, at its best, is decidedly better than much of the authorship we get nowadays. So few authors have brains enough or literary gift enough to keep their own end up in journalism that I am tempted to define 'journalism' as 'a term of contempt applied by writers who are not read to writers who are'. I do not apply the term to Mr. Shaw as one of disparagement. I merely mean that he concerned himself with music only as it came his way week by week in the shape of performances, and that he went no further into any subject than his couple of columns, or whatever it was, demanded of him. And if he was what the scholar would call a dilettante, he was at any rate a dilettante who knew his own little world of music inside out.

I do not suppose that Mr. Shaw could have written a reliable treatise on the relative quantities of chromatic dissonance in Cyprian de Rore and in Monteverdi, or on the evolution of the fugue, or on the influence of Hebrew melisma on plain-song, or even on the operas of Hasse. But he had at his finger-tips most of the works and the subjects about which he had to write as a concert- and opera-goer, especially the latter. He knew and understood the operas of the ordinary London repertory rather better than any of the people engaged in the singing or playing or conducting or producing of them did, with the possible exception of Maurel, who was not merely a singer, but had brains; and he turned the whole force of his lively intellect on to what he heard and saw. Finally, he wrote about these matters in a style that, for pace, for directness, for point, for wit and humour, for variety of colour, makes the best that is being written by the musical critics of today look third-rate. And so it comes about that these old articles of his are not only as readable but as valuable in 1932 as they were in 1890.

Indeed, more valuable in some ways, for we can do what their first readers could not—we can see them in the light of the forty years in between. A few of the performers with whom Mr. Shaw dealt are quite forgotten now; and it is a testimony to his fineness of perception that in very few instances does he exhibit any particular enthusiasm for these. On the other hand, he was astonishingly right with regard to people who were at that time just appearing above the horizon: from the beginning, for example, he sized up Paderewski so exactly, with all his virtues and all his faults, that nothing remains to be added to the estimate today. He made a few mistakes where composers were concerned. His contempt for Brahms could hardly have been greater had that unfortunate man spelt his name Shakespeare: perhaps in this case Mr. Shaw's Wagnerian prepossessions influenced his judgement.

He was inclined to over-estimate Gounod in comparison with Berlioz; but one surmises that what was given of Berlioz in London in those days was none too intelligently played, while Gounod's 'Faust' had the advantage of being presented by singers of some quality, to whom the opera had not yet become the hopelessly hackneyed and silly thing that the smaller British companies have made of it. In the main, Mr. Shaw's task as a judge of music was nothing like so difficult as that of the critic of the present day. A great epoch had just completed and entrenched itself. Wagner's supremacy was unquestionable; Verdi, who had by that time got as far as 'Otello', was at last showing his real mettle. Music and aesthetics were as yet unvexed by the unsettling doubts that were to creep in hardly more than a decade later; in musical, as in economic, theory a position of more or less stable equilibrium seemed to have been reached.

The inanities and vulgarities of jazz were not due for another twenty years or so. The principles of the classical German schools were as yet unassailed by the Russians in the East and Debussy in the West. There was a standard by which the goodness or badness of new music could be pretty accurately estimated at once; either it did what it set out to do as well, or almost as well, as a similar thing had been done by the best Germans or Italians, in which case it was good, or it didn't, in which case it was bad. Mr. Shaw had the supreme advantage of being able to tackle current problems of taste without any dead weight of critical convention upon him. Having been fortunate enough to evade the universities and the colleges, he saw things musical as they were, not as they would have appeared to him as a member of a clan, a clique, or a junta.

He was the symbol of the approaching rescue of music in England from the university and conservatoire groups that had been the arbiters of values until then. Elgar was soon to come along and demonstrate that an English composer could owe nothing whatever to the official 'heads' of music in this country and yet win an international reputation—a piece of flat disrespect to the schools and professors for which the professors, at any rate, have not forgiven him to this day. J. F. Runciman was soon to laugh the professors off the board—when he was not booting them off. Mr. Shaw turned upon the spectacle of the English musical world of the day an eye unclouded by tradition, a judgement unaffected by social or official considerations. He declined to take people like the Parrys and the

Stanfords and the rest of them seriously as composers, or the colleges as the providentially appointed trainers of the musical youth of the nation. And time has proved the rightness of nine contemporary estimates of his out of ten.

The most amusing and most instructive thing about this volume, perhaps, is the demonstration it affords that nothing ever really changes in this country. Alter the names in this sentence or that, and the record might as easily be that of 1850 or 1930 as of 1890. When Mr. Shaw was writing, London opera in general, and Covent Garden in particular, were very much what and where they still are. The general level of the singing was higher then; but the performances of the scratch companies of the 1890s were seemingly no nearer a reasonable ideal than those of recent years have been; the repertory was as stale, the direction and the ensemble were as bad, the productions and the scenery touched no higher level of intelligence. There was the same time-honoured talk of the urgent need for the establishment of opera in this country on a really sound basis; the same pathetic belief that one had only to go on talking long enough about these things for something to be done. There was the same cant as now about the marvellous virtues of our British orchestral players as readers—as an excuse, of course, for insufficient rehearsal and the consequent murdering of masterpieces. There were the same complaints about the carelessness and cynicism of popular concert and opera favourites when once they had established their position with us, as they thought, for all time. There was the same showing-up of the London orchestras by the Hallé people when they came to town—bringing with them, then as recently, a Berlioz of whom the London public had been shown too little. And so *ad infinitum.*

There is only one little matter in which the perfect correspondence between the two epochs fails. While the evils and absurdities remain the same, the apparatus for dealing with them has changed for the worse. They call for plainer speaking than is possible in these degenerate days. In Mr. Shaw's time the Press evidently had more courage and more freedom in the matter of criticism. He says nothing about the singers and players and conductors of that epoch that was not strictly true;

but I think I could point to at least a score of sentences in his book which in these days would have almost certainly led to a libel action, with the practical certainty of a verdict, given by twelve good men and true on a matter completely beyond their understanding, in favour of a stupid or intellectually dishonest plaintiff.

DA CAPO:

TO REPEAT OR NOT TO REPEAT?

10th March 1935

My Editor has sent me a letter from Mr. Oliver Strachey which apparently is too long for publication intact. Mr. Strachey, however, in a covering note, is good enough to say that if this should be the case my views on the subject would interest him.

Mr. Strachey begins with a protest against one feature of the recent performance of 'Acis and Galatea' by the B.B.C.—the omission of the da capo repeat from most of the arias. 'The Handelian aria', he says, 'was set out in a regular form; this consisted of a main section A, followed by a shorter section B in a different key, after which section A was repeated. . . . In almost every case the da capo was omitted, the return to the original key being signalised merely by a few bars played by the orchestra.' Mr. Strachey goes on to ask why this procedure was not condemned by the critics: 'any tampering with the structure and proportion of a work of art on this scale', he says, would be resented by 'the painter, sculptor, architect or poet'. As there is no public outcry against this mutilation of old music, Mr. Strachey opines that 'the advance that has taken place in the last forty years or so, especially in matters of tonality and form, has put us in the position of being unable really to appreciate the eighteenth-century efforts'. He follows this up with some sensible remarks on the difference between the free form, say, of Sibelius's seventh symphony, in which 'the relations and proportions involved are far too subtle to be pinned down and ticketed', and the more conventional form of the classical symphony.

As we have lost the eighteenth-century feeling in these matters, continues Mr. Strachey, and are bored by repetitions and by the too regular succession of tonic and dominant—forgetful that it was 'in spite of such futilities that the eighteenth century giants managed to produce great music'—the tendency is growing to present this old music in curtailed or adapted forms. But, he says, 'a work of art has a trick of being an organic whole. Try to abstract the content from the form, and you find it has vanished. . . . Faced with a work of art we must either take it or leave it—as it is. So it would be wiser perhaps to admit to ourselves that we simply do not like eighteenth century music, or like it only as Bishop Atterbury liked Milton.' (Atterbury, by the way, suggested that Pope should 'review and polish "Samson Agonistes",' and so, 'with a little trouble', 'improve' it 'into a perfect model and standard of tragic poetry'.)

I am afraid, however, that if we are to be thoroughly consistent in these matters we shall have to do rather more than merely play an old composition without the omission of a single note. We shall have to make sure, as well as we can, that the notes themselves sound exactly to our ears as they did to the composer's contemporaries. We shall have to reproduce faithfully the size and constitution of the old orchestras; and I doubt whether our modern ears would in all cases be gratified. Would Mr. Strachey, again, suggest that for last week's broadcast of Handel's opera 'Rodelinda' our gallant English male singers, some of whom no doubt have domestic responsibilities, should have been rekittened in order that the listener may hear more or less the kind of voice for which Handel wrote and which his audiences preferred to any other kind? I hardly think even a purist so exacting as Mr. Strachey would go as far as that.

Ought we to perform the old Italian madrigals today as they were performed in their own epoch, with the singers indulging to their hearts' content in coloratura modifications of their individual parts? Ought we to sing Handel's oratorios as they were sung in Handel's day, with the soloists indulging in all kinds of shakes and appoggiature and other coloratura embellishments? In the following musical example I give, at (a), the first bar of 'Comfort ye my people' (from the 'Messiah') as it appears in the score and as it is now sung, and at (b) the same bar as it was actually sung under Handel:

No. 1.

In the next example we see, at (a) and (b), the conclusion of the aria 'Every valley' as it is written and as it was sung:

If the 'Messiah' were to be sung today as it was sung in Handel's time, there would hardly be a bar of the solo parts that the plain man would recognise. The feeling of the eighteenth century for the expressive power of coloratura has vanished from the earth, never to return. Are we to restore the mere externals of this old manner for pure antiquarianism's sake, and so drive people away from the Handel oratorios, or ignore them and let people have a Handel they can understand and admire?

If, then, we cannot possibly go the whole hog in the matter of fidelity of reproduction of ancient masterpieces, it is surely just a matter of agreeing as to the extent of the carving that the animal must undergo for modern purposes. In theory I am wholly in agreement with Mr. Strachey on the subject of form, while finding myself compelled to part company from him occasionally in practice. We must distinguish, I think, between form in the higher sense of the term and mere formalism or pattern: the one has organic life, the other only machine-made symmetry. We cannot cut a bar out of a Beethoven symphony without letting the blood out of a living thing. Even works that are not quite first-class have the right to have the unity given them by the composer respected: I am wholly with a correspondent who wrote to me lately protesting against the way in which certain violinists cut the Tchaikovsky concerto, the view of some of these naïve creatures apparently being that we are there not to hear Tchaikovsky but to hear them, and that accordingly the passages in which they are not playing do not greatly matter. But the da capo repeat in the ancient arias is another affair altogether. The plain fact is that unless there is a good *inner* reason for the repeat it rather bores us today. We cannot cut the da capo out of a Gluck aria because to do so is to damage not only the musical tissue but the dramatic idea. There are hundreds of cases in Bach and Handel, however, in which the da capo means nothing more than that the composer complied lazily with a convention of his epoch that we have outgrown.

We in a modern audience must do one of two things in this matter. We must either possess our souls in what patience we can and submit to a long repeat that bores us—and perhaps, as a result, resolve never to undergo that experience again—or put our principles in our pocket and enjoy ourselves in our own way. The broad working rule in our concert halls, I think, is that if the aria is first-rate music the da capo is respected, but that if it is below the first-rate there is not much sense in going a second time through an experience that was not particularly thrilling the first time. There are arias of Handel in which the longest repeat has no terrors for me. There are others in which I say to the composer, as he writes 'da capo' in his score, puts down his pen, and leans back to take a pinch of snuff, 'No, Master! Emphatically no! I know in advance what you are going to say for the next two or three minutes. You have said it already at full length, and as I wasn't greatly interested in it the first time, you must excuse me if, instead of listening to it a second time, I take it as sung. You reply that the omission alters the proportions of the aria and upsets the balance of keys? I admit that; but, being a philosopher, I am always willing to put up with the lesser of two evils. Your job as a composer was to give organic life to your music. Whenever you do that I will not sacrifice a note of it: but when, in order merely to acquiesce in a slothful custom of your epoch, you ask me, the product of another epoch, to aid and abet you at the cost of my enjoyment, then, Master, you must forgive me if I respectfully decline. Your da capo is merely a long demonstration of the painfully obvious; and I can complete your circle swiftly in my imagination, without plodding over every inch of it again in actual fact.'

That, I fancy, is how most people regard this matter of the

da capo today; and they are justified not only by their feelings but by the history of music. For the whole essence of the post-Handelian developments in form was the recognition of the principle that while, for balance' sake, it may be necessary for a composer to return to his earlier matter, he must treat it, on its return, in a new way and draw new meanings from it, not merely say again, down to the last semi-quaver, what he has said in full already. Mr. Strachey's analogy with the other arts, I venture to say, is illegitimate. We may not be greatly impressed by an old picture the design of which is obtained by the simple and almost literal repetition on the right-hand side of something that has already been done on the left-hand side. But the design of a picture can be taken in at a glance, whereas in the case of music a long time-element comes into play; and that element gives time for a feeling of boredom to which the modern concert-goer is a little unwilling to submit himself.

MOZART AND SIBELIUS:

'FORM' AS SEEN IN HISTORICAL PERSPECTIVE

13th September 1936

In my last week's article I pointed out the important part played by the mental background in our judgements of music; a difference in the quality and the depth of this background can lead not only to different reactions by different individuals to the same work but to different reactions to it by the same individual at different times. It stands to reason that the professional student of music is more susceptible to these variations of opinion than the plain man. For the latter's background remains very much the same throughout his life: his horizon, broadly speaking, extends no further on the one side than the Bach-Handel epoch and no further on the other than about 1915, while within this limited area he listens over and over again each year to very much the same limited selection of the same standard works. He may have a dim sense that there was music before Bach, and that there has been music since Strauss, Debussy and Elgar; but though this other music may touch the fringe of his experience now and then it effects no readjustments in his general criteria: his background is fixed. The student with a longer historical perspective, on the other hand, sees the music of the last two centuries or so for just what it is—neither the first nor the final word in the art, but only an intermediate clause, and a somewhat limited clause at that.

For there never has been, and never will be, a music that makes full use of all the possibilities of the art. 'Progress' in these matters is partly an illusion: an advance in one direction is necessarily accompanied by a retrogression in another, so that there is a good deal to be said for the theory that the line of progress is not a straight one but a spiral. The human mind seems to be incapable of developing simultaneously, to their full theoretical extent, *all* the factors—melodic, harmonic, contrapuntal, rhythmic—of which music is composed: in each epoch it tends to fasten upon a particular problem of texture or of form and to work it out to the utmost of its powers, at the same time neglecting, comparatively, certain of the other factors. The special problem of the Mozart-Haydn epoch, for instance, was to work out the principles of large-scale construction in instrumental music. But it could only concentrate on this by paying relatively less attention to certain other things; with the result that a great deal that Bach had brought into music was temporarily lost. Each problem, in fact, can be dealt with only by narrowing it down and isolating it; and, as I have said, there has never yet been an age that has achieved progress in one direction in music without losing ground in other directions.

An age, for instance, in which the determining factor is harmony and one in which the determining factor is counterpoint will each look somewhat poverty-stricken when surveyed from the point of view of the other. The late eighteenth century, working in harmonic blocks in order to develop the possibilities of thematic variation for structural purposes (in the symphony, sonata, and so on), unconsciously and necessarily clipped the wings of melody. To be easily manipulated for the urgent special ends of that epoch, melody had to fall into neat little two- or four-bar symmetries; and, ironically enough, it is these simple symmetries that constitute 'melody' for most people today. But the eighteenth and nineteenth century melody, considered in and by itself, is a poor thing compared with the melody of plain-song or of Palestrina, which is infinitely freer.

Is it to be wondered at, then, that after a long absorption in plain-song or the older polyphonic music, one sometimes finds oneself listening to Mozart or Schubert with a faint momentary touch of exasperation, of weariness of the scissors-like click-clack of the limbs of the melody? I have called this reaction momentary because, of course, in the long run the special virtues of Mozart or Schubert and of their epoch make themselves felt again, and one no more condemns this type of art for its limitations in comparison with the art of Palestrina or of plain-song than one condemns the still older type for its limitations in comparison with the art of the classical period of the symphony and the song. But undoubtedly the historical background operates strongly at times in determining the critic's judgement; and it is for this reason that he may find himself, at some concert or other, regarding a generally admired song of Schubert's, let us say, as a rather infantile piece of prettiness, and perhaps being indiscreet to say so in print, to the annoyance of some reader who, lacking the historical perspective of the critic, has never seen the song in question against the same background as the critic has done on this occasion.

So, again, with the question of musical form. For most people, as for the writers of text-books and the conservatoires, 'form' means the kind of thing one finds at its highest perfection in Mozart, Beethoven and Brahms, but especially, perhaps, in Mozart. But on any broad view of art, form of the type we have in the first movement of a Mozart symphony is really a rather rudimentary thing; with its cut-to-length limbs and its symmetrical balance of parts on either side of certain axes it is merely the musical equivalent of that simple type of pictorial design which we find by the thousand in certain old pictures—a central figure, for example, with a balancing figure on either side of it, the total effect being that of a triangle or a parallelogram.

These simple types of what the painters call 'composition' predominate at certain early periods in the history of painting; and it is the task of later ages to improve upon them. This is done by various subtilisations of the basic design. The basis of the design of most pictures is one of the four simplest geometrical arrangements—(a) the circle, (b) the triangle, (c) the square, (d) the cross. In a relatively early stage of pictorial composition, the geometrical basis of the design is very evident —at times too evident. In later stages, balance of parts is obtained by less obvious symmetries in the arrangement. The principle of the steelyard, as an American writer has pointed out, now comes into operation. As the reader knows, while it needs two equal weights to maintain equilibrium at ends equidistant from a fulcrum, a small weight on the longer arm of the lever will suffice to counterbalance a much heavier weight on the shorter arm. This principle can be utilised in the composition of a picture; a large mass on the left-hand side may be perfectly balanced by something not much more than a point on the right-hand side, if this point be perfectly placed and perspectived, and emphasised by a particular light.

Something of the same principle may be seen to be in

operation in such a work as the seventh symphony of Sibelius. What puzzles the ordinary or the academic listener here is the absence of the simple and obvious mathematical symmetries to which he has grown accustomed in the classical symphony, and which he has come to regard as constituting 'form' *per se*. He accordingly decides that the Sibelius No. 7 is 'formless'. The difference between a Mozart symphony and the No. 7, however, is very much that between a picture of the first of the two types characterised above—the type in which the circle or triangle or square 'composition' is used in its most primitive mathematical form—and a picture of the second type, in which a higher unity and balance are obtained by less nakedly mathematical devices. The principle of the steelyard can be recognised in the Sibelius symphony in the use of that trombone phrase that recurs three times in the course of the work, apparently starting from nowhere: it pulls many times it apparent weight in the total structure by its peculiar character, the subtlety of its placing, the colour of it, the light that plays on it. The symphony is not formless in comparison with a Mozart first movement: on the contrary, it represents a much more highly organised form.

A passage in Goethe's treatise on morphology may help to make the point clearer. Goethe formulates the general law that 'the *more imperfect* a being is the more do its individual parts *resemble each other*, and the more do these parts *resemble the whole.* The *more perfect* the being is, the *more dissimilar are its parts.* In the former case the parts are more or less a repetition of the whole; in the latter case they are totally unlike the whole. The more the parts resemble each other, the less subordination is there of one to the other. *Subordination of parts indicates high grade of organisation.*' That is as true in the 'composition' of paintings and of symphonies as it is in biology or natural history. A Mozart first movement, in which the parts resemble each other and resemble the whole, however marvellous it may be as a specimen of its own historical genre, is none the less the representative of a relatively primitive genre. It illustrates merely a stage through which the symphony has to pass in order to attain to a higher stage of organisation. The higher type is seen in a work such as the Sibelius No. 7, in which there is the minimum of resemblance between the parts, and between any of these and the whole.

The reader will see for himself the importance of what I have called the mental background, the historical perspective, in our judgements of music. The listener who has never learned to conceive form under any other categories but those of the classical symphony will be inclined to see in a Mozart symphony the final perfection of form, and to sum up the Sibelius symphony as relatively formless; whereas the listener who brings to bear upon the problem of musical form his experiences in other arts, and his reflection upon these experiences, will see the Mozart symphony as not much more than the first or second step towards the freer and greater conception of form realised by Sibelius. It is not that the Mozart symphony is invalidated by its form, any more than Raphael's Holy Family, or his Three Graces, or his Sistine Madonna is invalidated by the obvious mathematical triangulism of the composition: it merely means that for a later age, of subtler mental processes and with a longer experience of art, the bare mathematics of design must make place for a subtler handling of the same basic problem.

THE TEMPORAL EQUATION:

INDIVIDUALS AND EPOCHS

30th June 1935

THOSE of us who worry over the many problems of musical criticism, and doubt more and more every day whether there is any rational way out of them, become still more perplexed when we turn our eyes from the personal aspect of the matter to what may be called the time-aspect of it. The sensitised-plate-reaction theory is satisfactory enough to critics who are not given to looking beyond their own instinctive reactions to the basic problems of criticism, but less completely satisfying to others. In the first place, sensitised-plate-reactions in the bulk, so far as they deal, or attempt to deal, with fundamental aesthetic values, merely cancel each other out: no two plates are sensitised in quite the same way or react in quite the same way, with the result that all the A types range themselves confidently on one side of the fence and all the Z types, with the same pathetic confidence, on the other.

In the second place, the same sensitised plate is differently sensitised, both in respect of quantity and in respect of quality, at different periods of its possessor's life. Few of us take the same view of any author or artist at fifty or sixty as we did at twenty or thirty. It is quite a common pastime among the sons of Belial to drag out from its well-merited obscurity something that a critic said about this composer or that thirty years ago, and show that it does not square with what he is saying today. The procedure is perfectly legitimate. But the reverse procedure, which would surely be equally legitimate, is never adopted: no one says to a critic, as he would be fully justified in doing, 'It is practically certain that what you think today about the composer X is not what you will be thinking twenty or thirty years hence. When that time comes, you will of course claim that your then views represent the truth of the matter and your present views were merely a stage of error through which you had to pass in order to reach the truth. But that being so, why should we read *now* what you have to say about X?' If the generality of people were to take this view of the matter, the result would be that everybody would be bravely and dogmatically writing or talking sensitised-plate criticism and nobody reading it or listening to it—perhaps not a bad state of affairs.

The humours of the situation increase when we turn from the individual critic of the hour to the epoch as critic. For epochs seem to have no more fundamental sense than individuals. We can all, as individuals, laugh at the critical assurance that will allow no validity to any personal equation but one's own: but no epoch has ever yet risen to the height of seeing that it also, *qua* epoch, has a temporal equation that is, or should be, a subject for laughter among thoughtful men. Each epoch plods along in the sublimely innocent belief that *its* sensitised plate is the only genuine article; and half the fun for later epochs, in matters of art, consists in telling earlier epochs just what they think of them and their critical judgements.

It never occurred to Winckelmann and his century to doubt the validity of the standards of value they applied to ancient Greek sculpture; even as late as the first decade or two of the nineteenth century the view was still held that things like the Apollo Belvedere, the Venus of Milo, and the Laocoön represented the highest achievements of Greek sculpture, while the Parthenon sculptures brought to England by Lord Elgin were either despised or patronisingly admired for the wrong reasons. Since the time of Winckelmann, however, there has been a steady slump in the aesthetic values of the sculptures over which he and his epoch rhapsodised; we have now arrived at the point when the most modern historians and critics assure us that the Venus of Milo 'has attained a somewhat undeserved position as one of the world's masterpieces of sculpture', or that 'as works of art' the Heracles of Glycon and the Belvedere Apollo 'are little short of abominable'; while Mr. Wilenski, in his racy book on *The Meaning of Modern Sculpture*, puts before us a photograph of a modern wax-and-indiarubber figure for shop windows and irreverently describes it as 'in the Praxitelean tradition'.

I am taking, for my present purpose, no side in these and similar controversies: I merely note, and ask the reader to note, the facts—that in addition to the personal equation in matters aesthetic there is such a thing as the temporal equation, and that just as other people's personal equations are an object of complacent compassion or derision to each of us, so the temporal equation of each epoch becomes sooner or later an object of compassion or derision for other epochs that are either the lucky possessors or the unfortunate victims (according to how you prefer to look at the matter) of a temporal equation of their own. We have only to keep our eyes and ears open in the concert room or the opera house today to realise that some old music is disparaged, and some admired for what would have seemed to its contemporaries the wrong reasons, simply because our temporal equation is not theirs. Most people today would be astonished to learn that the 'Seraglio' is an extremely serious opera with a few subsidiary comic situations: we read, for instance, in the Glyndebourne programme, that 'Osmin carries the opera on his shoulders: he is the central figure'—a pronouncement which, I fancy, would have made the eyebrows of Mozart and his librettist rise so high as to endanger the equilibrium of their wigs. The misunderstanding comes mainly from the fact that while Mozart's delicious comic music has a salt in it that preserves it for all time, much of the music of his serious arias is the expression of a purely local and temporal mentality to which the modern world has lost the key.

There is something in the mentality of each age that merely falls, so to speak, on the blind spot of the eye of a later age: our fathers took many things seriously that are jokes to us, and took a humorous view of many things that either do not amuse us in the least or repel us. It is difficult for us moderns, for example, to realise how seriously the dramatic motive of capture by Barbary pirates or the Turks was taken in the seventeenth century: the dramatic fiction had a certain gravity because the thing itself was so grave. Something of the validity of this motive still lingered on into the eighteenth century, as we see in the 'Seraglio'; while by the nineteenth century things had changed so much that Rossini, in 'L'Italiana in Algeri', could treat it all from the point of view of pure farce. (By a curious coincidence, while I was reflecting on this point last Sunday, and going through some ancient literature for evidence bearing on it, I read in my *Sunday Times* an account of a still existing charity that was founded by a London merchant some three hundred years ago for the benefit of unfortunate victims of the corsairs. Plays dealing with the fate of Europeans captured by the pirates are just a romantic joke to us now: but there was a time when the subject gave audiences a decided thrill.)

If, on the other hand, we want an example of how standards of humour can change from epoch to epoch, we may find it in the curious fact pointed out by a French writer of the nineteenth century that dramatists and audiences of Molière's day saw nothing repulsive in sons calmly discussing the maladies and imminent mortality of their fathers and candidly looking forward to the time when they would inherit their wealth. By an odd shift in the moral perspective of the theatre, the humours of a situation of this kind are now frowned upon in the case of fathers but accepted in the case of rich uncles. It is one of the most curious instances that can be cited of the changes that unconsciously come over the aesthetic mentality of men as the manners and morals of an epoch change.

The best illustration I have had for a long time of the influence of the temporal equation upon our judgement of music was afforded me the other evening at the Toscanini concert. During the 'Semiramide' overture every face in the audience was wreathed in smiles; as each supposedly humorous trait leaped out at us from the sparkling music, people instinctively looked round them to receive back from other eyes the delight that was bubbling in their own; when some particularly humorous touch flashed out, the universal feeling was that here the grand old joker that was Rossini was positively at his best. But alas for this point of view! 'Semiramide' is, or was in its own epoch, an opera of the most tragic seriousness. Few melodies seem, to us, so charged with the spirit of impish comedy as the first theme of the allegro section of the overture: it is not only that the melody itself sets us laughing but that we are sure Rossini was deliberately playing the antic for our benefit when he suddenly cut it short with that fortissimo crash on the diminished seventh, and then tiptoed down through those detached quavers to a resumption of his comic theme. But in the opera this theme (though there it appears in three-four time, instead of, as in the overture, in four-four) is of the most deadly seriousness. It was regarded in its own epoch as about the last word in tragic horror. The scene is in the tomb of King Ninus: the traitor Assur is about to be unmasked and meet his righteous doom: Rossini and his contemporaries saw not comedy but terrifying mystery in those pattering semiquavers with the perky upward flick at the end of them: and the diminished seventh and the stealthy following quavers were part and parcel of the recognised musical apparatus of the time for expressing horror.

And all this merely sends now a ripple of smiles through a modern audience, which is firmly convinced that Rossini was writing with his tongue in his cheek! So radically does the temporal equation change from epoch to epoch. We may be certain that it has changed in a hundred other ways, most of them so subtle that we are utterly unconscious of them, and that consequently many a piece of old music sounds very different in our ears from what it did in the ears of the composer and his contemporaries. For it is not with their ears but with their minds that men listen; and the mind of today is in many respects not the mind of a hundred or two hundred years ago. Not only is Smith's plate today sensitised in a very different way from Brown's, but both Smith's and Brown's are sensitised in a different way from those of their great-grandfathers. Will the day come when the nineteenth century view of Beethoven seems as absurd to the new criticism as the Winckelmann view of Greek art does to Wilenski?

LIVE EAGLES AND STUFFED ONES

2nd February 1936

Searching among my books the other day for one that had long been lost, I came at last to the top shelf of a cupboard—that knacker's yard, as it were, of every library, to which we consign the literary horses, mules and asses for which we have no further use, though some strain of sentimentality in us makes us keep putting off, perhaps for years, the day of death for them at the hands of the second-hand bookseller. I came across a number of those treatises on what used to be called 'musical form', analyses of Beethoven symphonies, of Mozart sonatas, of Bach fugues, and so on, to which we devote ourselves so dutifully in the innocent days of our youth; and, forgetting my original quest, I found myself turning over the leaves of some of them again, and wondering, as I have often done in recent years, how it is that these books afford us no criterion whatever by which we can determine the *aesthetic* value of a work. They show us in the minutest detail how a Bach fugue, let us say, is worked out; but they analyse with equal seriousness and apparently equal satisfaction a fugue that shows Bach's imagination working at high pressure hand-in-hand with his craftsmanship, and one in which, though the craftsmanship is admirably ingenious, the imagination has played a relatively small part. Then, descending the ladder, I caught sight of a volume of Hebbel's poetry which I had not seen for years: and opening this quite at random I lighted on an epigram that could not have applied better to the musical subject just then occupying my mind had the poet written it for that purpose.

It is entitled 'A Philosophical Analyst of Art', and runs thus:—

> Fangt ihm den Adler, er wird ihn zerlegen wie keiner, doch leider,
> Sieht er den hölzernen oft für den lebendigen an:

which, for my present purpose, may be rather freely rendered into English thus: 'Give him an eagle, and he will dissect it for you to perfection; but unfortunately he too often takes a stuffed bird for a live one.' And that, it seems to me, is the trouble with a good deal of our musical analysis: the methods employed and the results obtained are too often equally applicable to the stuffed eagle and to the living one. The old-fashioned analysis of 'form' is quite useful so far as it goes: but of itself it explains very little that really matters in the work of art, and supplies us with no material for an *aesthetic* valuation of it.

A simple illustration will make this clear. Following Hubert Parry, many an analyst, many a lecturer upon 'musical appreciation', has pointed out how admirably the unknown composer of the Londonderry Air has managed the second half of the song—how the melody makes a first attempt to rise, but sinks back further than the point from which it set out: how at the second attempt it rises again, still soars no higher, but, when it once more falls back, does so to a point slightly higher than the previous low one, a point, moreover, suggesting merely a *reculer pour mieux sauter*; and how, at the third attempt, it rises grandly to the highest point of the whole song, poses itself ecstatically there for a moment, and then makes a majestic descent to earth. All of which is perfectly true: but does it, after all, throw more than the most meagre light on the question of *why* the Londonderry Air is one of the loveliest melodies ever written? Of course it does not. This particular handling of a climax could be paralleled in a thousand other songs that have nothing like the aesthetic value of the Londonderry Air. The triumph of this latter, then, is not the result of its 'form': or at least not of its form alone, but of the suffusion of the form by something rich and rare that is not in the other songs. The only name we can give to this something is imagination.

I know of very few analyses of musical works in which the imaginative element is shown, as it ought to be, interpenetrating and vitalising the mere form. Perhaps the scarcity of this higher kind of analysis is due, in part, to the difficulty of quotation. For, unfortunately for us musicians, the quotation of music is a much more difficult and lengthy and therefore expensive matter than the quotation of a fragment of poetry or prose. But apart from this, one suspects that our professional analysts are not always as perceptive of the subtler felicities of the composer's imagination as they are to the more obvious 'formal' features of his work. And conversely, one further suspects, they are sometimes inclined to attach more importance to the mere formalities of composition than is the due of these. But here a difficulty arises. How are those of us who hold that in a certain instance the composer, his imagination having ceased for the moment to work at white heat, has sunk from form into mere formalism to persuade to our point of view those whose own imaginations do not work in quite the same way as ours?

This difficulty was brought home to me some time ago when I enlarged upon what I took, and shall always take, to be a defect in Brahms's handling, at certain points, of virtually all his first movements. My opponents argued that Brahms's procedure was perfectly clear—he took this theme and did so-and-so with it, and thus prepared the way for another theme. I am fully aware of all that: but my thesis is that in moments of this kind, though the procedure is logically explicable in terms of 'form', the imaginative heat has gone out of the music for the time being. There is no real inner continuity, only the outer semblance of continuity. Brahms, as I have put it before, at times like these merely goes on talking until he can think of something vital to say. The trouble is that whereas this kind of skilled carpentering is obvious enough in poetry or prose, where definite ideas are being dealt with, and where, consequently, a decline in value of the ideas can be detected at once and demonstrated, it is not so obvious in music, where the mere symmetry and the sensuous ring of the notes can sometimes give us a pleasure that blinds us to the temporary failure of the composer's *imagination* to work organically and, as the miners say, at depth.

At the head of one of the chapters of *The Antiquary* Walter Scott has one of those verses which he would fain have us believe were taken from old plays or poems, but which seem in many cases to have been his own ingenious invention. The verse in question runs thus:

> Go call a coach, and let a coach be called;
> And let the man who calleth be the caller;
> And in his calling let him nothing call
> But Coach! Coach! Coach! O for a coach, ye Gods!

Now the make-believe of this needs no demonstration: these

are merely sham-ideas, piled one on top of the other in a sham construction; for all the repetition and the variation there is no real progress—only the simulacrum of accumulation without the actuality of the real, the organic, cumulative. But make-believe of much the same kind, as I hold it to be, at certain transition-points in a Brahms first movement cannot so easily be *demonstrated*: apparently either one feels it to be make-believe or one does not. To me there is a good deal of this kind of sham-idea and sham-construction in many a modern symphony. When the earnestly-enquiring student said to Mephistopheles, 'But surely there ought to be an indivisible oneness of word and meaning?' the devil cynically advised him not to be too exacting in these matters: 'where meaning fails is just where words come in so handy!' For 'words' substitute 'notes' and classroom 'form', and you have, I think, an apt characterisation of those many passages in music—there is one in particular in Tchaikovsky's B flat minor piano concerto that might well be posted up in conservatoires as a dreadful example of how *not* to 'develop' a theme—in which, the imagination of the composer having ceased to function at depth for the time being, he fobs us off with mere mechanics. But if what Hebbel calls the 'philosophical analyst of art' cannot see, in cases of this kind, that what he is so learnedly dissecting is only a stuffed eagle, how can he be expected to be highly sensitive to what it is in the live eagle that makes it so magnificently alive?

EYES AND EARS

I

30th May 1943

THERE has been an interesting discussion lately in one of the musical journals on the subject of the place of score-reading in musical enjoyment. As usual in controversies of this kind there has been a good deal of straying into irrelevant side-issues; but even with regard to the main question there seems to me some confusion of thought.

One faction lays it down that as it is impossible to tell exactly what a score will sound like until we hear it, merely reading it can never be absolutely the same thing as listening to it. But who in his senses ever contended literally that it could? It is said that as the modern composer, by his own admission, often does not know in advance how a given page of his will sound, the outsider cannot hope to do so. That is perfectly true so far as it goes; but it does not by any means cover the whole field. In the case of ninety-five per cent of composers in the repertory this seeming difficulty can be taken in one's stride. Any trained musician who has heard one typical work of a given composer —such as Tchaikovsky, Sibelius, Rimsky-Korsakov, Strauss, Debussy, Ravel or Delius, to name only a few—some half-dozen times, and possesses any colour-memory at all, can get a pretty accurate idea of how another score of his will sound simply by reading it: the same formulae for colour-texture, the same devices for structural weighting or lightening, for brilliance, for sensuousness, etc., recur with unfailing regularity.

This is not to say, of course, that each of the scores of any one of these men sounds *precisely* like all his others; the further factors of subject, mood, and so forth come into consideration. But it is broadly true that the orchestration of the composers I have named, and of many others, is as truly a matter of the unwilled recurrences which I call fingerprints as their melody or harmony is. Each has his overriding personal *tic* of sound-procedure as of everything else. I will go so far as to say that if some super-scientist could so experiment with our minds as to cut out at will this element or that in our listening, and while we were listening to a particular work, obliterate our whole perception of it as melody, harmony and rhythm, leaving us only with an ebbing and flowing colour-wash of sound, we would still be able to name the composer without a moment's hesitation. What I am driving at in this connection is that reading the average score is not an act confined solely to the pages in front of us: it is a process in which all our previous hearings of the music of that particular composer co-operate in our subconsciousness, with the result that our colour-memory automatically translates the printed symbols into their sound-equivalents. It goes without saying that this inner reflection—for it is no more than that—will not be as *physically* intense as the reality: an actual trumpet-mass, for instance, can almost shatter our ear-drums, but the most accurate inner representation of the sound leaves us in no such danger as that.

To say, therefore, as some people do, that a mere reading of a score cannot possibly be *the same thing* as the physical impact of the colours on our physical ear is to waste time elaborating an elementary truism. Yet score-reading is absolutely indispensable, in more ways than one, to anyone to whom listening to music in the concert room is something more than a sort of ear-bath, anyone who wants really to know what, so to speak, the composer is talking about. The disparagers of score-reading seem to imagine that the pure essence of a work is embodied in the *sound* of it, with the corollary that when we have heard the sounds we have necessarily heard the work. I propose to try to show that this is pure delusion, that we can hear a given piece of music a hundred times and yet, if we do not know it also from the sight of the notes the composer has put on paper, get no further than the outer rim of his thought.

II

13th June 1943

FOLLOWING up my previous article on this subject, let us consider, first of all, the frank admission on the part of some composers that they themselves are not sure how a score of theirs will sound until they hear it. A man of crudely plain speech might say that this is a confession that they do not understand their job. Can we suppose, he would go on to say, that in two old works that were marvels of colour in their own day—the 'Freischütz' overture and the C major symphony—Weber and Schubert did not know exactly how the notes they were putting on paper would sound? Can we imagine Berlioz shamefacedly admitting that he did not know how his Requiem or 'Faust' or 'The Trojans' would sound? With Wagner, the whole orchestral texture of an opera changed in accordance with the milieu of the drama and the psychology of the characters: no one with any ear at all for sound could conceive the colour-complex of any five pages of 'Lohengrin' or the 'Götterdämmerung'—especially the second act—or 'Parsifal' recurring in one of the other works. Yet in each case Wagner, sitting at his desk, knew very well what the symbols he was putting down would sound like.

I myself, however, would not put it in that rough-and-tumble way. The simple truth seems to be that there are almost as many varieties of musical imagination and sound-perception as there are composers. In some of them there goes on during the whole time of artistic creation a subtle process corresponding to that of osmosis in chemistry: all the elements of the inner vision, line, colour, form, psychology and so on are instantaneously and inextricably interfused. In others the musical thinking is basically that of the draughtsman: the composer will of course find beautiful or appropriate colours for the adornment or heightening of his design, but substantially the thinking is from first to last in a sort of black-and-white. It therefore does not in the least follow that because a composer of today is a fine thinker in music he is also a born colourist. He is helped out technically in his scoring by the admirable text books of orchestration we now possess—a resource, by the way, not open to gifted pioneers like Weber and Schubert—and by his memory of what he has heard from childhood in the concert room and the opera house. The trouble is that he has under his fingers, in the orchestra of today, a fascinating but dangerous instrument of immense variety and still unexplored possibilities; and so he is often tempted to add two or three extra strands of colour to his score without being at all certain, if his musical thinking happens to be predominantly of the black-and-white order, what the total colour-mixture will sound like.

Some composers—Elgar was one—have the faculty of inner hearing much more strongly developed than others. One day when I called on him I found him reading a magazine article on a certain composer of today. He was very angry: 'The man evidently can't read music', he said of the writer of the article. I mildly suggested that this was going a bit too far. 'Well', he amended, 'he can't *hear* some of the things he quotes so admiringly. Look at that', and he pointed to one citation. 'On paper that looks wonderful, but it will sound horrible'; and when I heard the work I saw that he had been right. The composer in question is a lavish but far from infallible user of the too rich palette of the modern orchestra.

The bearing of all this on the problem of the benefits and difficulties of score-reading by the non-composer I will try to show in a final article on the subject.

III

20th June 1943

It is curious that none of the debaters of this subject ever seem to get to grips with the real question. They appear to imagine that certain people claim to be able to do what the modern composer sometimes admits his own inability to do—know at a glance exactly how a piece of complicated scoring will sound. That is so absurd that it is hardly worth wasting time over: the most practised score-reader can do no more than arrive, by prolonged study, at a notion of what the page will *sound* like. The real point, which is generally overlooked, is this: if a dead-sure inner sense of the colour-sound of a modern score is absolutely vital to an understanding of the work, then obviously the composer, if he himself lacks this sense, could not have carried out the train of thought that really constitutes the work. But he *has* written it. It has cohered and evolved organically in his imagination; therefore the physical sound of it was only one element of it among others, and not the basically determining element. Consequently the mental course taken by the composer in writing the work can be traversed in turn by the patient reader of the score: after a few hours he will get the same mental picture of the *music*, in detail and as a whole, that the composer had when writing it; and that is the seminal thing for him, as it was for the composer.

Far too much stress is laid, when this topic is under discussion, on the newest scores. Ninety-nine per cent of the music the plain man hears is not new but old; and it is principally in connection with the latter that it is important for him to develop the faculty of what we may call silent colour-hearing, so that when he reads a score, or better still, runs through the music in his mind apart from the score, he can recall accurately the physical sound of it, realising the work not as a dim abstraction of melodies and harmonies in no particular sound-medium but in all its varieties of colour. Some people no doubt lack that faculty altogether: this is a field of psychology that has not yet been scientifically studied as ordinary colour-blindness has been. But I believe that in a great many music lovers the faculty is latent; and I can assure them that it is well worth intelligent cultivation.

On this aspect of our problem I can touch only *en passant.* I need my final inch or two of space to stress something that makes assiduous score-reading absolutely essential to anyone who really wants to know what, so to speak, the composer is talking about. Actual listening in the concert room is indispensable, of course; but from this alone it is seldom possible to see a work entirely as the composer saw it. For one thing, it reaches the plain man through the medium of a performer, and that medium may be a weak or even a distorting one, for a performer, like a listener, can be 'fond of music' without really having a musical mind—that is to say, being able to think, for the time being, just as a composer thinks. I myself have heard, for instance, a performance of one of the greatest of the Beethoven quartets that was technically faultless, but in conception was purely infantile: Beethoven at his most tremendous was made to simper prettily like a smiling child plucking at its pinafore.

Moreover, even the most intelligent performance may sometimes be misrepresentative, by reason purely of the ineradicable defects of the instrument. This is peculiarly the case with the piano—the musical maid-of-all-work, as Liszt called it. No one who knows the arioso dolente of Beethoven's Op. 110 only from hearing it on the piano can be said to know more than the shell of it. What Beethoven had in his mind was an ideal *singing* voice, and the piano, with its percussive attack and its poor sustaining power, especially in the higher notes, simply cannot sing a melody of this kind with ideal legato and delicacy and variety of nuance. What the spirit that sang its dolorous song to Beethoven's inner ear was saying to him can be discovered only when we sing the melody to ourselves in a way that not even the best human throat or the best violin could do.

The illustration I have just given is the simplest conceivable. It could be multiplied a thousand-fold through all the ascending categories of musical complexity; and if that were done it would be seen that ears are not enough in music if we want to sense the work as the composer did when he was putting it on paper. We must supplement or correct the more or less generalised message of the ear by intensive study of the score.

MUSIC FOR EAR, OR EYE?

19th March 1944

TODAY, by way of light relief, I want to say something on a point that worried correspondents are very fond of raising: do some composers of 'modern' music really *hear* what they write, or is it just paper music, logically coherent to the eye but unconvincing to the ear? Well, there can be no cut-and-dried answer to that; sometimes a complex weaving of lines results in clear-speaking music, sometimes it reads more sensibly than it sounds. But for the pleasure of those people whom it comforts to believe that this or that 'modern' composer who exasperates them simply works out his patterns on paper without always knowing, or perhaps caring, what it will sound like I will tell a few stories today that may provide them with ammunition to fire at the objects of their dislike.

Many anecdotes circulate in musical circles of rehearsals and performances of 'modern' works in which something went wrong, whether by accident or design it is not for me to say. In one instance a clarionettist is said to have played a page or two consistently at the wrong pitch through his use of another clarionet than the one prescribed in the score: and the conductor never noticed it. Twenty-five years or so go there was a German story going the rounds of a first performance of a string quartet in which, at one point, the viola was for some time at the wrong pitch because the copyist of the parts had omitted to indicate that the instrument had shifted from the alto clef into the violin clef; and even the composer, who was present, is said not to have noticed that anything was wrong.

For the truth of these stories I cannot vouch personally. In two other cases, however, I can. One of the most eminent of living conductors told me, a few years ago, within an hour or two of the rehearsal of a certain new work by an equally eminent composer, that at one point he had been pulled up by an obvious discrepancy between what a certain player was playing and what was set down in the score. He appealed to the composer, who was on the platform, to say which was correct, score or part. The composer, who obviously did not know, tried to brush the question aside. The conductor insisted: 'It must be one or the other', he said. 'For my part I don't care which it is, but *both* can't be right.' The composer merely went red in the face and said, 'I tell you it's all right. Go on.' And that was that.

Another world-famous conductor told me that it once fell to his lot to conduct a piano concerto by a certain world-famous composer in which the latter was to play the solo part. They had a private rehearsal, the composer at the piano, the conductor following with the score. So little natural musical sense, apparently, did the work make here and there even for its creator that he kept bending over the piano, obviously spelling out the constituent notes of this chord or that, and sometimes hesitating so long over them that the conductor, who happens to be a very plainspoken man, lost his temper: 'X', he said, 'you are just a bluff.'

Finally, here is a story told not privately but in print—in a musical journal of 1926 which lies before me as I write—by the conductor Pierre Monteux *à propos* of his experiences as conductor of the Diaghileff ballets in Paris in 1924. The new 'Les Noces', he said, was to be conducted first of all by Stravinsky himself. Monteux naturally attended the rehearsals, score in hand. 'Much to my surprise', he says, 'I noticed that all the singers were singing their parts either one-third too high or one-fourth too low, and never the composer corrected them. The night of the performance . . . "Les Noces" with Stravinsky conducting, thunderous applause, but the singers were still singing one-third too high or one-fourth too low. The following day you can well imagine how surprised was Mr. Diaghileff when I demanded some new rehearsals for "Les Noces", and when he heard that all the singers had to learn their parts over.' And that, again, is that. The reader may be left to put what construction he likes on it all.

WHAT ARE TUNES?

23rd August 1953

A CORRESPONDENT in the South of England has sprung some pretty problems on me. His trouble is tunes. 'For years', he writes, 'I have bothered about them. What exactly is a tune? Does it consist of a certain number of bars arranged in a certain way? Are symphonic themes and Wagnerian motifs tunes? And so forth', he adds airily, as if he had not started trouble enough already.

But he goes on relentlessly: 'Then, having solved that problem, what is a good tune and what a bad one? Is there any definite answer to that question, or is it merely a question of taste or prejudice? I, for example, consider the following to be good tunes, but I can't say why'; and he reels off a list that ranges from the Londonderry Air to 'Knocked 'em in the Old Kent Road' and 'The Girl I Left Behind Me'. He could go on indefinitely, he continues, but the vastness of the field that opens out before the earnest inquirer appals him: 'So will you come to my aid, set out your views on the subject in a series of articles, and indicate, if possible, how an untrained person can separate the musical sheep from the goats.'

A series of articles is obviously beyond the scope of *The Sunday Times*, but I will try to answer one or two of my correspondent's questions.

I begin by dodging his first poser—'What exactly is a tune?'—taking refuge in the safe old wisecrack that while none of us may be able to say exactly what an elephant is, everyone knows an elephant when he sees one. The answer to his second query—'Are symphonic themes and Wagnerian motifs tunes?'—is easier. They are and they aren't. They are tunes (or some of them are) in the sense that they are recognisable shapely melodic units, but they differ from 'tunes' in the more exact sense of the term in that they have not come into existence purely and simply for their own sake but as starting-points for a larger whole. They are not self-contained small organisms, fully and harmoniously developed according to the special laws of their tiny being, but cells from which, under the right conditions of inner energy, temperature and environment, a large-scale organism may evolve.

As regards the goodness or badness of tunes I am afraid I can offer my correspondent no infallible touchstone, nor can anyone else. If we could we would have the key to all aesthetic judgement in our hands. Everyone agrees that 'Greensleeves', or the great tune in D major that cuts across the texture of the second movement of Beethoven's Ninth Symphony, or the tune of Schubert's Serenade, is a sheep, and a thing like 'O sole mio' a goat.

But *how* do we know? To that question there is no answer. The 'form' of the tune, on which nineteenth-century pedagogics laid such comical stress, has simply nothing at all to do with it; for tens of thousands of second-rate or third-rate tunes have precisely the same 'form' as this or that first-rate one. What intoxicates us is the odour of the rose, not the shape of it; and who can say positively why one rose smells more divinely than others of the same species in the same bed?

The old story of Mallarmé and the painter Degas is worth recalling in this connection. Degas, it appears, fancied himself as a poet as well; and one day he complained to Mallarmé that while he was chockfull of excellent ideas 'the poem wouldn't come out'. Mallarmé's reply went to the root of the matter: 'My dear fellow, poetry isn't written with ideas, it's written with words.' To see how true that is we have only to consider the resemblance and the difference between 'We're here today and gone tomorrow' and

We are such stuff
As dreams are made on; and our little life
Is rounded with a sleep.

The 'idea' is in both instances the same; it is the 'words' that make the difference. In Keats's first draft of 'A thing of beauty is a joy forever' the line had run 'A thing of beauty is a constant joy'. The poetic difference is vital; but how account for that vitality? So again with the two famous lines in Poe's 'To Helen':

To the glory that was Greece
And the grandeur that was Rome.

In an earlier edition these had run:

To the beauty of fair Greece
And the grandeur of old Rome.

The 'idea' is the same; the difference in poetic quality resides somewhere in the words. But where, precisely?

In the case of music we cannot, of course, make this distinction between idea and expression, for the two are inextricably interfused in the notes. We have no difficulty in deciding that the notes of the 'Joy' theme in the Ninth Symphony are incomparably better than any other theme made in the same rhythm out of the same six notes would have been; but *why* they are so infallibly right we simply cannot say. All we know is that some composers have a gift for doing the magical thing and others haven't. Some Frenchman or other, answering detractors of the great Napoleon, ironically conceded that lots of other generals knew as much about the art of war as the little Corsican did, but, he said, Napoleon had the knack of winning battles. So with Mozart, Rimsky-Korsakov, Schubert, Johann Strauss, Franz Lehár, and the unknown geniuses who produced all the world's best folk songs; they just had the knack of writing immortal tunes.

ST. PETER'S TOE:
CRITICISM AND AUTHORSHIP

20th February 1938

WHILE I was out of England a few weeks ago faint echoes reached me now and then of a controversy in London about some panels, acquired or to be acquired by the National Gallery, which were held to be, or not to be, by Giorgione. As well as I could make out from the occasional letters I saw on the subject, the position was really simplicity itself: if the panels were by Giorgione they were good panels and worth the money asked for them: if not, not—a position summed up long ago by Mr. Shaw in the remark of one of his characters that if a play was by a good author it is bound to be a good play.

With that simple conclusion, I gathered, most people were in complete agreement. But in the rare moments when my mind was not occupied with other and higher things—connected with the improbability of a given number turning up on the roulette wheel after I had discouraged it by staking on it—I found myself asking two questions: Are art connoisseurs as much at sea with regard to certain vital matters as we musical critics are with regard to music? And does it necessarily follow that because a work is known, beyond any possibility of doubt, to be by a great artist, it must be a great, or even a good, work?

The first of these two questions, of course, is pointed at the problem of what I have elsewhere called fingerprints. A real science of musical fingerprints is slowly coming into existence: it is beginning to be perceived that each composer betrays his hand by certain formulae of idiom or of procedure of which he himself is quite unconscious, but that recur with the inevitability of fate in everything that he does. The science is already so far advanced that it would have been the easiest thing in the world to prove the temerity of the claim—had it been persisted in—of a couple of ladies a few years ago that Puccini had cribbed some of his operas from manuscript works of theirs: unless the ladies, which is doubtful, had discovered Puccini's fingerprints and imitated them, and imitated them precisely in his way, the mere setting forth of these in an unbroken sequence from the 'Le Villi' of 1884 to the 'Turandot' of 1924 would have knocked the bottom out of their claim.

But the science is not yet advanced enough for us to be able to settle many questions of disputed authorship in music, because, for one thing, not nearly enough specialist work of this kind has been done upon the music of the minor composers. Is art criticism, at the moment, in the same position? I am aware that there have been several attempts by specialists to define the manner or mannerisms of this or that great painter; but the mere fact that no one can step forward and *prove* that these panels are or are not by Giorgione seems to me to suggest that the science of fingerprints has not as yet got even as far in the world of painting as it has in that of music.

The second of the two questions I have asked above is easier to answer, though in a way that hardly does credit to either our critical capacity or our critical honesty. Can there be the least doubt that suggestion plays far too large a part in the more standardised of our admirations? Are we not all inclined to see non-existent excellences in a given work merely because it bears a famous name? It has often struck me, when listening to some dull or trivial piece of music signed Bach or Mozart, for instance, that if any young composer of the present day were to seek our suffrages on the basis of something of his own anything like so bad as that, he would have the whole of the Press and of the public jeering at him. If one of these works had been originally given to the world under the name of some minor composer of its epoch it would not have the ghost of a chance of appearing in our concert programmes today; but let it only be attributed, even wrongfully, to a giant, and we unconsciously listen to it with all the weight of the great man's greater work dipping the balance in its favour.

'We taste nothing purely' was a favourite thesis of Montaigne's. That is certainly true of our musical appreciations: there is a great deal of music which we do not hear as it really is; whether we are aware of it or not, the great name dulls what should be the clean edge of our judgement. It is difficult for us to see many of the works of the past as they really are because of the enormous part that mass-suggestion plays in our attitude towards them. André Gide has hit off this tendency in a sentence which perhaps I have made use of before in this column: he compares the kind of immunity that some ancient works possess for us, owing to the associations, the century-old admirations, that have been worked into the very tissue of them, with the big toe of the statue of St. Peter, that has been worn smooth by centuries of the kisses of the faithful. A much better toe on a much better statue that has not had the advantage of these kisses, and of the self-hypnosis that accompanies them, receives less worship because it is seen precisely as it is.

This question of the power of association, of long-accumulated admiration, of self-hypnosis, is one to which criticism has not yet given adequate attention. I often wonder how, for instance, the finale of the Ninth Symphony would fare if we could see it just as it is, without our judgement of it being clouded in advance by all we have read about it and all we have been taught to believe about it. The reader will understand, I hope, that I am not suggesting that the movement is worthless: on the contrary, even in its faults it is the product of a great mind. What I do suggest is that we have some difficulty now in seeing it precisely as it is *qua* music because of the vast amount of cloud that has been created between the music and us by the rhapsodies of writers who keep shifting the criterion from the domain of aesthetics to that of metaphysics or heaven knows what else. Because Beethoven burst into a paean on the subject of joy, religion, human brotherhood and all the rest of it, he gets a number of good marks in a subject that has not the faintest connection with all this—that of art pure and simple.

I sometimes ask myself, again, what would have been said about Beethoven's procedure in the introduction to the finale had it been adopted not by Beethoven but, let us say, by Mahler. Let us suppose that Mahler, having written three masterly movements of a symphony and then, not knowing how the deuce to prepare for his finale—how to work in an 'Ode to Joy' that he had had in his mind for years—had begun the finale by quoting a fragment from each of the preceding movements, then made what Grove calls 'a horrible clamour', put a baritone up to say, 'O friends, not these tones! Let us sing something more agreeable and more joyful', and then dragged Schiller's poem in by the hair of its head. Had that happened, would not all the academics of today have been deriding Mahler for his 'incompetence' as a composer? As it is, does it not seem as if, while poor Mahler would not be allowed to do so much as look over the hedge, Beethoven is generously allowed not merely to steal the horse but to sell the spavined animal for more than it is really worth?

The intelligent reader, I hope, will observe that I am not dogmatising. I am merely asking a few questions that seem to me to go to the root of 'criticism'. Is criticism at its soundest when it estimates the aesthetic value of a statue's toe not by purely artistic considerations of what a toe ought to be, but by the smoothness conferred on it by the kisses of generations of the faithful?

MUSIC AS LANGUAGE AND THOUGHT

I

3rd October 1920

WHEN I was politely remonstrating the other day with certain literary men for implying that music was a mere skin-game, with which the intellect had next to nothing to do, I said something about music being 'a language and a body of thought'. Whereupon a correspondent wrote to me thus:—

> 'I wish you would develop the implications of that statement, so that those of us who are not musicians may learn of them as we do Shakespeare. Browning, Bernard Shaw, Runciman (*Saturday Review*) all worked at this theme, and you yourself most continuously of all. To me, with no musical skill whatever, music always suggests a problem in form. I wonder as I listen how the artist is going to continue—it is like in that to a chess problem or a difficult arrangement of balls at billiards. You see, it is to me merely form—no, not merely form, because there is colour as well. How this form expresses ideas other than elemental ones—a point Runciman is never tired of stating—is my difficulty. I am always up against it, always hoping that some day with attentive listening I shall be presented with music's secrets.'

Someone once wrote a book on *Varieties of Religious Experience.* I wish someone would write another on 'Varieties of Musical Experience'. Music and the hearing of it seem such simple, definite things to us all our lives, till one fine day we wake up and discover, to our astonishment, that other people do not hear it at all as we do. Even when they enjoy it as much as we do, they enjoy it in quite a different way; I have known people who thought the second act of 'Tristan' erotic in that pitiful lament over the nothingness of fleshly love! And there are minds that, though interested in music, are obviously only half musical. When I read Mr. Leigh Henry, for example, on Elgar or Beethoven or Strauss, I am reminded of a foreigner who has heard a poem read to him in a language he does not understand, and honestly wonders what on earth other people can see in it.

Put your dog before the finest picture in the world, and he will remain unmoved. For him it is not a picture, but just so many square feet of some uneatable substance or other in which he takes no interest. You cannot argue with him; you must just accept the fact that Providence has seen fit to deprive him of a faculty that more highly organised beings possess. A step higher in the musical scale we have the man who really does like the way a certain melody goes, but is deaf to the deeper psychological implications of it. He will think Bach's G string Aria or that haunting theme in Elgar's Quintet quite a pretty tune; but no amount of explanation on our part would make him understand how for us these tunes seem to reach to the confines of space. He wonders why on earth we make such a fuss over a mere couple of notes like the Fate theme in the Fifth Symphony; and it is no use our trying to convey to him that these notes in themselves are nothing, and would probably be nothing in anyone else's hands, but that in Beethoven's they epitomise a great part of the profoundest experience of the human race.

My present correspondent introduces me to a type of musical listener that is new to me. In one way he is to be envied. If he has the gift of visualising, so to speak, a whole musical work as a problem in form, he can do what thousands of people who call themselves musical cannot do. I suspect that one of the things that are wrong with the people who think Stravinsky a very great man and Beethoven a very little one is that they are constitutionally incapable of thinking contentedly over a large field. They prefer music that works in dabs and patches to music that goes on elaborating its thesis because it does not take so much intellectual effort to perceive a dab or a patch as to follow an argument. They cannot understand why some of us soon grow tired of this sort of music—unless it is first-rate of its kind, like Stravinsky at his best—because it points to a certain feebleness of intellect; nor can they understand what it is that fascinates us in a vast and finally controlled design like that of either of Elgar's symphonies.

If, then, my correspondent can really see the plan of a great piece of music steadily unfolding itself to the end, he is to be congratulated. What puzzles me is that he apprehends the music *only* as plan. Does literature, I wonder, appeal to him in the same way? I can hardly think so. From the greater literature there is to be had the same pleasure in architectonics as from the greater music. But I have never yet heard of anyone for whom this was the only pleasure that literature gave. Has there ever been anyone, for instance, who, as he ploughed his way through *War and Peace*, has merely felt curiosity as to how the literary chess problem works itself out? One *is* interested in this, of course, but also in something more. For the interplay of forces in a great drama novel is not merely an abstract one, like that of a machine. The work of art stirs emotions in us which the machine does not. I imagine that this correspondent, if I am right in taking his words literally, follows a piece of music much as the rest of us would follow a detective story. In the detective story pure and simple we have literary form pure and simple. The characters hardly exist as characters; all we are concerned with is the way they pull at and press on each other, and finally throw out the solution of a problem.

In the romance, the characters come a little nearer to the human beings we know; but the chief interest is still in the succession and clash of events, the wondering how it is all going to end, and the final satisfaction of this wonder. The detective story and the schoolboy's romance are chess problems played with men and women instead of with knights and pawns and bishops. But the great masters of fiction or the drama can work out these problems in terms not only of chess but of psychology and the poetry of works like the *Oedipus*, *Hamlet*, and *Othello*. Had Sardou written *Hamlet*, or Dumas *Lord Jim*, the incidents would have been the same, but he would have stopped at the incidents. For romance pure and simple, *Lord Jim* or *The Rescue* is as intriguing and exciting as anything of Stevenson's; but there is something more than romantic story-telling in them, something more than 'situation', something more than form. So it is with great music. A work like the Fifth Symphony does indeed give us the sort of pleasure in 'seeing how it all turns out' that *The Count of Monte Cristo* does. But it gives us something more in just that something more that *The Rescue* or *War and Peace* gives us.

I have not answered my correspondent's question as to how

the form of music 'expresses ideas other than elemental ones'. This I shall try to do next week.

II

10th October 1920

In the preceding article on this subject I tried to show, in answer to the correspondent who was interested in a piece of music only as the working out of a problem in musical form, that this pleasure in the working out of a form is implicit also in our appreciation of literature—most obvious in the case of the literature of mere construction, such as the detective story, but present also, subconsciously, in the most imaginative and psychological work.

There is, needless to say, a fair quantity of music—and quite good music, too—our pleasure in which comes wholly, or almost wholly, from seeing how the game is played, how the pattern is worked out. Music, in its structural aspect, is often compared with architecture. I sometimes think a better analogy would be with jewellery or wallpaper, where a 'unit' of design is built up into a pattern that the eye can embrace in its totality at once; though music, of course, has the immeasurable advantage of being able to show a unit at once the same and varied, there being nothing in the arts of visual design comparable, for instance, to the effect made by instantly repeating a musical figure in another key. If we want a perfect example in the smallest possible form of the delight that comes from hearing sound-units built up into a simple pattern like those evolved from the units of which, say, an elaborate gold pendant is built up, we have only to turn to Purcell's little Prelude to the Harpsichord Lessons.

The tiny piece 'means' nothing whatever: our joy in it comes solely and wholly from the effect of an 'up' here answering a 'down' there, and from the sense that the totality of notes makes something of the same balanced impression on the ear as a piece of simple linear design does on the eye.

There is a fair amount of music of this sort on a bigger scale; and if this were all that music is capable of, we should have no answer to the philosophers who deny it intellect. In a curious book, *Contre la Musique*, to which I have already referred, Victor de Laprade argues that music is the one art from which intellect and volition are absent. Its effect is partly sensuous, partly mathematical. As Laprade says, it is the only art to which animals, fools and idiots are to some degree susceptible—a proof that much of the pleasure it gives is purely physical. The remainder of the delight it gives us, he says, is that of the evolving pattern: certain of nature's own forces here fall into symmetrical lines in tones, as certain other of nature's forces fall into symmetrical lines in crystals, etc.

In literature, painting and architecture the creative artist is a free moral agent, starting out with an idea that is conceivable and expressible by itself, and consciously realising this idea in a given material. In the case of music there is no idea that is conceivable or expressible outside the composition itself; and although the composer seems to be consciously directing the course of the notes, he is in reality only unconsciously arranging the notes in patterns that are pre-ordained for him by those natural forces on which the rhythm of the cosmos depends.

To all which, of course, the answer is that poets and philosophers should not write about things they do not understand. They listen to music with a non-musical brain, and then deny that there can be anything more in it for a musical brain than for theirs. It never seems to occur to them to ask why, if music is only sound shaping itself into patterns much in the way that dust on a metal plate does when the plate is stroked with a violin bow, there are so many varieties, so many hierarchies, of composers.

Let me make use of an illustration that I have employed before to show that 'form' in music, in the ordinary sense of the term, counts for next to nothing. Suppose I copy out the first movement of Beethoven's Fifth Symphony, leaving lines underneath each line of Beethoven for a composition of my own. In these lines I do, in my own way, precisely what Beethoven has done in his. I cut my themes to the same length as his; I make my notes go up when his go up, and down when his go down. I begin my working-out, *reprise*, and so on, just where he does; and altogether I make my symphony, so far as the process of the notes is concerned, absolutely the same as his.

Will the *music* be therefore the same? Obviously not. My 'form' is as perfect as his, simply because it *is* his. What makes Beethoven's symphony better than mine is not any superiority in the pattern, but a superiority in the something that informs the pattern; and this informing something we call Beethoven's idea.

It will not do for the opponents of music to pounce upon the term 'idea' and say that we cannot legitimately use it in connection with a sequence of notes, inasmuch as the 'idea' cannot be expressed in words. Neither, for that matter, can the 'idea' of a painting or of a piece of architecture, yet no one would deny that St. Paul's incarnates a great idea, and a tin tabernacle a small one. Nor will it do, I think, to say that what we musicians mean by 'idea' in music would be better expressed by 'mood'. That is equally true, to a large extent, of poetry. Shakespeare's

'We are such stuff
As dreams are made on, and our little life
Is rounded with a sleep'

really contains no more and no better 'idea' than 'We're here today and gone tomorrow'. Shakespeare has simply felt a universal mood and given a certain verbal expression to it. The musician may feel the same universal mood, but *his* medium for expressing it is not words, but notes.

We must get rid of the notion that an 'idea' is not really an 'idea' unless it can be expressed in words. Words are only one medium for the utterance of what man thinks about life. To the musician, a piece of great music is as plain and coherent a reading of life as a poem can be. How otherwise could we discriminate between composers? How could we say that Bach was a great musical thinker and Balfe a small one, or that Beethoven's thought unfolds itself with a slow, inexorable logic over a half-hour's stretch, while another composer cannot think coherently for more than a page at a time? What does it matter whether the 'ideas' that music expresses are merely 'elemental', as my correspondent calls them, or other than elemental? The point is that they are ideas—musical ideas—and that there are degrees of value among musical ideas, and degrees of logic in the handling of them.

What I urged originally, as against some of the contributors to the *John o' London's Weekly* symposium, was not that music expresses ideas of the verbal sort, but that, in its own way, it is thought-expressive, that, for musicians, it is not a mere pleasurable aural massage, not a mere series of tonal patterns, but 'a language and a body of thought'. It can say, in its own way, things as airy or profound as anything that words can express. It was either Schopenhauer, or Wagner following Schopenhauer, who described Beethoven as 'speaking the highest wisdom in a language his reason does not understand'. Why should the man who can express himself only through the verbal language of reason assume that that is the only language of thought?

THE LATEST HORROR

5th July 1953

As I said a fortnight ago, I am a newcomer to television. I am finding it a source of great delight in some ways, and of horrors in another. At times it seems to confirm me in my general pessimistic opinion that it isn't worth while mankind sweating blood to put some wrong right, for when that has been done another is sure to come into sight that is worse than its predecessor. Progress is an illusion: man never is, but always to be, blest.

Let us take a very simple example. We can all of us remember the dark day of long ago when we realised that the crooner was not merely in our midst but had come to stay. We braced ourselves to endure that visitation; this, we said to ourselves with the courage of despair, is the limit. We were wrong, as usual; the Fates had up their sleeves a still worse affliction for us; after the male crooner came the female of the species.

And now there has come along something far, far worse than even the crooner. I refer to the television close-up of the female mouth. Here again we had been warned, so to speak; for years we have been unable to open a popular paper without wondering at the strange compulsion that makes the modern woman, as soon as she sees a camera pointed at her, put on a horse grin, apparently regarding her mouth as an instrument primarily devised by nature to afford in the twentieth century a free object-lesson in the basic facts of dentistry. Surely, we have often said to ourselves, if Helen of Troy had been in the habit of grinning in this chawbacon fashion in season and out of season there would have been no Trojan war; Menelaus would simply have said to the marauding Paris 'Keep her, my boy, keep her; rather you than me!' In that case, of course, we should never have had that immortal line of Marlowe's, 'Was this the face that stopped a thousand clocks?'; but there, we can't have everything.

But, as I have said, the television close-up of the mouth of the female singer going into action has brought us the worst horror of them all. In opera performances in the theatre I have been conscious now and then that a heroine's mouth was more widely open than was consistent with facial beauty, and I have admired the fortitude of the tenor or baritone in standing up as he did to the vast void in front of him when she passionately exhorted him to 'Look Into My Heart, Love' and provided him with every physical opportunity for doing so. In the theatre, however, distance, if it does not actually lend enchantment to the view, spares us some of the worst pains of disenchantment.

To drain the cup of horror to the dregs we have to go to the television close-up. What kindness do the gallant camera experts imagine they are doing us with this? What would we say to a Lieder singer who insisted on standing a mere twelve inches from us in our own music room and confronting us with a vast cavern of a mouth as she bellows at us 'Ich liebe dich' or 'Du meine Seele, du mein Herz'?

Yet even that procedure could not compete in hideous blatancy with the television close-up, in which, in the first place, the curvature of the picture exaggerates and burlesques some features of the singer's face, in particular broadening it and putting bulges on the cheekbones and widening the arch smile into a grin, making her look for all the world more like a ventriloquist's dummy than a human being, and in the second place affording us a view into the cavernous interior that already includes teeth and tongue and makes us ask ourselves with a shudder where, as science progresses, these personally conducted expeditions into the interior are going to end.

I have just been reading of 'a new lens of 80-inch focal length for television cameras' that is now on loan to the B.B.C. For the previous 40-inch lens, it appears, it was claimed that it 'could spot a fly on the face of a man half a mile away', while in one test 'the lattice work of an aerial mast three miles away was shown on the monitor screen in clear detail'. And now, I gather, these wonders are to be multiplied by two!

Shall we have them applied right away to the close-up of the female singer? I hope not; the present apparatus surely provides us with all the viewer needs in the way of mingled exasperation and ribald amusement in that field. The B.B.C.

must have a rich collection of these atrocities by now. I venture to suggest that it should preserve them as a Television Chamber of Horrors, and reel them off to us in quick succession for a quarter of an hour every now and then. Not only would that be grimly entertaining for us ordinary viewers, but the singers concerned would have a chance to see themselves as others have seen them on these dreadful occasions.

After some recent experiences I have been brooding tensely on the hilarious possibilities of tragic opera on television; but that is a subject that will have to wait.